The Default Provisions of Revised Article 9

Uniform Commercial Code

Timothy R. Zinnecker

Section of Business Law

American Bar Association

The materials contained herein represent the opinions of the authors and editors and should not be construed to be the action of the American Bar Association or the Section of Business Law unless adopted pursuant to the bylaws of the Association.

Nothing contained in this book is to be considered as the rendering of legal advice for specific cases, and readers are responsible for obtaining such advice from their own legal counsel. This book is intended for educational and informational purposes only.

Library of Congress Cataloging-in-Publication Data

Zinnecker, Timothy R.
    The default provisions of revised article 9 of the Uniform commercial code / Timothy R. Zinnecker.
    p. cm.
        ISBN 1-57073-759-2
    1. Security (Law)—United States. 2. Defaulty (Finance)—United States.
I. Title.

KF1050.Z56 1999
346.7307'4–dc21   99-052283

Cover design by Catherine Zaccarine

The Default Provisions of Revised Article 9 of the Uniform Commercial Code was first printed in *The Business Lawyer*, Volume 54, Number 3 (May 1999), and Volume 54, Number 4 (August 1999)

Discounts are available for books ordered in bulk. Special consideration is given to state and local bars, CLE programs, and other bar-related organizations. Inquire at Book Publishing, American Bar Association, 750 North Lake Shore Drive, Chicago, Illinois 60611.

03   02   01   00   5   4   3   2

CONTENTS

ACKNOWLEDGMENTS

David G. Epstein, Steve H. Nickles, Donald J. Rapson, Steven O. Weise, and Robert A. Zadek were extremely generous with their time, reviewing and offering many insightful comments on earlier drafts. Two of my favorite students, Trang-Dai Vu Hoang and William Scott Youngblood, provided invaluable research assistance. South Texas College of Law graciously provided a research stipend.

INTRODUCTION

The default provisions of Article 9 of the Uniform Commercial Code (U.C.C. or Code) strive to provide "flexible, effective, and efficient realization procedures."[1] The provisions fall short of achieving this noble goal, and blame rests squarely on the provisions themselves. The default statutes are not drafted with a great degree of rigidity and detail, but instead are loosely organized and informal.[2] Consequently, they fail to provide guidance on several fundamental issues.[3] These statutory gaps have prompted judicial intervention that has been "wasteful, expensive, inefficient, unfair and detrimental to secured financing."[4]

---

1. William E. Hogan, *The Secured Party and Default Proceedings Under the UCC*, 47 MINN. L. REV. 205, 253 (1962).

2. *See* 2 GRANT GILMORE, SECURITY INTERESTS IN PERSONAL PROPERTY § 43.1, at 1183 (1965) (noting that the default provisions reject the approach of "detailed statutory regulation," and instead "opt[ ] for a loosely organized informal, anything-goes type of foreclosure pattern"); *see also* Hogan, *supra* note 1, at 207 (observing the "remarkable absence of stringent requirements for mandatory public sales, detailed public notices, or other specific prohibitions").

Professor Gilmore was the primary drafter of the original Article 9. *See* BARKLEY CLARK, THE LAW OF SECURED TRANSACTIONS UNDER THE UNIFORM COMMERCIAL CODE ¶ 1.01[2][c], at 1-8 (rev. ed. 1993 & Supp. 1998).

3. Examples include the following: Is a guarantor a "debtor"? When will a secured party's repossession of collateral trigger a breach of the peace? Must a disposition notice be in writing? When is a disposition not commercially reasonable? Can a secured party's retention of collateral for an unreasonable period of time result in an involuntary waiver of any deficiency claim? Will a secured party's misconduct adversely affect its ability to pursue a deficiency claim?

4. Donald J. Rapson, *Default and Enforcement of Security Interests Under Revised Article 9*, 74 CHI.-KENT L.J. (1999) (forthcoming); *see also infra* notes 58, 286, and 590 and accompanying text (addressing whether a guarantor is a "debtor"); *infra* notes 184–96 and accompanying text (summarizing conduct that may breach the peace); *infra* notes 305–06 and accompanying text (discussing whether disposition notices must be written or whether they may be oral); *infra* notes 227–33 and accompanying text (analyzing commercial reasonableness); *infra* notes 576–81 and accompanying text (addressing involuntary strict foreclosure); *infra* notes 776–78 and accompanying text (reviewing effect of secured party's noncompliance on ability to recover deficiency claim).

The two sponsors of the U.C.C.—the National Conference of Commissioners on Uniform State Laws (NCCUSL)[5] and the American Law Institute (ALI)[6]—have issued a revised version of Article 9.[7] The most extensive changes have been made to the default provisions (which, for stylistic and substantive reasons, have expanded from seven to twenty-eight—an increase of 300%). With one exception,[8] this book examines each of these twenty-eight provisions.[9] It provides the inevitable (but hopefully useful) comparative analysis of current and revised law, offers drafting advice where appropriate, discusses perceived statutory weaknesses, and raises issues that may survive enactment. The

---

5. NCCUSL, an organization over a century old, is composed of representatives (Commissioners) from each state, the District of Columbia, Puerto Rico, and the U.S. Virgin Islands. Most Commissioners are appointed by the governor of the state; some derive appointment from their state's legislature or from another state body. All Commissioners are lawyers and serve without compensation. *See* Discussion, *Uniform State Laws: A Discussion Focused On Revision of the Uniform Commercial Code*, 22 OKLA. CITY U. L. REV. 257, 259 n.1 (1997).

6. The ALI, founded in 1923, has fostered improvement in the law through its Restatements of important areas of the common law. Its members currently exceed 2500, are primarily elected, and include "practitioners, judges, law professors, and others who have distinguished legal accomplishments." *Id.* at 260 n.2.

7. The Permanent Editorial Board for the Uniform Commercial Code (PEB) established a committee (PEB Study Group) in 1990 to study Article 9 and recommend any revisions it thought desirable. The PEB Study Group issued a report on Dec. 1, 1992. *See* PEB STUDY GROUP, UNIFORM COMMERCIAL CODE ARTICLE 9 (1992) [hereinafter PEB STUDY GROUP REPORT]. The PEB Study Group issued 30 default-related recommendations. *See id.* at 37–42 (recommendations only), 199–247 (recommendations and comments). On the PEB Study Group's recommendation, the PEB created a drafting committee (Drafting Committee) in 1993, charging it with the task of rewriting Article 9. William M. Burke chaired the Drafting Committee, and Professors Steven L. Harris (Chicago-Kent College of Law) and Charles W. Mooney, Jr. (University of Pennsylvania School of Law), served as co-reporters. The Drafting Committee met numerous times and issued several drafts of proposed Revised Article 9. Many of the drafts are available on the Internet. *See* NCCUSL, *Drafts of Uniform and Model Acts* (visited Oct. 25, 1999) <http://www.law.upenn.edu/library/ulc/ulc.htm>. Several of these drafts are cited in this book.

8. *See infra* note 109 (explaining omission).

9. The current version of Article 9, U.C.C. § 9-_____ (1995), is distinguished by the use of "current Article 9" or "current § _____" where appropriate. The revised version of Article 9, U.C.C. § 9-_____ (1999), is distinguished by the use of "Revised Article 9" or "revised § _____" where appropriate. This book cites to the official text and comments and not to text or comments in draft form, except where "Draft" is specifically cited.

book concludes that while the revised default provisions may be imperfect, they do significantly improve the flexibility, efficiency, and effectiveness of realization procedures for all interested parties and, therefore, are a notable improvement in the law.[10]

Timothy R. Zinnecker

10. This book makes no (direct) attempt to fuel the scholarly debates concerning (i) the utility of secured credit, (ii) the treatment afforded secured creditors in bankruptcy, and (iii) the degree to which a *commercial* code should apply to *consumer* transactions (and, if so, whether rules governing commercial and consumer transactions should be identical or different). A number of articles discuss the utility of secured credit. *See* David Gray Carlson, *On the Efficiency of Secured Lending*, 80 VA. L. REV. 2179 (1994); Lynn M. LoPucki, *The Unsecured Creditor's Bargain*, 80 VA. L. REV. 1887 (1994); Ronald J. Mann, *Explaining the Pattern of Secured Credit*, 110 HARV. L. REV. 625 (1997); Randal C. Picker, *Security Interests, Misbehavior, and Common Pools*, 59 U. CHI. L. REV. 645 (1992); Alan Schwartz, *The Continuing Puzzle of Secured Debt*, 37 VAND. L. REV. 1051 (1984); Robert E. Scott, *The Truth About Secured Financing*, 82 CORNELL L. REV. 1436 (1997); Robert E. Scott, *A Relational Theory of Secured Financing*, 86 COLUM. L. REV. 901 (1986); Paul M. Shupack, *Solving the Puzzle of Secured Transactions*, 41 RUTGERS L. REV. 1067 (1989); James J. White, *Efficiency Justifications for Personal Property Security*, 37 VAND. L. REV. 473 (1984). Numerous other articles debate the proper treatment to be afforded secured creditors in bankruptcy. *See* Lucian Arye Bebchuk & Jesse M. Fried, *The Uneasy Case for the Priority of Secured Claims in Bankruptcy: Further Thoughts and a Reply to Critics*, 82 CORNELL L. REV. 1279 (1997); Steven L. Harris & Charles W. Mooney, Jr., *Measuring the Social Costs and Benefits and Identifying the Victims of Subordinating Security Interests in Bankruptcy*, 82 CORNELL L. REV. 1349 (1997); Lynn M. LoPucki, *Should the Secured Credit Carve Out Apply Only in Bankruptcy? A Systems/Strategic Analysis*, 82 CORNELL L. REV. 1483 (1997); Steve H. Nickles, *Consider Process Before Substance, Commercial Law Consequences of the Bankruptcy System: Urging the Merger of the Article 9 Drafting Committee and the Bankruptcy Commission*, 69 AM. BANKR. L.J. 589 (1995); David M. Phillips, *Secured Credit and Bankruptcy: A Call for the Federalization of Personal Property Security Law*, 50 LAW & CONTEMP. PROBS. 53 (1987); Lawrence Ponoroff & F. Stephen Knippenberg, *The Immovable Object Versus the Irresistible Force: Rethinking the Relationship Between Secured Credit and Bankruptcy Policy*, 95 MICH. L. REV. 2234 (1997); Steven L. Schwarcz, *The Easy Case for the Priority of Secured Claims in Bankruptcy*, 47 DUKE L.J. 425 (1997); Steven L. Schwarcz, *Protecting Rights, Preventing Windfalls: A Model for Harmonizing State and Federal Laws on Floating Liens*, 75 N.C. L. REV. 403 (1997); James J. White, *No: It's a Populist Craving for a Petit Bourgeois Valhalla*, in *The Slippery Slope to Bankruptcy: Should Some Claimants Get a 'Carve-Out' from Secured Credit?*, BUS. LAW TODAY, Jan.–Feb. 1998, at 33; William J. Woodward Jr., *Yes: Reserve a Cushion of Free Assets for Unsecured Creditors*, in *The Slippery Slope to Bankruptcy: Should Some Claimants Get a 'Carve-Out' from Secured Credit?*, BUS. LAW TODAY, Jan.–Feb. 1998, at 32. Recent articles also discuss the propriety of including consumer transactions within the scope of Article 9 and whether consumer and commercial transactions should be governed by similar rules. *See* Michael M. Greenfield, *Article 9 and Consumer Transactions: The Need for Revision*, 48 CONSUMER FIN. L.Q. REP. 483 (1994); Fred H. Miller, *Consumers and the Code: The Search for the Proper Formula*, 75 WASH. U. L.Q. 187 (1997); Kathleen Patchel & Amelia H. Boss, *Consumer Transactions and the Code: Some Considerations*, 51 BUS. LAW. 1343 (1996).

REVISED § 9-601

Rights after Default; Judicial Enforcement; Consignor or Buyer of Accounts, Chattel Paper, Payment Intangibles, or Promissory Notes

A secured party's post-default rights under current Article 9 are found in part 5.[11] The post-default rights enjoyed by a secured party under Revised Article 9 are codified in part 6.[12] Most, but not all, of those rights are created by other provisions of part 6.[13] If the collateral consists of one or more bills of lading, warehouse receipts, or other documents of title, however, revised § 9-601 expressly permits the creditor to proceed either against the documents themselves or the goods described in the documents.[14] For example, a secured party that possesses a negotiable document of title for inventory stored by the debtor at a warehouse may, on the debtor's default, sell the document or, alternatively, surrender the document to the warehouse operator, obtain possession of the goods, and then sell the goods.[15]

Revised § 9-601 also permits a creditor to exercise non-Article 9 rights. For example, a creditor may reduce its claim to

---

11. *See* U.C.C. § 9-501(1) (1995) (opening sentence).

12. *See id.* § 9-601(a) (1999).

13. *See, e.g., id.* § 9-607 (permitting a creditor to pursue collection efforts against parties owing money to a debtor); *id.* § 9-609(b)(2) (permitting a creditor to take possession of collateral without judicial process); *id.* § 9-610 (permitting a creditor to dispose of collateral); *id.* § 9-620 (permitting a creditor to retain collateral in satisfaction of debt).

14. *See id.* § 9-601(a)(2). The secured party enjoys the same right under current Article 9. *See id.* § 9-501(1) (1995).

15. *See* 9 William D. Hawkland et al., Uniform Commercial Code Series § 9-501:5, at 632 (1997).

1

judgment and then have the collateral sold under a writ of execution.[16] A creditor that proceeds to liquidate the collateral under a writ of execution need not worry about complying with the procedural requirements of non-judicial collateral dispositions under part 6,[17] but this advantage may be meaningless if the value of the collateral is likely to decline during the time necessary to obtain the post-judgment writ and the debtor has no other marketable assets.[18]

Under current law, any judgment lien against the collateral relates back to the date of perfection, even if the secured party filed its financing statement on an earlier date.[19] Under revised § 9-601, the judicial lien relates back to the perfection date or the filing date, whichever is earlier.[20] This change mirrors the "first to file or perfect" priority rule[21] and, by providing a possibly earlier relation-back date, better protects a creditor whose security interest is perfected after, rather than at the moment when, the financing statement is filed (which may occur if the financing statement is filed before the security agreement is executed, the creditor extends any value, or the debtor acquires rights in the collateral).[22] This relation-back doctrine benefits the secured creditor

16. *See* U.C.C. § 9-601(a)(1) (1999). The secured party enjoys the same right under current Article 9. *See id.* § 9-501(1) (1995); *see also* Stewart v. Henning, 481 N.W.2d 230, 232 (N.D. 1992); Charles E. Brauer Co. v. NationsBank of Virginia, N.A., 466 S.E.2d 382, 386 (Va. 1996).

17. *See* U.C.C. § 9-601(f) (1999).

18. If the collateral is worth less than the secured debt, however, and the debtor has other marketable, non-exempt assets, then the creditor may conclude that its most prudent course of action is to ignore the collateral and instead pursue a judgment against the debtor and have the non-exempt assets sold under a writ of execution.

19. *See id.* § 9-501(5) (1995). One author suggests that the failure to relate the judgment lien back to the earlier of the two dates "was probably a drafting oversight." Eldon H. Reiley, *The Article 9 Revision Process and Interpretation of Original Article 9*, 31 UCC L.J. 261, 306 (1999).

20. *See id.* § 9-601(e) (1999). Subsection (e) also provides rules governing agricultural liens, which are not discussed in this book. *See infra* note 109.

21. *See* U.C.C. § 9-322(a)(1) (1999); *id.* § 9-312(5)(a) (1995).

22. *See id.* § 9-308(a) (1999) (providing a general rule that a security interest cannot be perfected before it has attached); *id.* § 9-203(a), (b) (indicating that a security interest attaches if the debtor has authenticated a security agreement that describes the collateral, the debtor has rights (or the power to transfer rights) in the collateral, and the creditor has given value); *cf id.* § 9-303(1) (1995) (stating a security interest must attach before it can be perfected); *id.* § 9-203(1) (indicating the steps of attachment).

in two ways. First, it negates any suggestion that the creditor somehow loses its original interest in the collateral and acquires a new interest that may be subject to a less favorable priority position in a dispute with a lien creditor or another secured creditor.[23] And second, if the debtor seeks bankruptcy protection shortly after the execution sale, the creditor's interest is less likely to be avoided as a voidable preference[24] because the sale itself does not trigger a transfer for antecedent debt[25] and the transfer date (a date earlier than the sale date) may fall outside the preference period.[26]

Revised § 9-601 states that the rights of part 6, whether statutory, contractual, or judicial, are cumulative and may be exercised simultaneously.[27] For example, a creditor may conduct an Article 9 disposition of repossessed collateral without forfeiting its right to bring a simultaneous or subsequent *in personam* action against the debtor.[28] Or, a creditor may pursue a judgment against the debtor without impairing its ability to concurrently or subsequently enforce its Article 9 rights in the collateral.[29]

Under current Article 9, a secured party that possesses collateral, whether before or after a default, has the rights and duties provided by § 9-207,[30] such as the limited right to operate the

---

23. *See id.* § 9-501 cmt. 6 (1995); *id.* § 9-601 cmt. 6 (1999).

24. *See generally* 11 U.S.C. § 547 (1994).

25. *See id.* § 547(b)(2); U.C.C. § 9-501 cmt. 6 (1995).

26. *See* 11 U.S.C. § 547(b)(4).

27. *See* U.C.C. § 9-601(c) (1999); *cf. id.* § 9-501(1) (1995) (indicating that rights and remedies are cumulative but not whether they may be exercised simultaneously). The creditor's ability to exercise its remedies cumulatively or concurrently may be subject to statutory or equitable limitations. *See, e.g.,* CAL. CIV. CODE §§ 1812.2, 1812.5 (West 1998) (forcing a creditor under a retail installment sales contract to either repossess and sell collateral and forego any possible deficiency action, or waive its rights in the collateral and seek an *in personam* judgment); Shedoudy v. Beverly Surgical Supply Co., 161 Cal. Rptr. 164, 166 (Ct. App. 1980) (invoking the doctrine of equitable marshalling); Coones v. FDIC, 848 P.2d 783, 797–98 (Wyo. 1993) (viewing creditor's pursuit of simultaneous remedies as harassment); U.C.C. § 9-601 cmt. 5 (1999) (requiring a secured party to act in good faith when simultaneously exercising remedies).

28. *See, e.g.,* Chase Manhattan Bank v. Natarelli, 401 N.Y.S.2d 404, 406–07 (Sup. Ct. 1977); U.C.C. § 9-615(d)(2) (1999) (imposing liability on obligors for any deficiency remaining after an Article 9 foreclosure sale).

29. *See, e.g.,* Fleming v. Carroll Publ'g Co., 621 A.2d 829, 835 (D.C. 1993).

30. *See* U.C.C. § 9-501(1) (1995) (fourth sentence).

collateral[31] and the duty to exercise reasonable care.[32] Under Revised Article 9, § 9-207 creates rights in favor of, and imposes duties on, a secured party when collateral is in its possession (such as inventory, equipment, or consumer goods) *or control* (for example, a deposit account, electronic chattel paper, investment property, or a letter-of-credit right).[33] A conforming change is reflected in revised § 9-601.[34]

As the first two words of revised § 9-601 indicate, the secured creditor cannot exercise its rights under part 6 until "[a]fter default."[35] The first-time visitor to Article 9 may be surprised to discover that, like its predecessor, part 6 does not define "default." Nor does any other provision of Article 9 or § 1-201

---

31. *See id.* § 9-207(4); *see also* Jorgensen v. Pressnall, 545 P.2d 1382, 1385–86 (Or. 1976) (permitting secured party to occupy mobile home in order to avoid water damage); McGinnis v. Wentworth Chevrolet Co., 645 P.2d 543, 546 (Or. Ct. App. 1982), *rev'd on other grounds*, 668 P.2d 365 (Or. 1983) (permitting creditor to remove vehicle from storage and drive it approximately 3000 miles during 26-month period); 2 GILMORE, *supra* note 2, § 42.11, at 1164 ("If a secured party takes possession of collateral which will deteriorate unless kept in use, he undoubtedly has a right to protect his own interest by using it and thus preserving its value.").

32. *See* U.C.C. § 9-207(1) (1995); *see also* Peoples State Bank & Trust Co. v. Krug (*In re* Krug), 189 B.R. 948, 959–61 (Bankr. D. Kan. 1995) (mem.) (concluding that a creditor which indiscriminately pastured bulls and females together breached duty to exercise reasonable care for purebred, registered, and registration-eligible cattle); Credit Alliance Corp. v. Timmco Equip., Inc., 507 So. 2d 657, 658–59 (Fla. Dist. Ct. App. 1987) (concluding creditor failed to exercise reasonable care when fire damaged loader); Royal West Airways, Inc. v. Valley Bank, 747 P.2d 895, 896–97 (Nev. 1987) (per curiam) (remanding to district court for determination of whether the creditor violated its custodial duties where the value of an airplane declined significantly after the creditor left it unattended and exposed to the elements, causing corrosion, rust, and tears to control surfaces, metal elements, and engines). Both versions of Article 9 permit a secured party and a debtor to contractually agree on the contours of "reasonable care" by adopting standards that are not manifestly unreasonable. *See* U.C.C. § 9-603(a) (1999); *id.* § 9-501(3) (1995). The term "reasonable" is not defined in the Code, but its excessive use prompted one author to write: "The word *reasonable*, effective in small doses, has been administered by the bucket, leaving the corpus of the Code reeling in dizzy confusion." David Mellinkoff, *The Language of the Uniform Commercial Code*, 77 YALE L.J. 185, 185–86 (1967).

33. *See* U.C.C. § 9-207 (1999). The steps necessary to "control" a deposit account, electronic chattel paper, investment property, and a letter-of-credit right are codified at *id.* §§ 9-104, 9-105, 9-106, and 9-107, respectively. *See also id.* § 9-102(a)(29) (defining "deposit account"); *id.* § 9-102(a)(31) (defining "electronic chattel paper"); *id.* § 9-102(a)(49) (defining "investment property"); *id.* § 9-102(a)(51) (defining "letter-of-credit right").

34. *See id.* § 9-601(b).

35. *Id.* § 9-601(a); *cf. id.* § 9-501(1) (1995) (explaining its application "[w]hen a debtor is in default").

(the "General Definitions") section of the U.C.C.) define this all-important term. Instead, the definition, which may be "as long as the creditor's arm and as broad as the counsel's imagination,"[36] is left to the agreement of the parties.[37] Why the Drafting Committee elected to reflect this deference to contract law through a statement in a comment rather than in one of the statutory provisions, or through an open-ended definition, is anyone's guess. Also worth noting in light of the perceived disparity in bargaining strength between secured creditors and consumer debtors is the failure of consumer advocates to persuade the Drafting Committee to limit "default" in consumer transactions to nonpayment of the debt and material impairment of collateral.[38] Nevertheless, secured creditors must be aware of state or federal law that may define "default" in such a narrow manner.[39]

Revised Article 9 does not attempt to address whether a creditor's post-default conduct can effectively waive a default if the

36. *See* 4 JAMES J. WHITE & ROBERT S. SUMMERS, UNIFORM COMMERCIAL CODE § 34-2, at 386 (4th ed. 1995).

37. *See* U.C.C. § 9-601 cmt. 3 (1999). The loan papers in many collateralized transactions define "default" in a manner that includes one or more of the following events: (i) the debtor fails to pay any of the debt when due; (ii) the debtor fails to comply with any covenant in any loan paper; (iii) the debtor becomes a party to (except as a claimant or creditor) or is made the subject of any proceeding under the Bankruptcy Code; (iv) the debtor fails to pay when due any other debt in excess (individually or collectively) of a specific amount; (v) any default exists under any other agreement to which the debtor is a party, the effect of which causes, or permits any other party thereto to cause, an amount in excess of a specific amount to become due and payable by the debtor before its stated maturity; and (vi) any representation or warranty made by the debtor contained in any loan paper was materially incorrect when made.

Absent any definition in the loan papers, a creditor may find that a "default" exists only if the debtor fails to pay any part of the secured debt. *See, e.g.,* Cofield v. Randolph County Comm'n, 90 F.3d 468, 471 (11th Cir. 1996); Jefferds v. Ellis, 486 N.Y.S.2d 649, 655 (Sup. Ct. 1985), *rev'd on other grounds*, 505 N.Y.S.2d 15 (App. Div. 1986).

38. The proposal "was generally rejected as being likely to breed frivolous litigation." Alvin C. Harrell, *UCC Article 9 Revisions Confront Issues Affecting Consumer Collateral*, 49 CONSUMER FIN. L.Q. REP. 256, 259 (1995).

39. *See, e.g.,* UNIF. CONSUMER CREDIT CODE § 5.109, 7A U.L.A. 152 (1999) (stating a default exists in a consumer credit transaction only if "the consumer fails to make a payment as required by agreement," or "the prospect of payment, performance, or realization of collateral is significantly impaired"). The Uniform Consumer Credit Code has been enacted in only five states: Colorado, Idaho, Iowa, Kansas, and Maine. *See id.* at 1. At least two other states have enacted a provision similar to Uniform Consumer Credit Code § 5.109. *See* MO. ANN. STAT. § 408.552 (West 1990); NEB. REV. STAT. § 45-1,105(5) (1993).

loan papers include a "no waiver" clause.[40] This issue, frequently litigated,[41] will continue to be resolved by law outside Article 9. Courts occasionally conclude that actions speak louder than words,[42] so prudence dictates that a secured party think twice before tolerating the debtor's failure to strictly comply with the terms of the loan papers.

A person that is either a consignor or a buyer of accounts, chattel paper, payment intangibles, or promissory notes falls within the definition of "secured party."[43] Nevertheless, with one exception, the rights and duties imposed by part 6 on a secured party do not apply to a buyer of such collateral or a consignor.[44] These parties are excluded from all but one of the provisions of part 6 because (i) buyers usually acquire the entire interest in the property and, therefore, should be permitted to enforce their rights in the property without regard to provisions enacted to protect a debtor's equitable interest, and (ii) other law governs the enforcement rights of a consignor.[45]

---

40. *See* U.C.C. § 9-601 cmt. 3 (1999). A typical "no waiver" (or "anti-waiver") clause, a boilerplate provision in most loan papers, follows:

> The acceptance by Lender at any time and from time to time of partial payment on the secured obligation shall not be deemed to be a waiver of any Default then existing. No waiver by Lender of any Default shall be deemed to be a waiver of any other then-existing or subsequent Default. No delay or omission by Lender in exercising any right or remedy shall impair that right or remedy or be construed as a waiver thereof, nor shall any single or partial exercise of any right or remedy preclude other or further exercise of that, or any other, right or remedy.

41. *See, e.g.,* Lewis v. National City Bank, 814 F. Supp. 696, 702 (N.D. Ill. 1993), *aff'd*, 23 F.3d 410 (7th Cir. 1994); B.P.G. Autoland Jeep-Eagle, Inc. v. Chrysler Credit Corp., 799 F. Supp. 1250, 1255–56 (D. Mass. 1992); Riley State Bank v. Spillman, 750 P.2d 1024, 1028 (Kan. 1988); Kessel v. Western Sav. Credit Union, 463 N.W.2d 629, 631 (N.D. 1990).

42. *See, e.g.,* Westinghouse Credit Corp. v. Shelton, 645 F.2d 869, 873–74 (10th Cir. 1981) (remanding for determination whether creditor's acceptance of payments habitually late by one to three months established course of performance that modified payment terms and "anti-waiver" clause of contract); Mercedes-Benz Credit Corp. v. Morgan, 850 S.W.2d 297, 299–300 (Ark. 1993) (concluding secured creditor's routine acceptance of delinquent payments effectively amended contractual payment and enforcement provisions); Moe v. John Deere Co., 516 N.W.2d 332, 338 (S.D. 1994) (holding creditor's repeated acceptance of late payments obligated creditor to notify debtor, before repossessing collateral, that debtor was expected to strictly comply with contract terms). *See also* 2 GILMORE, *supra* note 2, § 44.1, at 1214 ("[C]ourts pay little attention to clauses which appear to say that meaningful acts are meaningless and that the secured party can blow hot or cold as he chooses.").

43. *See* U.C.C. § 9-102(a)(72)(C), (D) (1999).

44. *See id.* § 9-601(g).

45. *See id.* § 9-601 cmt. 9.

REVISED § 9-602

WAIVER AND VARIANCE OF RIGHTS AND DUTIES

One of the basic tenets of the U.C.C. is freedom of contract. This principle is codified in current § 1-102, which permits parties to vary U.C.C. provisions by agreement.[46] This freedom is subject to a general limitation on the ability to disclaim Code-imposed duties of good faith, diligence, reasonableness, and care.[47] The principle is further subject to express limitations stated in other provisions of the U.C.C.[48] One provision is current § 9-501, which prohibits waivers or variances of specific rights given to the debtor, and selected duties imposed on the creditor, after default.[49] The drafters viewed § 9-501(3) as a codification of the "long-standing and deeply rooted attitude" that "agreements designed to cut down the debtor's rights and free the secured party of his duties" after default—when overreaching may reach its apex—should be viewed "with suspicion."[50] The concern with potential overreaching under Revised Article 9 remains, as evidenced by revised § 9-602, which, like its predecessor, expressly prohibits waivers and variances of specific rights and duties[51]

46. *See id.* § 1-102(3) (1995).
47. *See id.*
48. *See id.*
49. *See id.* § 9-501(3).
50. *See id.* § 9-501 cmt. 4; *see also* Walker v. Grant County Sav. & Loan Ass'n, 803 S.W.2d 913, 916 (Ark. 1991) ("One clear policy reason underlying Article 9 default provisions is the protection of post default debtors from the potential of overbearing tactics and intimidation by secured parties. After default the secured party is unquestionably in a position of control and even dominance.").
51. *See* U.C.C. § 9-602 & cmt. 2 (1999). This section is expressly subject to § 9-624, which provides three limited waivers. *See id.* (beginning "Except as otherwise provided in § 9-624"); *infra* notes 686–718 and accompanying text (discussing § 9-624).

(which are discussed elsewhere in this book as part of the analysis of the provision that creates the right or imposes the duty).

There are three notable differences between current § 9-501(3) and revised § 9-602. First, the revised list of statutes that create non-waivable rights and duties is much longer than the current list.[52] One reason is that some of the rights and duties existing under both versions of Article 9 are not expressly non-waivable under current Article 9 but are expressly non-waivable under Revised Article 9.[53] Also, part 6 creates additional non-waivable rights in favor of the debtor[54] and imposes more non-waivable duties on the secured party.[55]

Second, § 9-501(3) prohibits waivers or variances of rights given to a "debtor,"[56] a person who owes payment or other performance of the secured obligation, whether or not the person owns or has rights in the collateral.[57] Whether a guarantor is a "debtor" (and, therefore, a party either with non-waivable rights or to whom the secured party owes a non-waivable duty) is an issue frequently litigated under current Article 9.[58] That issue dis-

---

52. *Compare id.* § 9-501(3) (1995) (referencing seven provisions), *with id.* § 9-602 (1999) (referencing 20 provisions).

53. For example, current § 9-503 permits a creditor, after default, to seize collateral without judicial process if the creditor can do so without breaching the peace. *Id.* § 9-503 (1995). This duty, to act without breaching the peace, is not included among the non-waivable duties listed in § 9-501(3). Revised Article 9 continues to permit a creditor to seize collateral, after default, without judicial process so long as it does not breach the peace. *See id.* § 9-609(b)(2) (1999). Under Revised Article 9, this duty cannot be waived or varied. *Id.* § 9-602(6).

54. *See, e.g., id.* § 9-616(e) (1999) (creating, in favor of debtors and consumer obligors, the right to request and receive from the secured party an explanation of the calculated surplus or deficiency). This right is non-waivable under § 9-602(9).

55. *See, e.g., id.* § 9-615(f) (forcing the secured party to adopt a special method of calculating a deficiency or surplus if one of three listed parties is the transferee). This duty is non-waivable under § 9-602(8).

56. *Id.* § 9-501(3) (1995).

57. *See id.* § 9-105(1)(d).

58. *See, e.g.,* FDIC v. Payne, 973 F.2d 403, 409 (5th Cir. 1992); SNCB Corp. Fin. Ltd. v. Schuster, 877 F. Supp. 820, 827 (S.D.N.Y. 1994), *aff'd*, 71 F.3d 406 (2d Cir. 1995); Chrysler Credit Corp. v. B.J.M., Jr., Inc., 834 F. Supp. 813, 833 (E.D. Pa. 1993); Hollander v. California Mfg. Enters., Inc., 51 Cal. Rptr. 2d 694, 696 (Ct. App. 1996); May v. Women's Bank, N.A., 807 P.2d 1145, 1147–51 (Colo. 1991); United States v. Jensen, 418 N.W.2d 65, 65–67 (Iowa 1988); Ford Motor Credit Co. v. Thompson Mach., Inc., 649 A.2d 19, 21–22 (Me. 1994); McKesson Corp. v. Colman's Grant Village, Inc., 938 S.W.2d 631, 633 (Mo. Ct. App. 1997); Caterpillar Fin. Servs. Corp. v. Wells, 651 A.2d 507, 518–19 (N.J. Super. Ct. Law Div. 1994); Rabinowitz v. The Cadle Co. II, 993 S.W.2d 796,

appears under Revised Article 9, which not only redefines "debtor"[59] but also adds a new term, "obligor," that is defined in a manner that includes any guarantor.[60] Revised § 9-602 acknowledges the two terms by referring to rights given "to a debtor or obligor."[61]

Third, § 9-501(3) strongly implies, but does not expressly state, that a debtor cannot waive or vary the enumerated rights and duties.[62] Revised § 9-602 expressly states that "the debtor or obligor may not waive or vary the rules stated" in the referenced sections.[63] Revised § 9-602 does not, however, prohibit parties from agreeing to settle claims for prior conduct that may have violated or breached the specific rights or duties, even if the settlement agreement includes language that could be construed as a waiver.[64]

798–800 (Tex. App.—Dallas 1999); *see also* Beth C. Housman, Note, *Guarantors as Debtors Under Uniform Commercial Code § 9-501(3)*, 56 FORDHAM L. REV. 745, 749 n.34 (1988) (citing cases).

59. *See* U.C.C. § 9-102(a)(28) (1999).

60. *See id.* § 9-102(a)(59) (including within the definition of "obligor" any person that "owes payment or other performance of the obligation" or "is otherwise accountable in whole or in part for payment or other performance of the obligation").

61. *Id.* § 9-602.

62. *See id.* § 9-501(3) (1995) ("[T]he rules stated in the subsections referred to below may not be waived or varied . . . .").

63. *Id.* § 9-602 (1999).

64. *See id.* § 9-602 cmt. 3.

REVISED § 9-603

AGREEMENT ON STANDARDS CONCERNING RIGHTS AND DUTIES

Although current § 9-501 prohibits parties from waiving or varying specific rights and duties, the section permits parties to determine, by agreement, the standards by which the fulfillment of those rights and duties will be measured.[65] For example, current § 9-504 requires a secured creditor to send "reasonable notification" of most post-default collateral dispositions to a debtor.[66] In an attempt to define the contours of the quoted term,[67] creditors often include some variation of the following provision in their collateral documents: "Notice sent at least _____ calendar days prior to any action to which the notice relates is deemed reasonable notification." This agreed-upon standard is enforceable so long as it is not "manifestly unreasonable."[68]

---

65. *See id.* § 9-501(3) (1995).

66. *See id.* § 9-504(3).

67. Other than requiring (i) a notice of public disposition to state the time and place of disposition, and (ii) a notice of private disposition to include the time after which the disposition will occur, § 9-504(3) offers no guidance on the meaning of "reasonable notification."

68. *See id.* § 9-501(3); *see also* Mullins v. Horne, 587 P.2d 773, 776–77 (Ariz. Ct. App. 1978) (concluding provision in promissory note stating that notice mailed at least five days prior to collateral disposition *"shall be deemed reasonably and properly given"* was not manifestly unreasonable); First Bank and Trust Co. v. Mitchell, 473 N.Y.S.2d 697, 701 n.1 (Sup. Ct. 1984) ("Notice sent five days in advance of sale is the standard agreed to by the parties and is not manifestly unreasonable."). Creditors also have successfully drafted contractual standards for "commercially reasonable" dispositions under § 9-504(3). *See, e.g.,* Ford Motor Credit Co. v. Solway, 825 F.2d 1213, 1216–17 (7th Cir. 1987) (upholding contractual provision stating that any sale of collateral to the highest of at least three bidders would be deemed a commercially reasonable disposition).

This contractual freedom to define standards of performance in a manner not manifestly unreasonable continues under revised § 9-603.[69] There are two differences, however, between revised § 9-603 and its predecessor. First, current § 9-501 refers to rights given to a "debtor."[70] The language of revised § 9-603 acknowledges that part 6 gives rights to a "debtor" and an "obligor."[71]

And second, unlike current § 9-501, revised § 9-603 expressly prohibits parties from attempting to agree on what actions by a creditor, engaged in self-help repossession, will not breach the peace.[72] This express prohibition codifies the result reached in many cases where creditors unsuccessfully argued that they did not breach the peace during repossession because their actions were permitted by provisions in the loan documents.[73] The prohibition makes sense, as the goal of protecting

---

69. *See* U.C.C. § 9-603(a) (1999); *see also id.* § 1-102(3) (1995) (permitting parties to agree on the standards by which the performance of the U.C.C.-imposed, nonwaivable, obligations of good faith, diligence, reasonableness, and care are to be measured if the agreed-upon standards are not manifestly unreasonable). The "agreement" that establishes the standards need not be written. *See id.* § 1-201(3) (defining "agreement" as "the bargain of the parties in fact as found in their language *or by implication from other circumstances*," such as course of dealing, course of performance, or usage of trade) (emphasis added).

70. *See id.* § 9-501(3) (1995).

71. *See id.* § 9-603(a) (1999).

72. *See id.* § 9-603(b); *see also id.* § 9-609(b)(2) (imposing the duty to avoid breaching the peace); *id.* § 9-602(6) (prohibiting a waiver or variance of the duty); *cf. id.* § 9-503 (1995) (imposing the same duty); *id.* § 9-501(3) (omitting the duty from the list of duties that cannot be waived or varied); 9 HAWKLAND ET AL., *supra* note 15, § 9-503:3, at 680 ("Although the Code does not explicitly state that the debtor can waive his or her right to protest self-help repossession, any such waiver clause in a security agreement would probably not be enforceable.").

73. *See, e.g.,* Renaire Corp. v. Vaughn, 142 A.2d 148, 150 (D.C. 1958) ("While the contract gave the vendor the right to enter upon the premises it did not expressly give the right to break in in order to enter and we refuse to hold that it impliedly gave that right."); Girard v. Anderson, 257 N.W. 400, 402–03 (Iowa 1934) ("An agreement permitting a family's home to be broken open and entered [into] for the purpose of forcibly taking possession of property therein is contrary to good public policy and void to that extent."); Hileman v. Harter Bank & Trust Co., 186 N.E.2d 853, 854 (Ohio 1962) (holding that a clause permitting a chattel mortgagor to "make use of such force as may be necessary to enter upon, with or without breaking into any premises where the chattel(s) may be found and take possession thereof" did not authorize conduct that constituted a breaking and entering); *see also* Kimble v. Universal TV Rental, Inc., 417 N.E.2d 597, 601 n.4 (Ohio—Franklin County Mun. Ct. 1980) ("[I]t is probable that a contract . . . which authorized a repossession that constituted a breach of the peace, would violate public policy and would be unconscionable and unenforceable.").

life and property significantly outweighs any interest in preserving contractual expectations.

The definition of "manifestly unreasonable" is not found in revised § 9-603 or elsewhere in the U.C.C.[74] The term probably resides on the spectrum of reasonableness somewhere between "unreasonable" and "unconscionable." But knowing where to place the term between those two points remains uncertain. What is certain is that courts will be asked to engage in some line-drawing, not all courts will draw the line in the same place, and the line may move closer to "unreasonable" if the debtor is a consumer. Perhaps the flexible, or fact-sensitive, scope of the term will provide benefits otherwise destroyed by fixed and rigid contours, but those benefits come at the expense of uniformity and clarity—two of the stated purposes and policies of the U.C.C.[75]

---

74. Creditors may be pleased that the revision did not create, and make applicable to selected consumer transactions, a more stringent standard of "not unreasonable"—a proposal that was debated and rejected during the drafting process. *See* U.C.C. § 9-501(e) (Draft July 28–Aug. 4, 1995) (proposing a "not unreasonable" test in consumer secured transactions and a "not manifestly unreasonable" test in all other transactions). Not until two years later was the proposal abandoned in favor of a uniform "not manifestly unreasonable" test. *See id.* § 9-603 (Draft Aug. 7, 1997). Consumer representatives advocated a "not unreasonable" standard, contending "that the 'manifestly unreasonable' standard gives too much discretion to creditors to impose onerous standards on consumers." Alvin C. Harrell, *UCC Article 9 Drafting Committee March 1996 Meeting Considers Consumer-Related Collateral*, 50 Consumer Fin. L.Q. Rep. 95, 96 (1996). Although the Drafting Committee adopted a uniform "not manifestly unreasonable" standard, consumer representatives may take solace in the likelihood that a court may interpret the standard more strictly in consumer transactions than in commercial transactions. *See id.*

75. *See* U.C.C. § 1-102(2) (1995); *see also* William J. Woodward, Jr., *The Realist and Secured Credit: Grant Gilmore, Common-Law Courts, and the Article 9 Reform Process*, 82 Cornell L. Rev. 1511, 1522 (1997) ("[W]ithout 'uniformity,' the UCC loses its great appeal as a commercial statute."); *cf.* Fred H. Miller, *Realism Not Idealism in Uniform Laws—Observations from the Revision of the UCC*, 39 S. Tex. L. Rev. 707, 718 n.28 (1998) (summarizing the detriments of nonuniformity).

REVISED § 9-604

PROCEDURE IF SECURITY AGREEMENT COVERS REAL PROPERTY OR FIXTURES

In many loan transactions, the collateral includes both real and personal property. Usually the creditor's interest in personal property is created through the security agreement, and the interest in real estate is evidenced by a mortgage or deed of trust. Upon default, the creditor will pursue its rights against the personal property under Article 9 provisions and its rights against the real estate under applicable real property law. Occasionally, the interest in both types of collateral is created through a single document. Under current § 9-501, a creditor whose security agreement covers both types of collateral can proceed against the personal property under either the provisions of part 5 of current Article 9 or applicable real estate law, in which case the part 5 provisions are inapplicable.[76]

The secured party continues to enjoy the same option under revised § 9-604. The creditor can pursue its rights against the personal property under the provisions of part 6 of Revised Article 9 or in accordance with local property law.[77] Revised § 9-604

---

76. *See* U.C.C. § 9-501(4) (1995); *see also* FDIC v. Hulsey, 22 F.3d 1472, 1485 (10th Cir. 1994) (acknowledging that § 9-501(4) provides the creditor with "alternative ways to proceed if both real and personal property are involved"); United States v. Dawson, 929 F.2d 1336, 1340 (8th Cir. 1991) (observing that § 9-501(4) permits a creditor with an interest in both real and personal property to bring a single action against all of the collateral under real property law or separate actions against the real estate under real property law and the personal property under the U.C.C.); Lenape State Bank v. Winslow Corp., 523 A.2d 223, 228 (N.J. Super. Ct. App. Div. 1987) (holding that local real estate law governed, and U.C.C. was inapplicable to, disposition of real and personal property in single foreclosure action).

77. *See* U.C.C. § 9-604(a) (1999).

13

also expressly states what current § 9-501(4) implies: the creditor does not prejudice its rights against the real estate if it elects to exercise its U.C.C. rights against the personal property.[78] Which option should a creditor pursue? A prudent creditor will make its election only after becoming familiar with the relevant provisions of both the U.C.C. and the local property code and evaluating a host of factors, including: (i) the amount of the unpaid secured debt; (ii) the potential fair market value of the various types of collateral, both individually and collectively; (iii) any limits imposed by local non-U.C.C. law on the creditor's ability to pursue concurrent or subsequent actions; (iv) the rights afforded by the U.C.C. and real estate law; (v) the convenience and expediency of complying with the procedural and substantive requirements imposed on a creditor that wishes to exercise those rights; and (vi) the penalties that may be assessed against the creditor who fails to comply with those requirements.

Revised § 9-604 also offers guidance when the collateral is goods that are, or may become, fixtures.[79] The creditor may exercise any of its U.C.C. rights and remedies against the fixtures[80] or it can opt out of part 6 of Revised Article 9 and be governed by applicable real estate law.[81] The U.C.C. permits the creditor to remove the fixture from the real property after default,[82] subject to two significant statutory limitations. First, the creditor cannot remove the fixture without judicial process if doing so will

---

78. *See id.* § 9-604(a)(1); *see also Hulsey*, 22 F.3d at 1485 ("[B]y choosing to proceed under article 9 for the personal property, the FDIC was not thereafter precluded from foreclosing on the leasehold.").

79. The definition of "fixtures" remains substantially unchanged. *Compare* U.C.C. § 9-313(1)(a) (1995) (defining "fixtures" as goods that "become so related to particular real estate that an interest in them arises under real estate law"), *with id.* § 9-102(a)(41) (1999) (defining "fixtures" as "goods that have become so related to particular real property that an interest in them arises under real property law").

80. By expressly permitting the fixture financier to exercise any of its U.C.C. rights, revised § 9-604(b) effectively overrules cases holding that the only post-default U.C.C. remedy available to the fixture financier is removal. *See, e.g.,* Maplewood Bank & Trust v. Sears, Roebuck & Co., 625 A.2d 537, 540 (N.J. Super. Ct. App. Div. 1993) ("We are also persuaded that Sears is not entitled to any remedy, other than removal of the fixtures, based on equitable principles."), *aff'd,* 638 A.2d 140 (N.J. 1994).

81. *See* U.C.C. § 9-604(b) (1999).

82. *See id.* § 9-604(c).

breach the peace.[83] Second, as under current law, the creditor's interest must enjoy priority over the competing interest of any owner or encumbrancer of the real property.[84]

Just because a creditor can overcome these two statutory roadblocks to removal does not necessarily mean that the creditor should, or will, exercise that remedy. The creditor may voluntarily forego this right if removal is impracticable or cost-prohibitive, such as when the fixture is specially designed for the real estate and will have negligible value after removal.[85] Additionally, concepts of good faith and commercial reasonableness, equitable principles, or judicial interference may thwart removal of certain fixtures—such as a heating system from a Minneapolis elementary school in January or an air conditioning unit from a Phoenix nursing home in July—if health or safety would be adversely affected.[86]

The creditor that exercises its statutory right of removal is obligated to promptly reimburse any person, other than the debtor, with an interest in the real estate for the cost of repairing any physical injury to the real estate, but not for any diminution in value of the real estate caused by the absence of the fixture or the need to replace it.[87] For example, by removing a kitchen sink from a dwelling, the creditor may cause damage of $150 to the

---

83. See id. (permitting a creditor to remove a fixture "[s]ubject to the other provisions of this part"); id. § 9-609(b)(2) (permitting self-help repossession that does not breach the peace).

84. See id. § 9-604(c); cf. id. § 9-313(8) (1995). The priority scheme for fixtures has been relocated from current § 9-313 to revised § 9-334. Revised Article 9 does not define "encumbrancer." Presumably the term refers to a person with an "encumbrance," a term defined comparably under Revised Article 9 and current Article 9. See id. § 9-102(a)(32) (1999); id. § 9-105(1)(g) (1995).

85. See Morris G. Shanker, An Integrated Financing System for Purchase Money Collateral: A Proposed Solution to the Fixture Problem Under § 9-313 of the Uniform Commercial Code, 73 YALE L.J. 788, 805 (1964) (using an elevator as an example).

86. See id. at 804–05.

87. U.C.C. § 9-604(c) (1999). The creditor has the same obligation under current Article 9. See id. § 9-313(8) (1995); see also Coffee County Bank v. Hughes, 423 So. 2d 831, 834 (Ala. 1982) (holding that a mortgagee could recover damages for alleged physical injury to mortgaged property caused by removal of mobile home but not damages for decrease in market value of mortgaged property caused by absence of mobile home). The statute does not indicate which person is entitled to reimbursement if more than one person claims an interest in the real estate. In such a case, the fixture financier should consider depositing the appropriate amount with the court and bringing an interpleader action against all real estate claimants.

countertops and diminish the market value of the residence by $750; the creditor is obligated to pay only $150. The party entitled to reimbursement enjoys the statutory right to block removal until the creditor provides "adequate assurance" that it will honor its reimbursement obligation.[88] The quoted term is not defined, but presumably may take any mutually agreeable form, such as a cash deposit, letter of credit, or indemnification agreement. Once the creditor has provided adequate assurance, a party entitled to reimbursement should not unreasonably interfere with removal. Otherwise, the interfering party may be liable for conversion.[89]

A creditor that does not, or cannot, remove the fixture may conclude that its best course of action is to proceed judicially against the debtor, reduce its claim to judgment, and then enforce the judgment against the debtor's nonexempt assets.[90] Alternatively, a creditor that cannot remove a fixture because its interest is junior to one or more real estate claimants may be able to claim a share of any proceeds of any foreclosure sale of the real estate.[91] Even if the creditor is able to prove what percentage of the proceeds represents the value of the fixture, however, the creditor's claim may have "little value" after the holders of the prior real estate interests are paid and the costs of foreclosure are satisfied.[92] Although the creditor may argue that its interest in the fixture survives any foreclosure and remains effective against the real estate purchaser,[93] the argument may ring hollow if local real estate foreclosure law terminates all junior interests.

Two other options are available to the fixture financier that foregoes removal. First, the creditor may render the fixture unus-

---

88. U.C.C. § 9-604(c) (1999); *cf. id.* § 9-313(8) (1995) (requiring "adequate security").

89. *See* Leban Store Fixture Co. v. August Properties, 499 N.Y.S.2d 109, 110–11 (App. Div. 1986) (affirming judgment of $16,536 for conversion against landlord that unreasonably interfered with secured party's right to remove items sold to tenant).

90. *See* U.C.C. § 9-601(a)(1) (1999) (permitting secured party to proceed judicially against debtor); *see also* Stewart v. Henning, 481 N.W.2d 230, 232 (N.D. 1992) (holding creditor need not foreclose on its real and personal property liens before pursuing money judgment against debtor).

91. *See* 9 Hawkland et al., *supra* note 15, § 9-313:7, at 344.

92. *Id.*

93. *See* U.C.C. § 9-315(a)(1) (1999) (continuing the effectiveness of a security interest following disposition of collateral unless the creditor authorized the disposition free of the security interest).

able if it is equipment.[94] This may be an attractive option if removing and storing the equipment pending disposition is expensive, impractical, or both.[95] The statute does not expressly require the creditor to avoid breaching the peace,[96] but prudence suggests that the creditor not act in a manner that triggers tort liability.[97] And second, as under current law, the creditor may dispose of the fixture (whether or not rendered unusable) while it remains on the debtor's premises, in accordance with other applicable default provisions.[98]

---

94. *See id.* § 9-609(a)(2). The creditor enjoys the same right under current Article 9. *See id.* § 9-503 (1995). Because revised § 9-609 references "equipment," the creditor does not enjoy a statutory right to render unusable fixtures that may be consumer goods (e.g., refrigerators, water heaters, etc.).

95. *Id.* § 9-503 (1995).

96. *But see* 9 HAWKLAND ET AL., *supra* note 15, § 9-313:7, at 344 ("[W]hen the fixture is equipment, [the creditor should be able] to render it unusable if it can be done without a breach of the peace."); *cf.* U.C.C. § 2A-525 (permitting a lessor to take possession of goods or render them unusable without judicial process if action is taken without breaching the peace).

97. *See also* U.C.C. § 9-503 cmt. ("The authorization to render equipment unusable . . . would not justify unreasonable action by the secured party, since, under § 9-504(3), all his actions in connection with disposition must be taken in a 'commercially reasonable manner.' ").

98. *See id.* § 9-609(a)(2) (1999); *id.* § 9-503 (1995).

REVISED § 9-605

Unknown Debtor or Secondary Obligor

Revised Article 9 imposes many duties on a secured party, some of which are owed to a debtor,[99] a secondary obligor,[100] or a party that has filed a financing statement against the debtor.[101] It is conceivable that the secured creditor may fail to perform a duty owed to a party because it is not aware of that party's existence. For example, without the secured party's knowledge, the original debtor may have sold the collateral to a new owner that has become a "new debtor" under revised § 9-203(e) and as defined at revised § 9-102(a)(56). A secured party of record may have also acquired its status by purchasing a loan funded by the original secured party that failed to disclose to the new secured party the existence of a guarantor or other secondary obligor. Finally, a public official may provide the secured party with a search report against the debtor that erroneously omits one or more filings submitted by another secured party.

---

99. See, e.g., id. § 9-611(c)(1) (1999) (requiring a secured party to send a disposition notice to a debtor); id. § 9-616(b) (obligating a secured party to send an explanation of the calculated surplus or deficiency to a debtor in a consumer-goods transaction); see also id. § 9-102(a)(28) (defining "debtor").

100. See, e.g., id. § 9-611(c)(2) (requiring a secured party to send a disposition notice to any secondary obligor); id. § 9-621(b) (compelling a secured party to send a proposal of partial strict foreclosure to any secondary obligor); see also id. § 9-102(a)(71) (defining "secondary obligor").

101. See, e.g., id. § 9-611(c)(3)(B) (obligating a secured party to send a disposition notice to certain parties that have filed financing statements against the debtor); id. § 9-621(a)(2) (forcing a secured party to send a proposal of strict foreclosure to certain parties that have filed financing statements against the debtor).

In these and other similar situations, it seems unfair to ask the secured party to perform a duty in favor of an unknown party. Revised § 9-605 comes to the secured party's rescue. This new section relieves a secured party of its duty to a person that is a debtor or obligor unless the secured party "knows" (i) that a person is either a debtor or an obligor, (ii) the person's identity, and (iii) how to communicate with that person.[102] The section also relieves a secured party of its duty to any other secured party or a lienholder that has filed a financing statement against a person unless the secured party knows (i) that the person is a debtor, and (ii) the person's identity.[103]

An issue that may arise with some frequency is whether the secured party must take steps to acquire the requisite knowledge before it can claim the protection afforded by revised § 9-605. For example, a secured party may know that an individual is a debtor, know the debtor's identity (e.g., Timothy R. Zinnecker), and yet not know how to communicate with the debtor because the loan documents list either no address or a known stale address. Must the secured party review telephone books and on-line address listings before it is relieved of any duties owed to the debtor? Or may the secured party confine its knowledge to information provided solely by the loan papers? Presumably the non-waivable obligation to act in good faith[104] prevents the secured party from burying its

---

102. See id. § 9-605(1); see also id. § 1-201(25) (1995) ("A person 'knows' . . . of a fact when he has actual knowledge of it."). Revised § 9-628(a)(1) is a companion exculpatory provision. For much of the drafting process, the two companion provisions were significantly inconsistent: revised § 9-605 referenced "secondary obligor," and revised § 9-628 referenced "obligor." See, e.g., id. § 9-605 (Draft approved at NCCUSL Annual Meeting, July 30, 1998) (referencing "secondary obligor"); id. § 9-628(a) (referencing "obligor"). The author mentioned this inconsistency in a memorandum dated Sept. 2, 1998, and e-mailed to the co-reporters of the Drafting Committee on or about the same date, hoping that the text would be corrected or the inconsistency explained in the official comments which were not yet drafted. See Memorandum from Timothy R. Zinnecker, Associate Professor, South Texas College of Law, to Steven L. Harris and Charles W. Mooney, Jr. (Sept. 2, 1998) (on file with The Business Lawyer, University of Maryland School of Law) [hereinafter Zinnecker Memorandum]. The inconsistency was corrected in the next draft. See U.C.C. § 9-605 (Draft Nov. 16, 1998) (referencing "obligor").

103. See id. § 9-605(2) (1999). Revised § 9-628(a)(1) is a companion exculpatory provision.

104. See id. § 1-203 (1995) (obligating a party to perform and enforce every contract or duty created by the U.C.C. in good faith); id. § 1-102(3) (prohibiting a party

head in the sand. But whether, and to what extent, the secured party must take affirmative steps to acquire the requisite knowledge remains unclear.[105]

In addition to creating duties in favor of another secured party or lienholder that has filed a financing statement against the debtor,[106] Revised Article 9 also creates duties in favor of a party that holds a security interest perfected by compliance with a statute, regulation, or treaty.[107] If a secured party's knowledge of the existence of any party hinges on the accuracy of any information provided by the applicable official, then it seems reasonable to relieve the secured party of its duty toward that person if the information provided by the official fails to provide the secured party with the requisite knowledge (absent any independent knowledge). The Drafting Committee curiously did not draft revised § 9-605 accordingly.[108]

---

from disclaiming its duty to act in good faith); *id.* § 9-102(c) (1999) (incorporating Article 1 principles into Revised Article 9).

Current Article 9 does not define "good faith" but instead incorporates the Article 1 definition. Revised Article 9 adopts a new and broader definition. *Compare id.* § 1-201(19) (1995) (defining "good faith" as "honesty in fact in the conduct or transaction concerned"), *with id.* § 9-102(a)(43) (1999) (defining "good faith" as "honesty in fact and the observance of reasonable commercial standards of fair dealing"). This new definition follows the definition of "good faith" as applied to merchants under Article 2, as incorporated into Article 2A, and as used in revised Article 3, revised Article 4, Article 4A, and revised Article 8. *See id.* § 2-103(1)(b) (1995); *id.* § 2A-103(3); *id.* § 3-103(a)(4); *id.* § 4-101(c); *id.* § 4A-105(a)(6); *id.* § 8-102(a)(10). Revised Article 5 retains the narrower definition. *See id.* § 5-102(a)(7) & cmt. 3.

105. The author mentioned this concern to the Drafting Committee. *See* Zinnecker Memorandum, *supra* note 102, at 1.

106. *See supra* note 101.

107. *See, e.g.,* U.C.C. § 9-611(c)(3)(C) (1999) (obligating a secured party to send a disposition notice to certain creditors that have perfected a security interest by complying with selected statutes, regulations, or treaties); *id.* § 9-621(a)(3) (requiring a secured party to send a proposal of strict foreclosure to certain creditors that have perfected a security interest by complying with selected statutes, regulations, or treaties).

108. The author raised this issue with the Drafting Committee. *See* Zinnecker Memorandum, *supra* note 102, at 1–2. Revised § 9-605 could have been drafted as follows (new language italicized):

A secured party does not owe a duty based on its status as secured party . . . to a secured party or lienholder that has filed a financing statement against a person, *or to a secured party that has perfected a security interest against the person by complying with a statute, regulation, or treaty described in § 9-311(a),* unless the secured party knows: (A) that the person is a debtor; and (B) the identity of the person.

See id. § 9-605; *cf. id.* § 9-611(e) (providing a safe harbor for a secured party that relies on information provided in a report that omits a filed financing statement).

REVISED § 9-607[109]

COLLECTION AND ENFORCEMENT BY SECURED PARTY

The collateral in many secured transactions includes accounts, chattel paper, general intangibles, and instruments. The loan documents may specifically address whether the obligors should continue to remit payments on that collateral to the debtor or, instead, the secured party. Whether or not the secured party and debtor contractually agree on collection procedures, current Article 9 expressly provides the secured party with collection rights after default. Under current § 9-502, a secured party is permitted to notify an account debtor, or any obligor on an instrument serving as collateral, to make payment to the secured party, whether or not the security arrangement permitted the debtor to receive payment before default.[110] Additionally, the creditor may take control of any identifiable proceeds of the collateral,[111] such as cash or checks.[112]

109. Noticeably absent from this book is any discussion of revised § 9-606 ("Time of Default for Agricultural Lien"). *See id.* § 9-606. The scope of Revised Article 9 includes agricultural liens. *See id.* § 9-109(a)(2); *see also id.* § 9-102(a)(5) (defining "agricultural lien"). Because the author has no practical or academic experience with statutory, agricultural-related security interests, the author has elected not to discuss revised § 9-606 or any other provision of part 6 dealing solely with agricultural liens.

110. *See* United States v. Delco Wire and Cable Co., 772 F. Supp. 1511, 1521 (E.D. Pa. 1991); U.C.C. § 9-502(1) (1995); *see also* U.C.C. § 9-105(1)(a) (defining "account debtor" as a person "obligated on an account, chattel paper or general intangible").

111. *See* U.C.C. § 9-502(1) (1995); *id.* § 9-306(2) (preserving the creditor's interest "in any identifiable proceeds").

112. Debtors may commingle cash proceeds with other cash not representing proceeds. Most courts have held that commingling does not automatically destroy identifiability and have invoked equitable tracing methods to determine which commingled proceeds remain identifiable. *See* 9 HAWKLAND ET AL., *supra* note 15, § 9-306:3, at 37–38. Revised Article 9 affirms these decisions. *See* U.C.C. § 9-315(b)(2) (1999). For a discussion of the most common equitable tracing method—the lowest intermediate balance rule—see Robert H. Skilton, *The Secured Party's Rights in a Debtor's Bank Account Under Article 9 of the Uniform Commercial Code*, 1977 S. ILL. U. L.J. 120, 140–43. *See also* U.C.C. § 9-315 cmt. 3 (1999) (referencing the "lowest intermediate balance rule" as a permissible equitable principle).

A secured party continues to enjoy these rights under revised § 9-607.[113] The section also provides the creditor with additional rights. For example, a creditor may notify any party that owes a performance obligation (as contrasted with a payment obligation) to the debtor on any of the collateral and request that party to render performance to, or for the benefit of, the creditor.[114] Furthermore, the creditor is not limited to *notifying* a party that owes a payment or performance obligation to the debtor. The section expressly permits the creditor to *enforce* those obligations by exercising any rights that the debtor may have against the obligated party.[115] To illustrate:

- Bank has a security interest in Retailer's accounts. Retailer sells a unit of inventory to Buyer on credit, creating an account. Retailer defaults on its obligations to Bank. Bank may notify Buyer to make payment directly to Bank. Bank also may exercise any of Retailer's contractual and other rights against Buyer if Buyer fails to honor its payment obligation.
- Bank has a security interest in Retailer's equipment, including a photocopier purchased from Seller that fails to operate properly. Retailer defaults on its obligations to Bank. Bank may enforce Retailer's breach of warranty action against Seller.[116]
- Bank has a security interest in Retailer's intellectual property. Competitor is conducting its business in a manner that infringes on one of Retailer's patents. Retailer defaults on its obligations to Bank. Bank may seek an injunction against Competitor.[117]

---

113. *See* U.C.C. § 9-607(a)(1)–(2) (1999); *see also id.* § 9-102(a)(3) (defining "account debtor" as "a person obligated on an account, chattel paper, or general intangible" but excluding "persons obligated to pay a negotiable instrument, even if the instrument constitutes part of chattel paper").

114. *See id.* § 9-607(a)(1). Under the common law, the ability of the assignee to enforce an obligor's performance may be limited if (i) enforcement in favor of the assignee will materially change the obligor's duty, materially increase the burden or risk imposed on the obligor by the underlying contract, materially impair the obligor's chance of obtaining return performance, or materially reduce the value of the return performance; or (ii) the assignment is prohibited by statute, public policy, or contract terms. *See* RESTATEMENT (SECOND) OF CONTRACTS § 317(2) (1981); E. ALLAN FARNSWORTH, CONTRACTS § 11.4 (2d ed. 1990); *cf.* U.C.C. § 2-210(2) (1995).

115. *See* U.C.C. § 9-607(a)(3) (1999).

116. *See id.* § 9-607 cmt. 3.

117. *See id.*

The notification and enforcement rights awarded by revised § 9-607 do not adversely impact rights that a third party may have (either under the U.C.C. or otherwise) against the debtor or the secured party.[118] For example, Buyer may discharge its payment obligation on an account by remitting a check directly to Retailer, instead of Bank, if Bank has not honored Buyer's request for "reasonable proof" of Bank's security interest in the account.[119] Also, Bank may have a security interest in a negotiable promissory note in Retailer's possession executed by Buyer and payable to the order of Retailer. Although Buyer is obligated to pay Retailer, Buyer may avoid paying Bank if Bank's lack of possession prevents it from qualifying as a "person entitled to enforce" the note.[120] Or Bank may have a security interest in a letter of credit issued for the benefit of Retailer. But just because Retailer has the right to submit a draw request to, and receive payment from, the issuer of the letter of credit does not necessarily mean that Bank enjoys the same right.[121]

A secured party that attempts to enforce a payment or performance obligation must proceed in a "commercially reasonable manner" if the secured party has chargeback or recourse rights.[122]

---

118. *See id.* § 9-607(e) & cmt. 6; *see also* Rapson, *supra* note 4 (discussing enforcement rights under leases and licenses.

119. *See* U.C.C. § 9-406(c) (1999).

120. *See id.* § 3-301 (1995) (defining "person entitled to enforce" an instrument in a manner that requires possession in most instances).

121. *See id.* § 5-112(a) (generally prohibiting anyone other than the beneficiary from drawing, or otherwise demanding performance, under a letter of credit that does not provide otherwise); *see also id.* § 9-409 (1999) (rendering ineffective, under subsection (a), any contractual term or rule of law, custom, or practice, that restricts assignment of letter-of-credit rights, but preserving, under subsection (b), letter-of-credit law and practice that limits the right of a beneficiary to transfer its right to draw or otherwise demand performance under the letter of credit); *id.* § 9-102(a)(51) (excluding from the definition of "letter-of-credit right" a beneficiary's right to demand payment or performance under the letter of credit).

122. *Id.* § 9-607(c) (1999); *see also id.* § 9-502(2) & cmts. 2–3 (1995); 9 HAWKLAND ET AL., *supra* note 15, § 9-502:03, at 737–38 (explaining why the U.C.C. imposes a duty of commercial reasonableness on a secured party that has chargeback or recourse rights but not a secured party without those rights); CC Fin., Inc. v. Ross, 301 S.E.2d 262, 264 (Ga. 1983) ("The apparent reason for the requirement of commercial reasonableness is to assure, where the secured assignee of receivables undertakes to collect on accounts, that the assignee act with the same degree of prudence which the original account creditor would exercise.").

This duty cannot be waived or varied.[123] Revised Article 9 does not define "commercially reasonable manner," but does provide some guidance in limited situations. For example, the mere fact that a secured party could have obtained a greater amount by collecting or enforcing the obligations at a different time or in a different method does not prevent the secured party from proving that it acted in a commercially reasonable manner.[124] Additionally, a secured party's collection or enforcement efforts are commercially reasonable if those efforts are pre-approved in a judicial proceeding or by a bona fide creditors committee, a representative of creditors, or an assignee for the benefit of creditors.[125]

Usually, however, the task of crafting the contours of permissible conduct will fall on the courts.[126] As under current law, parties

---

123. See U.C.C. § 9-602(3) (1999); cf. id. § 9-501(3) (1995) (prohibiting the waiver of rights and duties under § 9-502 only if those rights and duties require accounting for any surplus proceeds of collateral). One author believes that the failure to include the duty to act in a commercially reasonable manner among the nonwaivable duties listed in current § 9-501(3) is "a drafting error." See CLARK, supra note 2, ¶ 4.04[1], at 4-68 to 4-69; see also PEB STUDY GROUP REPORT, supra note 7, at 208 (recommending that the duty to collect in a commercially reasonable manner be non-waivable).

124. See U.C.C. § 9-627(a) (1999).

125. See id. § 9-627(c).

126. See, e.g., In re Braten Apparel Corp., 68 B.R. 955, 965 (Bankr. S.D.N.Y. 1987) (noting that the mere possibility of better collection results through alternative methods does not establish commercial unreasonableness, stating that "conformity with reasonable commercial practices among others collecting receivables would establish that a collection effort was done in a commercially reasonable manner," and holding that the creditor liquidated receivables in a commercially reasonable manner where evidence revealed full-time collection personnel prepared collection folders for each account, corresponded in writing and by telephone with account debtors as necessary, instituted litigation where appropriate, reviewed results of efforts and planned follow-up activities on a daily basis, kept substantial accounting records, and prepared regular progress reports); In re Emergency Beacon Corp., 48 B.R. 341, 349 (S.D.N.Y. 1985) (noting that "[t]he wide discrepancy between the $650 actually received from collections and the $16,000 top estimated value of the receivables signals a need for close scrutiny," but stating that "a seemingly low return is usually not dispositive of the issue of commercial reasonableness"); Fedders Corp. v. Taylor, 473 F. Supp. 961, 977 (D. Minn. 1979) ("If the requirement of commercial reasonableness as applied to liquidation of accounts receivable means anything it must mean at a minimum that Fedders was obligated to account to defendants as to the final disposition of the receivables."); Western Decor & Furnishings Indus. v. Bank of Am., 154 Cal. Rptr. 287, 290 (Ct. App. 1979) (determining that the creditor liquidated the debtor's receivables with face value of approximately $183,000 in a commercially reasonable manner even though creditor notified only 335 of the 356 account debtors and collected only $12,347); Kearney State Bank & Trust Co. v. Scheer-Williams, 428 N.W.2d 888, 895 (Neb. 1988) (concluding that the evidence supported jury's determination that liquidation of accounts receivable was commercially reasonable); DeLay First Nat'l Bank & Trust Co. v.

to the transaction can attempt to mitigate the degree of judicial involvement by agreeing on parameters of permissible conduct through the use of standards that are not manifestly unreasonable.[127] For example, the parties might contractually agree that the secured party acts in a commercially reasonable manner if it (i) expends resources, subject to a dollar or percentage cap, in an effort to collect from financially troubled account debtors and (ii) compromises or settles claims against selected categories of account debtors who assert defenses or counterclaims, whether meritorious or not.[128] A creditor that fails to act in a commercially reasonable manner in exercising its collection or enforcement rights is subject to several potential penalties, including court-ordered modification or termination of the collection and enforcement rights,[129] liability to the aggrieved party for actual damages,[130] and a reduction or elimination of any deficiency claim.[131]

A creditor that attempts to enforce its collection and enforcement rights against third-party obligors may incur a variety of fees and expenses. This section permits a creditor to deduct from any collections all reasonable expenses incurred in the collection and enforcement process, "including reasonable attorney's fees and legal expenses."[132]

Jacobson Appliance Co., 243 N.W.2d 745, 751 (Neb. 1976) (holding that the bank failed to prove it acted in commercially reasonable manner where record indicated bank did not attempt to collect all accounts but instead sent two letters on some accounts and thereafter took no further action on any accounts); Interchange State Bank v. Rinaldi, 696 A.2d 744, 750–51 (N.J. Super. Ct. App. Div. 1997) (rejecting as "legally untenable . . . or unsupported by the evidence" the debtor's assertion that the creditor's failure to give notice of receivables liquidation was commercially unreasonable); Manufacturers & Traders Trust Co. v. Pro-Mation, Inc., 497 N.Y.S.2d 541, 542 (App. Div. 1985) (holding that creditor acted in commercially reasonable manner by notifying parties obligated on debtor's accounts receivable and instructing them to remit payments to creditor).

127. *See* U.C.C. § 9-603(a) (1999); *see id.* § 9-501(3) (1995).

128. *See* WILLIAM H. LAWRENCE ET AL., UNDERSTANDING SECURED TRANSACTIONS § 18.03, at 368 (1997).

129. *See* U.C.C. § 9-625(a) (1999).

130. *See id.* § 9-625(b).

131. *See id.* § 9-626(a)(3), (4).

132. *See id.* § 9-607(d); *cf. id.* § 9-502(2) (1995) (permitting a creditor to "deduct his reasonable expenses of realization from the collections"). As used in revised § 9-607(d), "reasonable attorney's fees and legal expenses" includes "only those fees and expenses incurred in proceeding against account debtors or other third parties." *Id.* § 9-607 cmt. 10 (1999).

Occasionally the collateral includes a real estate note.[133] If the debtor-holder has defaulted on its obligations to the secured party, the secured party may desire to exercise the debtor's rights in the real estate, including the right to proceed with a nonjudicial foreclosure.[134] Unless it has a recordable interest in the property, the creditor may not be able to exercise that right. Revised § 9-607 addresses this concern.[135] The creditor may record a copy of the security agreement that creates or provides for the security interest in the obligation secured by the real estate, accompanied by the creditor's sworn affidavit stating that a default has occurred and that the creditor is entitled to conduct a nonjudicial foreclosure against the real property, in the appropriate real estate office.[136] Even if the creditor satisfies the requirements of revised § 9-607, the creditor should review the local real estate law and comply with any additional requirements that it may impose. Additionally, the creditor may wish to include in its loan papers a provision in which the debtor acknowledges that the creditor, after default, may exercise nonjudicial rights of foreclosure against the real estate.[137]

---

133. The current and revised versions of Article 9 both exclude interests in real estate from their coverage. *See id.* § 9-104(j) (1995); *id.* § 9-109(d)(11) (1999). But both versions govern security interests in payment obligations secured by real estate interests. *See id.* § 9-102(3) & cmt. 4 (1995); *id.* § 9-109(b) (1999).

134. As the secured party's rights derive from those of the debtor, the secured party can exercise rights against the real property only if the debtor could then do so. *See id.* § 9-607 cmt. 8 (1999).

135. The concern also might disappear if the creditor can obtain a recordable assignment from the debtor. Prudence dictates that the creditor request the assignment *before* default. Thereafter, the debtor—already in default under at least one provision of the loan documents—may be unwilling to cooperate, even if the loan documents include a traditional "cooperation clause," such as "Debtor shall promptly authorize, execute, acknowledge, deliver, file, and record any additional writing as Secured Party may deem reasonably necessary or appropriate to preserve, protect, or enforce its interest in the Collateral or any other contractual, equitable, or statutory right or remedy."

136. *See* U.C.C. § 9-607(b) (1999).

137. An example follows: "Debtor acknowledges that upon Default, Secured Party may exercise any and all rights then or thereafter available to Debtor against any real estate interest created by any mortgage or deed of trust executed in favor of Debtor that secures repayment of any Collateral, including, without limitation, the right to conduct a nonjudicial foreclosure of any such real estate interest." Several drafts of Revised Article 9 contemplated that the secured party's ability to exercise nonjudicial rights of foreclosure had to be evidenced in the recorded security agreement, not the recorded sworn affidavit. *See, e.g., id.* § 9-607(b) (Draft Oct. 1997) (requiring creditor to file or record "a copy of the security agreement that entitles the secured party to exercise those rights" of nonjudicial foreclosure).

Unlike its predecessor, Revised Article 9 governs security interests in selected deposit accounts.[138] Revised § 9-607 provides a creditor with self-help remedies against deposit accounts in which the creditor's security interest is perfected by "control."[139] If the deposit account is maintained with the secured party, the secured party has "control"[140] and, upon default, may apply the balance of the account against the secured obligation.[141] If the account is maintained with another depositary institution, the creditor may obtain "control" in one of two ways. First, the debtor, creditor, and depositary institution may agree that, without the debtor's consent, the depositary institution will honor the creditor's instructions directing disposition of funds in the account.[142] Second, the account can be restyled, presumably with the debtor's consent, in a manner that reflects the creditor

---

138. *Compare id.* § 9-109 cmt. 16 (1999) ("Except in consumer transactions, deposit accounts may be taken as original collateral under this Article."), *with id.* § 9-104(*l*) (1995) ("This Article does not apply . . . to a transfer of an interest in any deposit account . . . .").

Revised Article 9 defines "deposit account" as "a demand, time, savings, passbook, or similar account maintained with a bank. The term does not include investment property or accounts evidenced by an instrument." *Id.* § 9-102(a)(29). A "bank" is defined as "an organization that is engaged in the business of banking. The term includes savings banks, savings and loan associations, credit unions, and trust companies." *Id.* § 9-102(a)(8); *cf. id.* § 9-105(1)(e) (1995) (defining "deposit account" as "a demand, time, savings, passbook or like account maintained with a bank, savings and loan association, credit union or like organization, other than an account evidenced by a certificate of deposit").

139. *See id.* § 9-607(a)(4)–(5) (1999).

140. *See id.* § 9-104(a)(1).

141. *See id.* § 9-607(a)(4).

142. *See id.* § 9-104(a)(2). The three-party agreement must be an authenticated record. *Id.*; *see id.* § 9-102(a)(7), (69) (defining "authenticate" and "record," respectively). The agreement to honor the creditor's instructions may be subject to any agreed-upon condition (e.g., "Creditor's instruction must be accompanied by a statement that Debtor is in default under the loan documents.") other than the debtor's consent. *Id.* § 9-104 cmt. 3. Because the debtor's ability to direct disposition of funds from the account is not automatically terminated when a creditor has control over the account, *see id.* § 9-104(b), a creditor should include a provision in the three-party agreement that addresses the debtor's ability to withdraw funds from the account. Otherwise, the creditor's post-default demand for funds may be an exercise in futility. Additionally, the creditor should consider requesting a provision that limits the institution's ability to exercise any right of set-off or recoupment. With one exception, these rights are not adversely affected by the creation or perfection of a security interest in the deposit account, the institution's knowledge of the security interest, or the institution's receipt of instructions from the creditor. *See id.* §§ 9-340, 9-341.

as the institution's "customer" on the account.[143] If the creditor has achieved control in either manner, the creditor may instruct the depositary institution to pay the balance in the account to, or for the benefit of, the creditor.[144] Because the provision is silent on how quickly the institution must honor the request, the creditor may wish to reach agreement with the institution on this matter when control is first established.

143. *See id.* § 9-104(a)(3); *see also id.* § 4-104(a)(5) (1995) (defining "customer" as "a person having an account with a bank or for whom a bank has agreed to collect items"); *id.* § 9-102(b) (1999) (incorporating the Article 4 definition of "customer" into Revised Article 9).

144. *See id.* § 9-607(a)(5) (1999).

REVISED § 9-608

APPLICATION OF PROCEEDS OF COLLECTION OR ENFORCEMENT; LIABILITY FOR DEFICIENCY AND RIGHT TO SURPLUS

Although current § 9-502 provides the secured party with collection rights, the section offers little guidance on how any proceeds collected are to be applied.[145] The statute permits the creditor to deduct "reasonable expenses of realization from the collections,"[146] and requires the creditor to "account to the debtor for any surplus,"[147] but does not address such issues as whether junior or senior creditors are entitled to any of the collected proceeds, how the secured party should handle any noncash proceeds that it receives, and when the secured party may deduct its legal fees and expenses. These issues, as well as others, are addressed by revised § 9-608.

Under revised § 9-608, a secured party must apply cash proceeds received from exercising its collection or enforcement rights under revised § 9-607 as follows. First, the creditor may satisfy its reasonable expenses of collection and enforcement.[148] The creditor also may recoup its reasonable attorneys' fees and legal expenses incurred in proceeding against the

---

145. One of the principal architects of Article 9 believed that the payment scheme of § 9-504(1) governs application of proceeds collected under § 9-502. *See* 2 GILMORE, *supra* note 2, § 44.8, at 1251.

146. U.C.C. § 9-502(2) (1995).

147. *Id.* Absent a contrary agreement, the secured party is entitled to keep surplus proceeds if the underlying transaction was a sale of accounts or chattel paper.

148. *See id.* § 9-608(a)(1)(A) (1999). These expenses of collection and enforcement include reasonable attorney's fees and expenses incurred in proceeding against account debtors and other third parties. *See id.* § 9-607(d) & cmt. 10.

debtor or any obligor *if the loan documents so provide* and recoupment is not prohibited by law.[149] Whether expenses of any nature are "reasonable" will vary from case to case, but common sense suggests that the expenses incurred should not be disproportionate to either the amount attempted to be collected or enforced or the amount of the unpaid secured debt. Second, the creditor may apply the proceeds against any debt that was secured by the collateral that generated the proceeds.[150] Third, the creditor must remit any remaining proceeds to any party with a *subordinate* security interest in, or lien on, the collateral that generated the proceeds if the creditor has received from that party an authenticated demand before the proceeds are completely distributed.[151] However, the creditor that requests, but does not timely receive, reasonable proof of the subordinate security interest or lien need not honor that party's demand.[152] Fourth, the creditor must return any remaining cash proceeds to the debtor[153] unless the underlying

149. *See id.* § 9-607 cmt. 10. The emphasized language should prompt creditors to revise their standard loan documents accordingly. Even then, creditors may run afoul of state statutes that limit, or prohibit, recoupment of attorneys' fees. *See, e.g.,* Northwestern Nat'l Bank v. American Beef Packers, Inc. (*In re* American Beef Packers, Inc.), 548 F.2d 246, 247–48 (8th Cir. 1977); Harper v. Wheatley Implement Co., 643 S.W.2d 537, 540–41 (Ark. 1983); White v. Associates Commercial Corp., 725 S.W.2d 7, 9 (Ark. Ct. App. 1987); First Nat'l Bank v. Schroeder, 355 N.W.2d 780, 782–83 (Neb. 1984).

150. *See* U.C.C. § 9-608(a)(1)(B) (1999). Implicit is the understanding that the creditor may not apply proceeds to unsecured debt or collateralized debt not secured by the proceeds. For example, Bank may make a $1000 unsecured loan to Debtor, a $2000 purchase-money loan to Debtor secured only by equipment purchased with the loan proceeds, and a $5000 loan secured by the Debtor's accounts. Debtor defaults on all three payment obligations. If Bank is fortunate enough to collect payments from account debtors in excess of the unpaid $5000 loan, Bank cannot apply the excess against the unpaid amounts of either the $1000 unsecured loan or the $2000 purchase-money loan. Instead, any excess must be remitted to subordinate creditors under revised § 9-608(a)(1)(C) or the debtor, as surplus, under revised § 9-608(a)(4).

151. *See id.* 9-608(a)(1)(C); *see also id.* § 9-102(a)(7) (defining "authenticate"). A creditor that receives authenticated records from multiple creditors should bring an interpleader action against those creditors and deposit the relevant amount with the court.

152. *See id.* § 9-608(a)(2).

153. *Id.* § 9-608(a)(4); *cf. id.* § 9-502(2) (1995) (stating that "the secured party must account to the debtor for any surplus"). The obligation to remit surplus proceeds to the debtor cannot be waived or varied under either version of Article 9. *See id.* § 9-501(3)(a); *id.* § 9-602(5) (1999).

transaction is a sale of accounts, chattel paper, payment intangibles, or promissory notes.[154]

This payment scheme noticeably excludes from the list of potential recipients any creditor whose security interest in, or lien on, the collateral that generated the proceeds enjoys priority over the security interest of the collecting creditor. Senior creditors may be distraught over the text of § 9-608,[155] but the official comments should allay their concerns.[156] Notwithstanding any contrary results suggested by the language of revised § 9-608 (e.g., "A secured party *shall* apply . . . cash proceeds . . . in the following order . . . ."[157]), the application scheme "does not affect the

---

154. *See id.* § 9-608(b) (1999). Under § 9-502(2), if the underlying transaction is a sale of accounts or chattel paper the debtor is entitled to proceeds (and is liable for any deficiency) "only if the security agreement so provides." *Id.* § 9-502(2) (1995). No similar language appears in revised § 9-608(b). The omission of such language may suggest that subsection (b) cannot be contractually modified. That is not the intended construction. For a while, revised § 9-608(b) included the phrase "only if its agreement so provides." *See, e.g., id.* § 9-608(b) (Draft Oct. 1996). The language was subsequently deleted "as unnecessary" because revised § 9-602, which limits freedom of contract, does not include revised § 9-608(b) among its list of statutes that create non-waivable rights and duties. *See id.* § 9-608(b) & cmt. ("Changes from Prior Draft") (Draft Mar. 1998); *see also id.* § 9-602(4)–(5) (1999) (referencing subsection (a), but not subsection (b), of revised § 9-608).

155. A creditor whose security interest or lien enjoys a rank *equal* to the interest of the collecting creditor also is excluded from the distribution scheme of revised § 9-608. The date and time of filing a financing statement or recording a lien will often dictate priority of the interests, so interests of equal rank should occur infrequently. Parties may contractually agree that their competing interests enjoy equal priority, notwithstanding the priority dictated by their respective filings. However, most creditors that go to the trouble of contractually altering their priority also contractually agree on how proceeds are to be applied. Therefore, concerns raised by competing interests of equal rank may be more academic than realistic.

156. One can make a plausible argument for excluding senior claimants from the payment scheme of revised § 9-608. A creditor with a senior security interest in or lien on accounts, chattel paper, instruments, and similar collateral should be cognizant of the risk that the debtor will neither remit payments to the creditor nor buy additional collateral (e.g., inventory) with the payments. A creditor that fails to control collections implicitly assumes that risk and is not placed in a worse position if a junior creditor obtains an interest in the collateral and then collects payments directly from the account debtors and other parties. A senior creditor that assumes these risks should not be surprised at being excluded from the payment scheme of revised § 9-608, especially when the creditor can so easily mitigate the risk by (i) demanding that account debtors and other obligors remit payments directly to the creditor (or a lockbox that the creditor controls), and (ii) monitoring the activities of the debtor, account debtors, and other obligors to ensure compliance.

157. *Id.* § 9-608(a)(1) (1999) (emphasis added).

priority of a security interest in collateral which is senior to the interest of the secured party who is collecting or enforcing collateral under Section 9-607."[158] Whether a junior secured party enjoys priority in collected proceeds is dictated by several non-default provisions of Revised Article 9. Fortunately, these provisions are referenced in comment 5 to revised § 9-607, which, in turn, is cross-referenced in comment 5 to revised § 9-608.

A creditor that receives noncash proceeds[159] instead of cash proceeds is subject to the duties imposed by revised § 9-207,[160] such as exercising reasonable care in handling and preserving the collateral[161] and keeping the collateral identifiable.[162] A creditor may elect not to apply the noncash proceeds against the unpaid debt unless failure to do so is commercially unreasonable.[163] A creditor that does apply the noncash proceeds against the unpaid debt must do so in a commercially reasonable manner.[164] For example, a creditor that receives a promissory note from an account debtor may, if not commercially unreasonable, simply hold the note and reduce the debtor's unpaid balance only as the maker remits payments. Alternatively, the creditor may, in a commercially reasonable manner, apply the principal portion of the note against the amount owed by the debtor to the creditor.[165] The duty to act in this manner cannot be waived or varied,[166] but the parties may, through adoption of standards that are not manifestly unreasonable, attempt to contractually

---

158. *Id.* § 9-608 cmt. 5; *cf.* PEB STUDY GROUP REPORT, *supra* note 7, at 222 (recommending that a junior creditor is entitled to retain collected proceeds free of the senior creditor's interest only if the junior creditor acts in good faith and without knowledge that the collections violate the rights of the senior creditor). *See generally* Rapson, *supra* note 4 (discussing collections by subordinate secured creditors).

159. *See* U.C.C. § 9-102(a)(58) (defining "noncash proceeds").

160. *See id.* § 9-601(b); *cf. id.* § 9-501(1) (1995) (stating that a secured party has the rights, remedies, and duties provided in § 9-207).

161. *See id.* § 9-207(a) (1998); *cf. id.* § 9-207(1) (1995) (obligating a secured party to exercise reasonable care with respect to collateral in its possession).

162. *See id.* § 9-207(b)(3) (1999); *cf. id.* § 9-207(2)(d) (1995) (stating that a "secured party must keep the collateral identifiable").

163. *See id.* § 9-608(a)(3) (1999).

164. *Id.*

165. *Id.* § 9-608 cmt. 3.

166. *See id.* § 9-602(4).

define what conduct is deemed commercially reasonable.[167] For example, the parties may agree that upon receipt of a promissory note from an account debtor the secured party will immediately apply an agreed-upon percentage of the principal against the debtor's unpaid obligation.

Absent any contrary agreement, a creditor retains the ability to pursue a deficiency action against the debtor and any other obligor if proceeds collected and applied do not extinguish the debtor's entire unpaid obligation.[168] No obligor is liable for any deficiency in a transaction involving the sale of accounts, chattel paper, payment intangibles, or promissory notes, however, unless the loan documents so provide.[169]

167. *See id.* §§ 9-603(a), 9-608 cmt. 4

168. *See id.* § 9-608(a)(4); *cf. id.* § 9-502(2) (1995) (imposing liability on a debtor for any deficiency).

169. *See id.* § 9-608(b) (1999); *see also supra* note 154.

REVISED § 9-609

SECURED PARTY'S RIGHT TO TAKE POSSESSION AFTER DEFAULT

The right to engage in self-help repossession "is a remedy of ancient and honorable lineage."[170] Two policies underlie this valuable right: (i) creditors are able to seize collateral without resorting to judicial process, which can be expensive and time-consuming; and (ii) debtors have access to credit at lower costs.[171] The drafters of current Article 9 included self-help among the creditor's post-default rights.[172] A creditor continues to enjoy the right to seize collateral without judicial process under Revised Article 9, subject to three limitations. This right and its limitations are found in revised § 9-609.[173]

---

170. Soia Mentschikoff, *Peaceful Repossession Under the Uniform Commercial Code: A Constitutional and Economic Analysis*, 14 WM. & MARY L. REV. 767, 767 (1973). For an excellent article that traces the development of the self-help remedy from its origin in Greek and Roman law, see James R. McCall, *The Past as Prologue: A History of the Right to Repossess*, 47 S. CAL. L. REV. 58 (1973).

171. *See* Williams v. Ford Motor Credit Co., 674 F.2d 717, 719 n.4 (8th Cir. 1982); Riley State Bank v. Spillman, 750 P.2d 1024, 1029 (Kan. 1988). *See generally* James J. White, *The Abolition of Self-Help Repossession: The Poor Pay Even More*, 1973 WIS. L. REV. 503; Robert W. Johnson, *Denial of Self-Help Repossession: An Economic Analysis*, 47 S. CAL. L. REV. 82 (1973); Mentschikoff, *supra* note 170, at 769–70 (suggesting numerous economic and other consequences that would result if automobile financiers were forced to repossess collateral by judicial process).

172. *See* U.C.C. § 9-503 (1995).

173. Additional non-U.C.C. limitations may exist. *See, e.g.*, N.Y. PERS. PROP. LAW § 413(12)(c) (McKinney Supp. 1999) (permitting self-help repossession against selected consumer debtors only if the debtor consents to the repossession in a "substantially contemporaneous writing"). Furthermore, a party may successfully repossess collateral only to have its possession challenged by a senior claimant. *See* U.C.C. § 9-609 cmt. 5 (1999).

First, as under current Article 9, a creditor cannot seize the collateral unless a default exists.[174] Therefore, before exercising its self-help remedy a creditor should review the loan documents to determine that the debtor is indeed in default.[175] Otherwise, the creditor may be liable for conversion or wrongful repossession.[176]

Second, even if a default exists, the contract terms may limit the creditor's ability to take possession of the collateral. This contractual limitation is recognized by § 9-503 through its opening language: "Unless otherwise agreed . . . ."[177] This phrase has been deleted from revised § 9-609(a),[178] presumably because the Drafting Committee viewed the language as unnecessary because the U.C.C. permits the secured party and the debtor to contractually modify their behavior,[179] subject to express prohibitions not applicable here.[180] Therefore, prior to repossessing any collateral, the creditor should determine that the loan documents neither prohibit self-help nor require satisfaction of any

---

174. *See id.* §§ 9-609(a)(1), 9-609(b)(2); *id.* § 9-503 (1995); *see also* United States v. Fullpail Cattle Sales, Inc., 617 F. Supp. 73, 75 (E.D. Wis. 1985) (noting that the creditor's right to possess collateral turned on whether debtors were in default); Fulton v. Anchor Sav. Bank, 452 S.E.2d 208, 213–17 (Ga. Ct. App. 1994) (reversing trial court's grant of summary judgment in favor of repossessing creditor where evidence raised genuine issues of material fact concerning existence of default).

175. *See* Ash v. Peoples Bank, 500 So. 2d 5, 7 (Ala. 1986) (concluding that debtors' failure to maintain insurance on van triggered default that made creditor's subsequent repossession lawful); First Nat'l Bank v. Beug, 400 N.W.2d 893, 896 (S.D. 1987) (noting that debtor's failure to make payments on note constituted a default that permitted creditor to repossess equipment).

176. *See, e.g.,* Warren v. Ford Motor Credit Co., 693 F.2d 1373, 1376 (11th Cir. 1982) (affirming a verdict that creditor's vehicle repossession amounted to conversion where evidence indicated debtor had not yet defaulted); Bank of Cabot v. Bledsoe, 653 S.W.2d 144, 146 (Ark. Ct. App. 1983) (affirming the trial court's conclusion that creditor wrongfully repossessed vehicle in absence of default). *But see* Jean Braucher, *The Repo Code: A Study of Adjustment to Uncertainty in Commercial Law,* 75 Wash. U. L.Q. 549, 591–92 (1997) (contending that conversion is a "conceptually wrong" remedy for a breach of the peace).

177. *See* U.C.C. § 9-503 (1995).

178. The language was not deleted until late in the drafting process. *Compare id.* § 9-609 (Draft Oct. 1997) (including the language), *with id.* § 9-609(a) (Draft Jan. 1998) (deleting the language).

179. *See id.* § 1-102(3) & cmt. 2 (1995).

180. *See id.; id.* § 9-602 (1999).

conditions precedent. Otherwise, the creditor may be charged with conversion or wrongful repossession.[181]

The third, and most frequently litigated, limitation on the creditor's self-help remedy is the requirement that the creditor not breach the peace.[182] Noted jurist Sir William Blackstone offered the following justification for this restraint:

> If therefore he can so contrive it as to gain possession of his property again, without force or terror, the law favours and will justify his proceeding. But, as the public peace is a superior consideration to any one man's private property; and as, if individuals were once allowed to use private force as a remedy for private injuries, all social justice must cease, the strong would give law to the weak, and every man would revert to a state of nature; for these reasons it is provided, that this natural right of recaption shall never be exerted, where such exertion must occasion strife and bodily contention, or endanger the peace of society.[183]

The drafters of current Article 9 intentionally declined to define "breach of peace,"[184] and the term remains undefined in

---

181. *See, e.g.,* Klingbiel v. Commercial Credit Corp., 439 F.2d 1303, 1307 (10th Cir. 1971) (concluding that the creditor's failure to give contractually required notice prior to repossessing vehicle triggered wrongful repossession and conversion); Zimprich v. North Dakota Harvestore Sys., Inc., 461 N.W.2d 425, 427–29 (N.D. 1990) (concluding that the creditor's post-default repossession of feed-storage system constituted conversion when creditor had agreed to defer exercising its right to repossess); Frierson v. United Farm Agency, Inc., 672 F. Supp. 1272, 1276–77 (W.D. Mo. 1987) (holding that the creditor who failed to comply with notice requirement in loan documents could neither seize funds in bank account nor ignore garnishment summons), *rev'd in part on other grounds*, 868 F.2d 302 (8th Cir. 1989).

182. *See* U.C.C. § 9-609(b)(2) (1999). The same limitation exists under current Article 9. *See id.* § 9-503 (1995). The duty to avoid breaching the peace cannot be waived or varied under Revised Article 9. *See id.* § 9-602(6) (1999); *cf. id.* § 9-501(3) (1995) (failing to list § 9-503 as a statute that creates a duty that cannot be waived or varied); PEB STUDY GROUP REPORT, *supra* note 7, at 208–09 (recommending that "Section 9-501(3) be revised to make it clear that the 'no breach of peace' right and duty cannot be waived").

183. 3 WILLIAM BLACKSTONE, COMMENTARIES ON THE LAWS OF ENGLAND 4–5 (Legal Classics Library 1983) (1768); *see also* Sam A. Simmerman & John Variola, Case Comment, Ford Motor Credit Company v. Byrd: *Is Repossession Accomplished by the Use of Stealth, Trickery, or Fraud a Breach of the Peace Under Uniform Commercial Code Section 9-503?*, 40 OHIO ST. L.J. 501, 504 (1979) ("Another policy implicit in the breach of the peace restriction is that a democratic government favors resolution of disputes through institutions and not by individual, extrajudicial activity.").

184. As one author has stated:

In establishing the § 9-503 procedure the Code draftsmen intended to build upon the prior history of the self-help remedy and not to create any new rights or obligations. Thus, the choice of the term "breach of peace" was not inadvertent. Nor

Revised Article 9.[185] The task of fashioning the contours of the term has fallen to the courts.[186] Although the inquiry is fact-sensitive, and no two cases present identical facts,[187] the following guidelines can be gleaned from the case law.

- A creditor will not breach the peace if the debtor is present and voluntarily consents to the repossession.[188]
- A creditor will breach the peace if the debtor is present and objects to the repossession.[189]

was it an oversight in draftsmanship that the proponents of Article 9 failed to define breach of peace.
Eugene Mikolajczyk, Comment, *Breach of Peace and Section 9-503 of the Uniform Commercial Code—A Modern Definition for an Ancient Restriction*, 82 DICK. L. REV. 351, 354–55 (1978).

185. Some states, however, have a statutory definition. *See, e.g.,* WYO. STAT. ANN. § 6-6-102(a) (Michie 1997) ("A person commits breach of the peace if he disturbs the peace of a community or its inhabitants by unreasonably loud noise . . . .").

186. Revised Article 9 prohibits the parties from attempting to define the parameters of permissible conduct, even through standards that are not manifestly unreasonable. *See* U.C.C. § 9-603(b) & cmt. 2 (1999).

187. A glimpse at the case law reveals that a breach of the peace arises most often when a vehicle is repossessed—an event that occurs approximately 500,000 times each year. *See* Harrell, *supra* note 38, at 256.

188. *See, e.g.,* Brown v. Indiana Nat'l Bank, 476 N.E.2d 888, 893 (Ind. Ct. App. 1985); 4 WHITE & SUMMERS, *supra* note 36, § 34–7, at 418 ("If the debtor voluntarily and contemporaneously consents to a repossession it cannot be a breach of the peace."). Whether the consent of a third person is effective may depend on such factors as the apparent authority and age of that person, as well as the relationship between that person and the debtor. *See id.* at 419.

189. *See, e.g.,* Fulton v. Anchor Sav. Bank, 452 S.E.2d 208, 213 (Ga. Ct. App. 1994); Dixon v. Ford Motor Credit Co., 391 N.E.2d 493, 497 (Ill. App. Ct. 1979); Census Fed. Credit Union v. Wann, 403 N.E.2d 348, 351–52 (Ind. Ct. App. 1980); First & Farmers Bank v. Henderson, 763 S.W.2d 137, 140–41 (Ky. Ct. App. 1988); Hester v. Bandy, 627 So. 2d 833, 840–41 (Miss. 1993); Morris v. First Nat'l Bank & Trust Co., 254 N.E.2d 683, 686–87 (Ohio 1970); Hollibush v. Ford Motor Credit Co., 508 N.W.2d 449, 453 (Wis. Ct. App. 1993); 9 HAWKLAND ET AL., *supra* note 15, § 9-503:3, at 678 ("[I]f the debtor protests the secured party's repossession . . . a breach of peace will be imminent, and self-help repossession should no longer be an alternative for the secured party."); 4 WHITE & SUMMERS, *supra* note 36, § 34–7, at 421–22 ("When the creditor repossesses in disregard of the debtor's unequivocal oral protest, most courts find the creditor guilty of a breach of the peace. . . . A rule that an oral protest is sufficient to foreclose non-judicial repossession is wise because it does not beckon the repossessing creditor to the brink of violence."); Braucher, *supra* note 176, at 574 ("The law imposes the obligation to withdraw on the party in a better position to react coolly—the one who has not been surprised and who is just doing a job."). *But see* Williams v. Ford Motor Credit Co., 674 F.2d 717, 720 (8th Cir. 1982) (concluding that a vehicle can be repossessed if the debtor is present but fails to object); Chrysler Credit Corp. v. Koontz, 661 N.E.2d 1171, 1174 (Ill. App. Ct. 1996) (rejecting "[the defendant's] invitation to define 'an unequivocal oral protest' " as a breach of the peace in the absence of any evidence that the debtor "implied violence at the time of or immediately prior to the repossession by holding a weapon, clenching a fist, or even vehemently arguing toe-to-toe with the repossessor so that a reasonable repossessor would understand that violence was likely to ensue if he continued with the vehicle repossession").

- A creditor will not breach the peace by removing collateral from a parking lot, street, driveway, or open garage.[190]
- A creditor will breach the peace by removing collateral from a restricted area.[191]
- A creditor will breach the peace if a peace officer is present during the repossession and a confrontation between the creditor and debtor occurs.[192] This is true even if the peace officer is present at

190. *See, e.g.,* Butler v. Ford Motor Credit Co., 829 F.2d 568, 568 (5th Cir. 1987) (removing truck from driveway); *In re* Hamby, 19 B.R. 776, 779–80 (Bankr. N.D. Ala. 1982) (removing car from parking lot); Ash v. Peoples Bank, 500 So. 2d 5, 6 (Ala. 1986) (removing van from public street); Reno v. General Motors Acceptance Corp., 378 So. 2d 1103, 1105 (Ala. 1979) (removing car from supermarket parking lot); Oaklawn Bank v. Baldwin, 709 S.W.2d 91, 92 (Ark. 1986) (removing truck from driveway); Raffa v. Dania Bank, 321 So. 2d 83, 84 (Fla. Dist. Ct. App. 1975) (removing car from driveway); Pierce v. Leasing Int'l, Inc., 235 S.E.2d 752, 755 (Ga. Ct. App. 1977) (removing car from open garage attached to residence); Jordan v. Citizens & Southern Nat'l Bank, 298 S.E.2d 213, 214 (S.C. 1982) (removing truck from driveway); Ragde v. Peoples Bank, 767 P.2d 949, 950 (Wash. Ct. App. 1989) (removing cars from driveway).

191. *See, e.g.,* Laurel Coal Co. v. Walter E. Heller & Co., 539 F. Supp. 1006, 1007 (W.D. Pa. 1982) (removing bulldozer after cutting chain used to lock fence); Henderson v. Security Nat'l Bank, 140 Cal. Rptr. 388, 391 (Ct. App. 1977) (removing car after breaking lock on garage door); Girard v. Anderson, 257 N.W. 400, 400 (Iowa 1934) (removing piano from house in absence of debtors but in accordance with contract terms); Riley State Bank v. Spillman, 750 P.2d 1024, 1030 (Kan. 1988) (removing collateral from business premises after locksmith unlocked door and removed and replaced locks); Bloomquist v. First Nat'l Bank, 378 N.W.2d 81, 86 (Minn. Ct. App. 1985) (removing collateral from business premises after climbing through cracked, but taped shut, window pane and opening garage door secured by deadbolt lock); Martin v. Dorn Equip. Co., 821 P.2d 1025, 1026 (Mont. 1991) (removing collateral from ranch by using bolt cutters to cut padlock on chained gate); Kimble v. Universal TV Rental, Inc., 417 N.E.2d 597, 601–03 (Ohio—Franklin County Mun. Ct. 1980) (removing television after forcibly entering locked apartment); Davenport v. Chrysler Credit Corp., 818 S.W.2d 23, 30 (Tenn. Ct. App. 1991) (removing vehicle from enclosed garage where vehicle had been chained to a post with a logging chain and two padlocks); General Elec. Credit Corp. v. Timbrook, 291 S.E.2d 383, 384 (W. Va. 1982) (removing mobile home after breaking lock on door). *But see* Polivy v. Air One, Inc., 700 A.2d 71, 73 (Conn. App. Ct. 1997) (cutting chains to gain access to airplane did not trigger breach of peace because chains had been installed by mechanic that had disclaimed any right to possession); Global Casting Indus., Inc. v. Daley-Hodkin Corp., 432 N.Y.S.2d 453, 454, 456 (Sup. Ct. 1980) (holding that creditor's use of locksmith to gain access to collateral located on business premises was not a breach of the peace because debtor had executed security agreement that "authorize[d] and empower[ed] Bank, with the aid and assistance of any person, to enter upon the premises").

192. *See, e.g.,* Harris v. City of Roseburg, 664 F.2d 1121, 1125–27 (9th Cir. 1981) (holding that police officer's verbal confrontation with debtor during vehicle repossession precluded summary judgment on issue of state action); MacLeod v. C & G Inv. Group (*In re* MacLeod), 118 B.R. 1, 2 (Bankr. D.N.H. 1990) (concluding that repossession was unlawful where policeman awakened debtor and told him to remain in his house and not "do something stupid" during an imminent repossession); Walker v. Walthall, 588 P.2d 863, 866 (Ariz. Ct. App. 1978) ("[T]he introduction of law enforcement officers into the area of self-help repossession, regardless of their degree of participation or non-participation in the

the creditor's request to prevent any potential violence, because the peace officer's presence chills the debtor's right to object to the repossession.[193]

- A creditor that repossesses a motor vehicle containing the owner's personal effects may be liable for conversion unless the contract permits the creditor to seize personal effects; even if the contract permits seizure of personal effects, the creditor must make them available to the owner once possession of the vehicle is secured, and the creditor cannot make their return contingent on payment of the unpaid debt.[194]

actual events, would constitute state action, thereby invalidating a repossession without a proper notice and hearing."); *First & Farmers Bank*, 763 S.W.2d at 140 (concluding that the presence of the deputy sheriff, armed and in full uniform, during creditor's confrontation with debtor prevented lawful repossession); Waisner v. Jones, 755 P.2d 598, 602 (N.M. 1988) (holding that the presence of military security police during creditor's confrontation with debtor during repossession on military base prevented lawful seizure); Stone Mach. Co. v. Kessler, 463 P.2d 651, 652–53, 655 (Wash. Ct. App. 1970) (finding breach of the peace where sheriff, in uniform and wearing his badge and sidearm, told debtor, "[w]e come [sic] to pick up the tractor"). *But see* United States v. Coleman, 628 F.2d 961, 964 (6th Cir. 1980) (ruling that the mere presence of police in patrol car parked around corner from site where creditor repossessed vehicle without confronting debtor did not constitute state action); *First & Farmers Bank*, 763 S.W.2d at 137, 143 (McDonald, J., concurring) ("It is one thing to hold that an officer of the law may not *participate* in a self-help repossession. It is quite another to say that he may never be present as a neutral observer."); *Walker*, 588 P.2d at 866–67 (Eubank, J., dissenting) (arguing that mere presence of peace officer who took no part in repossession negotiations between creditor and debtor did not trigger breach of peace).

193. *See MacLeod*, 118 B.R. at 3; *Stone Mach. Co.*, 463 P.2d at 651, 654–55; *see also* Braucher, *supra* note 176, at 581 (observing that "a repossession using a law officer is not self-help, and thus it is not authorized by UCC section 9-503, making it unlawful," absent judicial approval).

194. *See, e.g.*, Thompson v. Ford Motor Credit Co., 550 F.2d 256, 258–59 (5th Cir. 1977) (holding that an exculpatory provision in a contract saved creditor from liability for allegedly converting personal items in repossessed vehicle); Larranaga v. Mile High Collection & Recovery Bureau, Inc., 807 F. Supp. 111, 114–15 (D.N.M. 1992) (finding a creditor liable for conversion of personal property in repossessed vehicle in absence of any contractual language); Oaklawn Bank v. Baldwin, 709 S.W.2d 91, 92 (Ark. 1986) (ruling that owners of personal property in repossessed vehicle were entitled to trial on conversion theory); Ford Motor Credit Co. v. Herring, 589 S.W.2d 584, 586 (Ark. 1979) (holding that contract terms did not shield creditor from liability for intentionally withholding personal items in repossessed vehicle from debtor who demanded return after creditor had secured possession of vehicle); Southern Indus. Sav. Bank v. Greene, 224 So. 2d 416, 418–19 (Fla. Dist. Ct. App. 1969) (concluding that the creditor was liable for losing cash and jewelry hidden in trunk of repossessed car); Newman v. Basin Motor Co., 644 P.2d 553, 556 (N.M. Ct. App. 1982) (concluding that contractual provision permitting creditor to seize items in repossessed motor vehicle did not protect creditor from liability for wrongfully repossessing and selling trailer attached to vehicle); Jones v. General Motors Acceptance Corp., 565 P.2d 9, 12 (Okla. 1977) (stating that a contractual provision authorizing seizure of personal items in repossessed vehicle did not save creditor from liability for wrongful retention).

- The creditor's duty to avoid breaching the peace is non-delegable; the creditor remains liable for the conduct of any independent contractor hired to perform the repossession.[195]
- A creditor that breaches the peace may be liable for punitive damages.[196]

195. *See* Clark v. Associates Commercial Corp., 877 F. Supp. 1439, 1444–45 (D. Kan. 1994); General Fin. Corp. v. Smith, 505 So. 2d 1045, 1047–48 (Ala. 1987); Sammons v. Broward Bank, 599 So. 2d 1018, 1019–21 (Fla. Dist. Ct. App. 1992); Fulton v. Anchor Savs. Bank, 452 S.E.2d 208, 213–14 (Ga. Ct. App. 1994); Nichols v. Metropolitan Bank, 435 N.W.2d 637, 640–41 (Minn. Ct. App. 1989); Robinson v. Citicorp Nat'l Servs., Inc., 921 S.W.2d 52, 54–55 (Mo. Ct. App. 1996); DeMary v. Rieker, 695 A.2d 294, 301–02 (N.J. Super. Ct. App. Div. 1997); Mauro v. General Motors Acceptance Corp., 626 N.Y.S.2d 374, 376–77 (N.Y. 1995); Williamson v. Fowler Toyota, Inc., 956 P.2d 858, 861 (Okla. 1998); McCall v. Owens, 820 S.W.2d 748, 751–52 (Tenn. Ct. App. 1991); MBank El Paso, N.A. v. Sanchez, 836 S.W.2d 151, 152–53 (Tex. 1992). *But see* Kouba v. East Joliet Bank, 481 N.E.2d 325, 328 (Ill. App. Ct. 1985) (stating that employer usually is not liable for acts of independent contractors but could be liable for failing to exercise reasonable care in selecting a competent contractor or ordering or directing the injurious act); Hester v. Bandy, 627 So. 2d 833, 843 (Miss. 1993) (holding that creditor can be liable for acts of independent contractor "when one employs another to perform a task in which a serious danger to person or property, a crime, or some tort can reasonably be anticipated in its performance"); MBank El Paso, 836 S.W.2d at 158–60 (Hecht, J., dissenting) (arguing that Article 9's self-help remedy provision does not create a nondelegable duty). As noted by Professor Braucher, "lenders have responded to this legal development by increasingly insisting that their independent contractors obtain liability insurance coverage for most breaches of the peace." Braucher, *supra* note 176, at 560.

196. *See, e.g.,* Klingbiel v. Commercial Credit Corp., 439 F.2d 1303, 1309–10 & n.15 (10th Cir. 1971) ($7500); Chrysler Credit Corp. v. Turner, 553 So. 2d 64, 67 (Ala. 1989) ($15,000); Big Three Motors, Inc. v. Rutherford, 432 So. 2d 483, 487 (Ala. 1983) ($15,000); Vogel v. Carolina Int'l, Inc., 711 P.2d 708, 711 (Colo. Ct. App. 1985) ($73,000); Deavers v. Standridge, 242 S.E.2d 331, 334 (Ga. Ct. App. 1978) ($1000); *First & Farmers Bank,* 763 S.W.2d at 139 ($75,000); *Bloomquist,* 378 N.W.2d at 86–87 (remanding for determination of damages, which may include punitives); Zimprich v. North Dakota Harvestore Sys., Inc., 461 N.W.2d 425, 427 (N.D. 1990) ($20,000); *Kimble,* 417 N.E.2d at 601–03 ($4000); *Williamson,* 956 P.2d at 863 ($15,000); Mitchell v. Ford Motor Credit Co., 688 P.2d 42, 44 (Okla. 1984) ($60,000); 2 GILMORE, *supra* note 2, § 44.1, at 1213 (noting that "[j]uries love to award punitive damages" for certain breaches of the peace). *But see General Fin. Corp.,* 505 So. 2d at 1049 (Torbert, C.J., concurring specially) ("Without proof that a creditor knew that an independent contractor was going to breach the peace in repossessing the collateral or ratification of the independent contractor's conduct, punitive damages should not be recoverable."); *Henderson,* 140 Cal. Rptr. at 392–93 (refusing to assess punitive damages against creditor that did not authorize, ratify, or participate in, wrongful acts of repossessor); MBank El Paso, 836 S.W.2d at 155–58 (Cook, J., dissenting) (arguing that creditors should not be held strictly liable for wrongful acts of independent contractors); CLARK, *supra* note 2, ¶ 4.05[2][c][ii], at S4-50 to S4-51 (arguing that the dual purposes of awarding punitive damages—punishment and deterrence—are not advanced when a creditor is held liable for an independent contractor's actions that the creditor did not authorize). *See generally* Jonathan M. Purver, Annotation, *Punitive Damages For Wrongful Seizure Of Chattel By One Claiming Security Interest,* 35 A.L.R.3d 1016 (1971 & Supp. 1995).

With all of the foregoing case law at its disposal, it is somewhat surprising that the Drafting Committee declined to eliminate, if not reduce, the vagueness of the "breach of the peace" standard through codification of the less controversial holdings.[197] As recently noted by one author, statutory elaboration and clarification would encourage better compliance and provide more certainty.[198]

A creditor that cannot seize collateral without breaching the peace, or who wishes to obtain the collateral with no risk of liability for violating that duty, enjoys the statutory right to take possession of collateral with judicial assistance.[199] For example, a

197. Two helpful statements are found in revised § 9-609 cmt. 3 (1999). First, "courts should hold the secured party responsible for the actions of others taken on the secured party's behalf, including independent contractors engaged by the secured party to take possession of collateral." *Id.* Second, "[t]his section does not authorize a secured party who repossesses without judicial process to utilize the assistance of a law-enforcement officer." *Id.*

198. *See* Braucher, *supra* note 176, at 615–16. Professor Braucher proposed that § 9-503 be amended by including some variation of the following two clauses:

  (b) In taking possession of collateral by self-help, it is a breach of the peace for the secured party, without the contemporaneous permission of the debtor, to:
    (1) enter a locked or unlocked residence, garage or commercial building;
    (2) break, open or move any lock, gate or other barrier to enter enclosed real property;
    (3) enter upon residential real property, including a driveway, before 8 o'clock antemeridian or after 9 o'clock postmeridian;
    (4) proceed with a repossession if the debtor, a member of the debtor's household or an employee of the debtor is present and objects by words or actions or requests that the repossession not take place;
    (5) attempt a repossession by a trick that will or is likely to involve a confrontation with the debtor, a member of the debtor's household or an employee of the debtor; or
    (6) otherwise create an unreasonable risk of violence.
  (c) If a secured party or its independent contractor in the course of taking possession of collateral by self-help breaches the peace or uses law officers without the benefit of judicial process, the secured party shall be liable to the debtor for the fair market value of any property taken, and the debt shall be canceled.

Id. According to Steven O. Weise, an American Bar Association advisor to the Drafting Committee, "the Drafting Committee specifically considered the proposals in [Professor Braucher's] article and concluded that it would not be productive to have specific rules." Memorandum from Steven O. Weise to Timothy R. Zinnecker (Mar. 22, 1999) (on file with *The Business Lawyer*, University of Maryland School of Law) [hereinafter Weise Memorandum].

199. *See* U.C.C. § 9-609(a)(1), (b)(1) (1999); *cf. id.* § 9-503 (1995) (permitting the creditor to "proceed by action"); *id.* § 1-201(1) (defining " '[a]ction' in the sense of a judicial proceeding to include[ ] recoupment, counterclaim, set-off, suit in equity and any other proceedings in which rights are determined").

creditor may bring an action against the debtor, receive a favorable judgment, obtain a writ of execution, and, with the assistance of the sheriff or other proper official, seize the collateral over the objections of the debtor.[200] Also, a creditor may attempt to repossess collateral by complying with local replevin or sequestration procedures.[201] Although the time and expense necessary to accomplish judicial seizure may make this option appear less attractive than self-help, prudence suggests that repossession by judicial process may be the preferred course of action if any possibility exists that self-help repossession cannot be accomplished without breaching the peace.[202]

Under current Article 9, the secured party can require the debtor to move the collateral to a mutually convenient location "[i]f the security agreement so provides."[203] The secured party enjoys the same right under Revised Article 9 "[i]f so agreed, and in any event after default."[204] Although Revised Article 9 no longer requires a written agreement, the secured party should consider addressing the matter contractually before the debtor defaults and becomes uncooperative. Any provision should dictate not only one or more acceptable locations[205] but also the promptness with which the debtor must respond to the creditor's request. A creditor may find this right attractive if the collateral is likely to decline in value (from market forces, debtor misconduct, or otherwise) if it remains at its present location. Additionally, a creditor might request movement if the collateral is located at several places, especially if it believes that relocation to a cen-

---

200. *See, e.g.,* Dakota Bank & Trust Co. v. Reed, 402 N.W.2d 887, 888 (N.D. 1987).

201. *See, e.g.,* Del's Big Saver Foods, Inc. v. Carpenter Cook, Inc., 603 F. Supp. 1071, 1075–76 (W.D. Wis. 1985), *aff'd,* 795 F.2d 1344 (7th Cir. 1986); Sedalia Mercantile Bank & Trust Co. v. Loges Farms, Inc., 740 S.W.2d 188, 192 (Mo. Ct. App. 1987).

202. Absent a debtor's consent, repossession by judicial process will, by necessity, be the only option available to some creditors (e.g., those with a security interest in inventory and equipment kept by a debtor in a store, warehouse, or other closed facility).

203. U.C.C. § 9-503 (1995).

204. *Id.* § 9-609(c) (1999).

205. Just because a new location is "reasonably convenient" under revised § 9-609(c) does not necessarily make the new location commercially reasonable. As the new location must be "reasonably convenient" to both parties, the debtor should be estopped from challenging its commercial reasonableness. But such challenges may be brought by others, such as another secured party.

tral place will attract more potential buyers and possibly higher bids at any foreclosure sale. A secured party must realize, however, that any relocation request may be an exercise in futility. A debtor already in default may not be troubled if its refusal triggers another default, especially when retaining physical control of the collateral may represent the debtor's most powerful post-default weapon in its relationship with the creditor. If the debtor refuses to cooperate, the creditor should attempt to enforce this right with the aid of injunctive relief.[206]

Like its predecessor, Revised Article 9 requires a creditor that possesses collateral to exercise "reasonable care" in its custody and preservation[207] and to preserve the identifiability of non-fungible collateral.[208] The secured party may use or operate the collateral for the purpose of preserving it or its value,[209] and all reasonable expenses (including any insurance or taxes) incurred by the creditor in possessing, preserving, using, or operating the collateral become part of the secured obligation.[210]

---

206. *See, e.g.,* Clark Equip. Co. v. Armstrong Equip. Co., 431 F.2d 54, 57 (5th Cir. 1970) (affirming trial court's issuance of injunctive order requiring debtor to move equipment located in five states to a central location). *See also* Bookout v. Atlas Fin. Corp., 395 F. Supp. 1338, 1340 (N.D. Ga. 1974) (relying on *Clark* to invoke equitable principles and appoint receiver to conserve collateral), *aff'd sub nom.* Bookout v. First Nat'l Mortgage & Discount Co., 514 F.2d 757 (5th Cir. 1975); *cf.* Stern v. South Chester Tube Co., 390 U.S. 606, 609–10 (1968) (concluding that the shareholder could seek mandatory equitable relief against corporation that repeatedly denied statutory access to books and records).

207. *See* U.C.C. § 9-207(a) (1999); *id.* § 9-207(1) (1995); *see also supra* note 32.

208. *See* U.C.C. § 9-207(b)(3) (1999); *id* § 9-207(2)(d) (1995); *see also* Aspen Enters., Inc. v. Bodge, 44 Cal. Rptr. 2d 763, 769 (Ct. App. 1995) (concluding that a secured party could commingle repossessed tires with its general inventory as secured party kept repossessed tires identifiable and the tires were fungible).

209. *See* U.C.C. § 9-207(b)(4)(A) (1999); *id.* § 9-207(4) (1995); *see also supra* note 31.

210. *See* U.C.C. § 9-207(b)(1) (1999); *id.* § 9-207(2)(a) (1995); *see also* J. T. Jenkins Co. v. Kennedy, 119 Cal. Rptr. 578, 583 (Ct. App. 1975) (concluding that § 9-207(2) permitted secured party to recover $6200 paid to extinguish fuel tax lien on repossessed truck); First City Div. of Chase Lincoln First Bank v. Vitale, 510 N.Y.S.2d 766, 770 (App. Div. 1987) (remanding for determination of reasonableness of repossession and relocation expenses of $30,447); Davis v. Small Bus. Inv. Co., 535 S.W.2d 740, 744–45 (Tex. Civ. App.—Texarkana 1976, writ ref'd n.r.e.) (denying recovery of expenses of $23,060 absent proof that charges were reasonable); 2 GILMORE, *supra* note 2, § 42.6, at 1139 (distinguishing a secured party's payments made to protect its own interest from those made to protect the debtor's interest).

A creditor that elects not to repossess equipment may render it unusable,[211] which may be attractive when repossessing and storing equipment is expensive, impractical, or both,[212] and the creditor is concerned that the debtor may conceal, misuse, or dispose of the equipment.[213] Current Article 9 does not expressly prohibit the creditor from breaching the peace when rendering equipment unusable.[214] Revised Article 9 expressly requires the creditor to avoid breaching the peace.[215] Finally, as under current law, the creditor may dispose of collateral in accordance with other applicable default provisions whether or not the creditor has taken possession of the collateral or rendered it unusable.[216]

211. *See* U.C.C. § 9-609(a)(2) (1999). The creditor enjoys the same right under current Article 9. *See id.* § 9-503 (1995).

212. *See id.* § 9-609 cmt. 6 (1999); *id.* § 9-503 cmt. (1995); *see also* First Republic Corp. of Am. v. BayBank, 677 N.E.2d 1146, 1148 (Mass. 1997) ("The estimate given for the cost of removing and storing the equipment was over one-half of the actual value of the equipment itself, making a move impractical for any of the parties involved.").

213. *See* 9 HAWKLAND ET AL., *supra* note 15, § 9-503:6, at 684–85.

214. *But see id.* § 9-313:7, at 344 ("[W]hen the fixture is equipment, [the creditor should be able] to render it unusable if it can be done without a breach of the peace."); U.C.C. § 9-503 cmt. (1995) ("The authorization to render equipment unusable . . . would not justify unreasonable action by the secured party, since, under Section 9-504(3), all his actions in connection with disposition must be taken in a 'commercially reasonable manner.' "); *cf. id.* § 2A-525(2), (3) (permitting a lessor to take possession of goods or render them unusable without judicial process if action is taken without breaching the peace). For a case in which a secured party was convicted of criminal trespass and aggravated theft after rendering heavy equipment unusable by entering the debtor's premises and removing vital parts, see *State v. Pranger*, 822 P.2d 714 (Or. Ct. App. 1991).

215. *See* U.C.C. § 9-609(a)(2), (b)(2) (1999). This clarification occurred very late in the drafting process. *Compare id.* § 9-609 (Draft approved at NCCUSL Annual Meeting, July 30, 1998) (prohibiting a secured party from breaching the peace during self-help repossession under subsection (b)(2) but not while rendering equipment unusable under subsection (d)(1)), *with id.* § 9-609(b)(2) (Draft Nov. 16, 1998) (requiring the secured party to avoid breaching the peace when rendering equipment unusable under subsection (a)(2)). *See also* Zinnecker Memorandum, *supra* note 102, at 2 ("Can the secured party breach the peace while rendering equipment unusable under 9-609(d)(1)?").

216. *See* U.C.C. § 9-503 (1995); *cf. id.* § 9-609(a)(2) (1999).

REVISED § 9-610

DISPOSITION OF COLLATERAL AFTER DEFAULT

Under current § 9-504, a creditor enjoys the post-default right to "sell, lease or otherwise dispose of any or all of the collateral."[217] The creditor continues to enjoy this right under revised § 9-610, which also expressly states that licensing is a permitted form of disposition.[218]

Current law permits the secured party to dispose of the collateral "in its then condition *or* following any commercially reasonable preparation or processing."[219] Despite the disjunctive nature of the language, some courts have held that creditors are required to take commercially reasonable steps to prepare or process collateral before disposal, and that failure to do

---

217. *See id.* § 9-504(1) (1995).

218. *See id.* § 9-610(a) (1999). Licensing may be an attractive option for disposing of particular types of collateral, including: patents, copyrights, trademarks, and similar intellectual property; film and music collections; and computer software. In simple terms, licensing is the grant of a limited right of use, with the licensor retaining ownership and control.

Licenses can be exclusive or non-exclusive; limited in duration, territory, products, services, and otherwise; may be royalty-bearing or royalty-free, for a finite sum, a mix of royalty and lump sum, or other types of consideration; and, in general, may be as expansive or limited as the parties to a license agree.

Steven M. Weinberg, *Overview of the Law and Business of Licensing Copyrights, Trademarks and Publicity Rights, in* ADVANCED SEMINAR ON LICENSING AGREEMENTS 1998, at 9, 15 (PLI Patents, Copyrights, Trademarks, and Literary Property Course Handbook Series No. G4-4033, 1998).

219. U.C.C. § 9-504(1) (1995) (emphasis added).

so may impair the creditor's ability to recover a deficiency.[220] The retention of the language in its then-present form was a source of debate during the early stages of the drafting process,[221] but the Drafting Committee soon reached a consensus: the language would remain intact in the same statutory

---

220. *See, e.g.,* Chavers v. Frazier (*In re* Frazier), 93 B.R. 366, 371 (Bankr. M.D. Tenn. 1988) (holding that the creditor's failure to inspect and overhaul jet engines prior to sale of Lear jet constituted commercially unreasonable behavior), *aff'd,* 110 B.R. 827 (M.D. Tenn. 1989); Farmers & Merchants Bank v. Barnes, 705 S.W.2d 450, 452–53 (Ark. 1986) (concluding that the creditor failed to sell excavator in commercially reasonable manner when it failed to spend $1000 to paint it, fix leaks, and replace broken windows, worn-out pins, and worn-off teeth); Franklin State Bank v. Parker, 346 A.2d 632, 635 (N.J. Dist. Ct. 1975) (holding that the creditor acted improperly in selling vehicle without making such minor repairs as replacing missing spark plugs, points, condenser, and carburetor air filter); Weiss v. Northwest Acceptance Corp., 546 P.2d 1065, 1071–73 (Or. 1976) (noting relevance of evidence indicating that cleaning and washing logging equipment prior to sale could have resulted in higher sales price); First Bank v. VonEye, 425 N.W.2d 630, 637 (S.D. 1988) (citing Westgate State Bank v. Clark, 642 P.2d 961, 970 (Kan. 1982), for authority that "when the cost of preparing the collateral for sale is small, in comparison to the extra money it is likely to generate, the creditor should spend the extra money"). *But see* C.I.T. Corp. v. Duncan Grading & Constr., Inc., 739 F.2d 359, 361 (8th Cir. 1984) (citing statutory language for the proposition that a creditor "may, but is not required to, repair, improve, or otherwise spruce up the collateral before it is sold"); 4 WHITE & SUMMERS, *supra* note 36, § 34-14, at 451–52 ("We believe the cases are an incorrect reading of the statute. After all, the person complaining of the secured creditor's failure to paint, repair or the like, is usually the debtor—the very person who allowed the collateral to deteriorate in the first place.").

221. *See* U.C.C. § 9-504 cmt. 3 (Draft July 28–Aug. 4, 1995). The draft stated that

> [t]he Drafting Committee has not reach[ed] a consensus on whether a secured party is entitled to sell collateral without preparation or processing in all cases or whether preparation or processing is required if it would not be commercially reasonable to forego it. Accordingly, the draft places brackets around the language that appears to give a secured party the freedom to forego preparation or processing even if the omission would not [be] commercially reasonable. If the bracketed language ["in its then condition or following any commercially reasonable preparation or processing"] is deleted from subsection (a), new language ["If commercially reasonable, a secured party may dispose of collateral . . . in its then condition or following preparation or processing . . . ."] . . . should be added to make clear that preparation and processing are required if necessary to the commercial reasonableness of a disposition. Alternatively, the issue could be clarified in an Official Comment along the following lines:
>
>> A secured party is not entitled to dispose of collateral "in its then condition" when, taking into account the costs and probable benefits of preparation or processing and the fact that the secured party would be advancing the costs at its risk, it would be commercially unreasonable to dispose of the collateral in its then condition.

Id.

location.[222] Other than replacing "then condition" with "present condition," the final version of the renumbered statute reflects that decision.[223] Therefore, creditors are advised not to interpret the statutory language literally, but instead to evaluate the probable benefits likely to result from preparing or processing the collateral. If the creditor believes that the benefits may outweigh the costs, then the creditor should consider preparing or processing the collateral to avoid allegations that its disposition was not commercially reasonable.[224] For example, a creditor should spend $75 to tune a repossessed piano if the creditor believes that, as a result of the tuning, the sales price may increase by $500. But a creditor should forego replacing the keyboard at a price of $1000 if the creditor believes that taking such action will increase the sales price by only $600.

The success of any prediction of potential return may turn more on luck than on a fair assessment of existing commercial realities. And knowing at what point between costs and benefits a court will draw the line of commercial reasonableness remains uncertain.[225] Nevertheless, because the amount of any deficiency may be adversely affected by behavior that is commercially unreasonable,[226] a creditor should seriously consider spending the money necessary to prepare or process the collateral for disposition if the probable benefits outweigh the costs. Furthermore, in anticipation of likely challenges from the debtor, the

---

222. *See id.* § 9-504 cmt. 3 (Draft July 12–19, 1996).
The Drafting Committee was concerned that if the quoted language were added to the list in subsection (f) ["If commercially reasonable, a secured party may dispose of collateral . . . in its then condition or following preparation or processing . . . ."], courts might be unnecessarily quick to impose a duty of preparation or processing on the secured party. Accordingly, the Drafting Committee chose to retain the language in subsection (a).
Id.

223. *See id.* § 9-610(a) (1999).

224. Under both the current and revised versions of Article 9, all aspects of disposition must be "commercially reasonable." *See id.* § 9-504(3) (1995); *id.* § 9-610(b) (1998); *infra* notes 227–31 and accompanying text (discussing this requirement).

225. But "courts should not be quick to impose a duty of preparation or processing on the secured party." *Id.* § 9-610 cmt. 4 (1999).

226. *See id.* § 9-626. *See also* First Fidelity Acceptance v. Hutchins, 717 A.2d 437, 439 (N.J. Super. Ct. Law Div. 1998) (concluding creditor's decision to spend $1655 to repossess and refurbish car that sold for only $500 at foreclosure sale was not commercially reasonable and limited amount of deficiency).

creditor should document how and why it concluded whether to prepare or process the collateral prior to disposition.

Like its predecessor, Revised Article 9 allows the creditor to dispose of the collateral by public or private proceedings, by one or more contracts, as a unit or in parcels, and at any time and place, but every aspect of the sale must be "commercially reasonable."[227] The term is not defined by the U.C.C., but proof that the secured party could have achieved a better price by disposing of the collateral at a different time or by a different method does not, by itself, prevent the secured party from proving that its conduct was commercially reasonable.[228] In the absence of very limited situations,[229] the contours of "commercial reasonableness" are dictated by the facts of each case.[230] And one need only look as far as the nearest treatise to conclude that the term has been the subject of an overwhelming amount of litigation.[231] No doubt the issue of commercial reasonableness will remain a frequent visitor to the courthouse under Revised Article 9. Whether the Drafting Committee should be praised or pilloried for promoting litigation through its continued use of an undefined term[232] depends on whether

227. *See id.* § 9-610(b); *id.* § 9-504(3) (1995).

228. *See id.* § 9-627(a) (1999); *id.* § 9-507(2) (1995).

229. *See id.* § 9-627 (1999) (stating that dispositions are deemed "commercially reasonable" in limited situations); *cf. id.* § 9-507(2) (1995) (same).

230. One case offers 17 factors (including "[o]ther factors") that should be given "equal weight" in determining whether a disposition was commercially reasonable. *See* Crosby v. Reed (*In re* Crosby), 176 B.R. 189, 195–96 (B.A.P. 9th Cir. 1994), *aff'd*, 85 F.3d 634 (9th Cir. 1996); *see also* William Mark Rudow, *Determining the Commercial Reasonableness of the Sale of Repossessed Collateral*, 19 UCC L.J. 139, 140–58 (1986) (analyzing 12 factors).

231. *See, e.g.,* CLARK, *supra* note 2, ¶¶ 4.08[1]–[8], at 4-113 to 4-172; 9 HAWKLAND ET AL., *supra* note 15, §§ 9-504:4 to 9-504:10, at 709–60; 4 WHITE & SUMMERS, *supra* note 36, §§ 34-10 to 34-16, at 429–58. *See also* Richard C. Tinney, Annotation, *What is "Commercially Reasonable" Disposition of Collateral Required by UCC § 9-504(3)*, 7 A.L.R.4th 308, 313 (1981); *cf.* Donald J. Rapson, *Who Is Looking Out For The Public Interest? Thoughts About The UCC Revision Process In The Light (and Shadows) of Professor Rubin's Observations*, 28 LOY. L.A. L. REV. 249, 258–59 (1994) (criticizing the nebulous concept of "commercial reasonableness").

232. Litigation on one contentious, price-related issue should be reduced somewhat by revised § 9-615(f), a provision that addresses the commercial reasonableness of using a disposition price to calculate a deficiency or surplus if that price results from a disposition by the foreclosing secured party to itself, a related party, or a secondary obligor. *See* U.C.C. § 9-615(f) (1999).

one prefers the certainty provided by rules or the flexibility afforded by standards.[233]

Under both current and Revised Article 9, the duty to dispose of collateral in a commercially reasonable manner cannot be waived or varied.[234] The parties may adopt contractual standards that define commercially reasonable conduct, however, if those standards are not manifestly unreasonable.[235] No doubt some debtor advocates will argue that this provision improperly erases the line between "commercially reasonable" and "commercially unreasonable" behavior and redraws it between "commercially reasonable" and "manifestly unreasonable" conduct.[236] And consumer advocates will contend that the provision cloaks creditors with the authority to *unilaterally* dictate the standards by which their conduct will be governed because consumers are bereft of any bargaining power.[237] Nevertheless, creditors that prefer to control their own destiny, rather than placing themselves at the complete mercy of the

---

233. For an interesting discussion of the "rules versus standards" debate in the context of a rather famous (or infamous, depending on your team loyalty) professional sports incident, see Robert A. Hillman, *What the Knicks Debacle of '97 Can Teach Students About the Nature of Rules*, 47 J. LEGAL EDUC. 393 (1997); *see also* Louis Kaplow, *Rules Versus Standards: An Economic Analysis*, 42 DUKE L.J. 557, 621 (1992) (suggesting that rules should govern frequent behavior and standards should regulate infrequent behavior). *But see* Pierre Schlag, *Rules and Standards*, 33 UCLA L. REV. 379, 430 (1985) (concluding that the debate is a worthless undertaking).

234. *See* U.C.C. § 9-602(7) (1999); *id.* § 9-501(3) (1995).

235. *See id.* § 9-603(a) (1999); *id.* § 9-501(3)(b) (1995).

236. *See* Greenfield, *supra* note 10, at 485; *see also* Mark Snyderman, *What's So Good About Good Faith? The Good Faith Performance Obligation in Commercial Lending*, 55 U. CHI. L. REV. 1335, 1342 (1988) (noting a distinction between "a proscription against 'not manifestly unreasonable' behavior and a requirement that contract performance behavior meet 'reasonable commercial standards' "); *cf.* U.C.C. § 1-203 (1995) (obligating a secured party to act in "good faith"); *id.* § 9-102(a)(43) (1999) (defining "good faith" as "honesty in fact *and the observance of reasonable commercial standards of fair dealing*") (emphasis added).

237. *See* Greenfield, *supra* note 10, at 485–86; *cf.* 2 GILMORE, *supra* note 2, § 44.3, at 1221 ("No one will deny that the consumer security agreement is a contract of adhesion or that the consumer needs protection."). If the consumer is truly without any bargaining power, then perhaps the standards remain unenforceable, not because they are manifestly unreasonable but because they were not reached "by agreement" as required by revised § 9-603. Professor Greenfield acknowledges this argument, but believes that "it is too subtle and too easily missed by lawyers and judges who are not steeped in the UCC." Greenfield, *supra* note 10, at 485–86.

courts, should take advantage of this statutory invitation to contractually define commercially reasonable conduct.[238] Possible matters that might be addressed include minimum and maximum preparation and processing costs, acceptable times and places of sale, the content and mode of any publicity, and the speed with which the creditor must sell the collateral.

Like current § 9-504, revised § 9-610 permits a secured party to purchase collateral at a public disposition and, in limited situations, at a private disposition.[239] Why restrict the creditor's right to purchase at its own sale unless the sale is public? As Professor Gilmore explained, "At a 'public sale,' it may be hoped, there will be that lively concourse of bidders which will protect the secured party from his own weakness and drive the price up to those Himalayan peaks of fair value and true worth."[240] Current Article 9 does not define "public sale" or "private sale,"[241] so that task has fallen to the courts. Most cases have held that restricting access to the sale creates a private sale, even if the invited attendees engage in competi-

---

238. *See, e.g.,* Ford Motor Credit Co. v. Solway, 825 F.2d 1213, 1216–17 (7th Cir. 1987) (holding that the contract provision, which provided that creditor's sale to highest cash bidder would be a commercially reasonable means of disposal if creditor solicited bids from three or more dealers in the type of repossessed collateral, was not manifestly unreasonable); Ford Motor Credit Co. v. DeValk Lincoln-Mercury, Inc., 600 F. Supp. 1547, 1551–52 (N.D. Ill. 1985) (same); Liberty Bank v. Honolulu Providoring Inc., 650 P.2d 576, 579–80 (Haw. 1982) (observing that creditor failed to comply with provision, not manifestly unreasonable, requiring creditor to provide debtor with notice at least five days prior to sale); Wippert v. Blackfeet Tribe, 695 P.2d 461, 464 (Mont. 1985) (concluding that creditor complied with contract provision, not manifestly unreasonable, requiring creditor to give written notice to debtor at least five days prior to any sale); *cf.* Walker v. Grant County Sav. & Loan Ass'n, 803 S.W.2d 913, 916 (Ark. 1991) (holding that "[the] agreement . . . must be in writing"). The ability to "agree" on the timeliness of notice has been constrained. *See infra* notes 316–36 and accompanying text (discussing U.C.C. § 9-612 (1998)).

239. *See* U.C.C. § 9-610(c) (1999); *id.* § 9-504(3) (1995).

240. 2 GILMORE, *supra* note 2, § 44.6, at 1242; *see also* 1A PETER F. COOGAN ET AL., SECURED TRANSACTIONS UNDER THE UNIFORM COMMERCIAL CODE § 8.06[2][c], at 8-110 to 8-111 (1991) ("It is inappropriate for the secured creditor to establish the value of the collateral by negotiating with himself, so the Code sensibly prohibits the secured party's buying at a private sale unless there is some external guide . . . to fix the price.").

241. *Cf.* U.C.C. § 2-706 cmt. 4 (1995) (indicating that a public sale is "a sale by auction" and a private sale "may be effected by solicitation and negotiation conducted either directly or through a broker").

tive bidding.[242] Additionally, courts have held that a "public invitation" is an essential element of a public sale.[243] Furthermore, selling collateral to the general public by "sealed bids" has created a private sale,[244] whereas conducting an auction "with reserve" has not.[245]

242. Most of the "restricted access" cases have involved sales of vehicles at "dealers only" auctions. *See, e.g., Solway*, 825 F.2d at 1217–18; Chrysler Credit Corp. v. Curley, 753 F. Supp. 611, 617 n.12 (E.D. Va. 1990); Beard v. Ford Motor Credit Co., 850 S.W.2d 23, 27–29 (Ark. Ct. App. 1993); John Deery Motors, Inc. v. Steinbronn, 383 N.W.2d 553, 555–56 (Iowa 1986); Garden Nat'l Bank v. Cada, 738 P.2d 429, 431–32 (Kan. 1987); Coy v. Ford Motor Credit Co., 618 A.2d 1024, 1028–29 (Pa. Super. Ct. 1993). *See also* Morrell Employees Credit Union v. Uselton, 28 U.C.C. Rep. Serv. (Callaghan) 269, 272–74 (Tenn. Ct. App. 1979) (concluding that restricting access to corporate employees and members of credit union created private sale); *cf.* RESTATEMENT OF SECURITY § 48 cmt. c (1941) ("A public sale is one to which the public is invited by advertisement to appear and bid at auction for the goods to be sold."); Hogan, *supra* note 1, at 226 ("There is some indication that 'public' is a literal requirement and that everyone must be allowed to be present and to make an offer."). *But see* 1A COOGAN ET AL., *supra* note 240, § 8.06[2][c], at 8-111 (arguing that a dealer's auction, regularly scheduled and conducted, and where competitive bidding is present, should be a public sale because market forces operate unimpeded); LAWRENCE ET AL., *supra* note 128, § 18.02[A] [3], at 351 ("The hallmark of a public sale should be the competitive nature of the sale, not whether the public is invited.").

243. *See, e.g.,* Stewart v. Taylor Chevrolet, Inc. (*In re* Webb), 17 U.C.C. Rep. Serv. (Callaghan) 627, 631 (S.D. Ohio 1975) (holding that a sale was private in absence of evidence that "the public was invited by newspaper advertisement, poster, bulletin, or broadside, or by radio or television announcement"); Lavender v. AmSouth Bank, N.A., 539 So. 2d 193, 195 (Ala. 1988) (noting the presence of several factors that created public sale, including public invitation through newspaper advertisement); Bolen v. Mid-Continent Refrigerator Co., 411 N.E.2d 1255, 1259 (Ind. Ct. App. 1980) (holding that the placement of notice in two local newspapers satisfied the requirement of public invitation); Lloyd's Plan, Inc. v. Brown, 268 N.W.2d 192, 196 (Iowa 1978); Bank of Houston v. Milam, 839 S.W.2d 705, 708 (Mo. Ct. App. 1992) (finding a public sale after noting three notices of sheriff's sale were posted in public places); Pioneer Dodge Center, Inc. v. Glaubensklee, 649 P.2d 28, 30 (Utah 1982) ("The requirement of a public invitation is essential for a public sale . . . . It is fundamental that a public sale presupposes posting public notices or advertising."); *see also* 2 GILMORE, *supra* note 2, § 44.6, at 1242 ("If the sale has not been appropriately publicized, it would not be a public sale no matter where it was held or how it was conducted."); J. E. Keefe, Jr., Annotation, *What Constitutes A "Public Sale,"* 4 A.L.R.2d 575, 575 (1949); Boyd J. Peterson, Annotation, *Secured Transactions: What is "Public" or "Private" Sale Under UCC § 9-504(3),* 60 A.L.R.4th 1012, 1018 (1988).

244. *See* Cheshire v. Walt Bennett Ford, Inc., 788 S.W.2d 490, 494 (Ark. Ct. App. 1990); Boatmen's Nat'l Bank v. Eidson, 796 S.W.2d 920, 923 (Mo. Ct. App. 1990); *see also* Hogan, *supra* note 1, at 227 ("Furthermore, the term 'public sale,' may carry with it the notion of an auction where the price is successively raised through a series of offers; thus, sealed bids may not suffice."). *But see* Bank of Am. v. Lallana, 960 P.2d 1133 (Cal. 1998) (holding that disposition of debtor's automobile by sealed bid at public auction was public sale).

245. *See* Liberty Nat'l Bank v. Greiner, 405 N.E.2d 317, 321 (Ohio Ct. App. 1978).

To some extent, Revised Article 9 codifies existing case law. "Public disposition" (like its predecessor "public sale") is not defined in the text, but the official comments reveal that the term is intended to refer to a disposition "at which the price is determined after the public has had a meaningful opportunity for competitive bidding."[246] The term "meaningful opportunity" is "meant to imply that some form of advertisement or public notice must precede the sale (or other disposition) and that the public must have access to the sale (disposition)."[247] Neither revised § 9-610 nor its accompanying comments discuss the intended meaning of "private disposition," which leads to the inference that the term encompasses any disposition that is not a "public disposition."

As before, the creditor can purchase collateral at a private disposition if the collateral "is customarily sold on a recognized market."[248] Most courts have narrowly construed the term "recognized market," finding that it exists only where sales involve many fungible items with nonexistent or immaterial differences, haggling and competitive bidding are absent because price is controlled by neutral forces, and current price quotations of comparable items are readily available.[249] Revised Article 9 adopts a similar narrow construction, defining "recognized market" as a market "in which items sold are fungible and prices are not subject to individual negotiation."[250] No one should object to a creditor purchasing collateral at a private sale if the collateral is customarily sold on a recognized market because the commercial

---

246. U.C.C. § 9-610 cmt. 7 (1999).

247. *Id.* For much of the drafting process, "meaningful opportunity" implied access to "the public (or the commercially relevant segment of the public)." The parenthetical was deleted very late in the drafting process. *Compare id.* § 9-610 cmt. 7 (Draft Nov. 16, 1998) (including the parenthetical), *with id.* (1999) (omitting the parenthetical).

248. *Id.* § 9-610(c)(2) (1999); *id.* § 9-504(3) (1995).

249. *See* Aspen Enters., Inc. v. Bodge, 44 Cal. Rptr. 2d 763, 772 (Ct. App. 1995); Cooper Invs. v. Conger, 775 P.2d 76, 80 (Colo. Ct. App. 1989); Havins v. First Nat'l Bank, 919 S.W.2d 177, 183 (Tex. App. Ct.—Amarillo 1996, no writ).

250. U.C.C. § 9-610 cmt. 9 (1999).

reasonableness of the creditor's purchase price is so easily measured against an objective benchmark.[251]

Whether a "recognized market" exists for specific collateral has been frequently litigated. Courts have consistently held that stocks, bonds, and other publicly traded investments are customarily sold on a "recognized market."[252] Revised Article 9 affirms these decisions through its use of the New York Stock Exchange as an example of a "recognized market."[253] Courts have reached inconsistent results in the numerous cases involving motor vehicles[254] and livestock.[255] Revised Article 9 will bring some consistency in future cases, as it states: "A market in which prices are individually negotiated or the items are not fungible is not a recognized market, even if the items are the subject of widely disseminated price guides or are disposed of through dealer auctions."[256] Under this statement, a "recognized market"— at least as that term is used in Revised Article 9—does not exist for automobiles or livestock, for no two cars and no two animals

251. A creditor's sale, whether to itself or another party, of collateral normally sold on a recognized market may be statutorily reasonable. *See id.* § 9-627(b).

252. *See, e.g.,* FDIC v. Blanton, 918 F.2d 524, 528 (5th Cir. 1990); Finch v. Auburn Nat'l Bank, 646 So. 2d 64, 65–66 (Ala. Civ. App. 1994); Hersch v. Citizens Sav. & Loan Ass'n, 194 Cal. Rptr. 628, 630 (Ct. App. 1983); Northern Trust Co. v. Burlew, 525 N.E.2d 1123, 1126 (Ill. App. Ct. 1988); Washburn v. Union Nat'l Bank & Trust Co., 502 N.E.2d 739, 742 (Ill. App. Ct. 1986); Marine Midland Bank-Rochester v. Vaeth, 388 N.Y.S.2d 548, 550 (Sup. Ct. 1976).

253. *See* U.C.C. § 9-610 cmt. 9 (1999).

254. *See, e.g.,* Chrysler Credit Corp. v. H & H Chrysler-Plymouth-Dodge, Inc., 927 F.2d 270, 273 (6th Cir. 1991) (no); Norton v. National Bank of Commerce, 398 S.W.2d 538, 540 (Ark. 1966) (no); Community Management Ass'n v. Tousley, 505 P.2d 1314, 1315–16 (Colo. Ct. App. 1973) (no); Beneficial Fin. Co. v. Reed, 212 N.W.2d 454, 459 (Iowa 1973) (no); Nelson v. Monarch Inv. Plan, 452 S.W.2d 375, 376–77 (Ky. Ct. App. 1970) (no); Ford Motor Credit Co. v. Russell, 519 N.W.2d 460, 465 (Minn. Ct. App. 1994) (yes); L.C. Arthur Trucking, Inc. v. Evans, 13 U.C.C. Rep. Serv. 2d (Callaghan) 623, 625 (Va. Cir. Ct. 1990) (yes); Mount Vernon Dodge, Inc. v. Seattle-First Nat'l Bank, 570 P.2d 702, 712 (Wash. Ct. App. 1977) (yes).

255. *See, e.g.,* Wippert v. Blackfeet Tribe, 695 P.2d 461, 464 (Mont. 1985) (no); State Bank v. Hansen, 302 N.W.2d 760, 765 (N.D. 1981) (no); First Nat'l Bank v. Kehn Ranch, Inc., 394 N.W.2d 709, 714–15 (S.D. 1986) (yes); Havins v. First Nat'l Bank, 919 S.W.2d 177, 183–84 (Tex. App.—Amarillo 1996, no writ) (yes, but not in this case); Cottam v. Heppner, 777 P.2d 468, 473 (Utah 1989) (yes).

256. U.C.C. § 9-610 cmt. 9 (1999).

are identical. With few exceptions, courts have hesitated to find a recognized market for most other collateral.[257] This trend should continue if courts are mindful of the purpose underlying this narrow exception to the general rule prohibiting a creditor from buying collateral at a private disposition.

Another limited exception under the current and revised versions of Article 9 permits the creditor to purchase collateral at a private disposition if the collateral is "the subject of widely distributed standard price quotations."[258] Neither version offers any insight into the intended meaning of the phrase. Nor does either version suggest answers to two questions asked by Professor Gilmore: (i) To what degree must price quotations be disseminated before they are "widely distributed"? and (ii) When do price quotations become "standard"?[259] One author has suggested that collateral falls within the exception if prices realized in actual sales of comparable property are currently available by quotation.[260] That interpretation is plausible and would be in line with the policy underlying any limited exception to the general prohibition against creditor purchases at private sales. Yet, it is difficult to imagine collateral that would fall within this exception (at least

---

257. *See, e.g.,* SMS Fin., L.L.C. v. ABCO Homes, Inc., 167 F.3d 235, 243–44 (5th Cir. 1999) (used bowling alley equipment); Smith v. Mark Twain Nat'l Bank, 805 F.2d 278, 289 (8th Cir. 1986) (certificates of deposit and repurchase agreements); In re Bro Cliff, Inc., 8 U.C.C. Rep. Serv. (Callaghan) 1144, 1149 (Bankr. W.D. Mich. 1971) (inventory of air conditioners, televisions, and stereos); Canadian Community Bank v. Ascher Findley Co., 280 Cal. Rptr. 521, 533–34 (Ct. App. 1991) (oil rig); Cooper Invs. v. Conger, 775 P.2d 76, 80–81 (Colo. Ct. App. 1989) (restaurant equipment and furniture); 1st Charter Lease Co. v. McAl, Inc., 679 P.2d 114, 115 (Colo. Ct. App. 1984) (computer hardware); Hertz Commercial Leasing Corp. v. Dynatron, Inc., 427 A.2d 872, 876 (Conn. Super. Ct. 1980) (photocopier); Roberts v. First-Citizens Bank & Trust Co., 478 S.E.2d 809, 813 (N.C. Ct. App. 1996) (certificate of deposit); M.P. Crum Co. v. First Southwest Sav. & Loan Ass'n, 704 S.W.2d 925, 927 (Tex. App.—Tyler 1986, no writ) (residential mortgages). But see Clark v. EZN, Inc., 67 Cal. Rptr. 2d 403, 405 (Ct. App. 1997) (concluding that distributorship was a "recognized market" for foldable steel ramps that attach to back of truck tailgates); Aspen Enters., Inc. v. Bodge, 44 Cal. Rptr. 2d 763, 771–73 (Ct. App. 1995) (holding that the jury could conclude from evidence that "recognized market" existed for new tires); American Parts Sys., Inc. v. T & T Automotive, Inc., 358 N.W.2d 674, 677 (Minn. Ct. App. 1984) (finding a "recognized market" for auto parts).

258. U.C.C. § 9-610(c)(2) (1999); *id.* § 9-504(3) (1995).

259. *See* 2 GILMORE, *supra* note 2, § 44.6, at 1244.

260. *See* Richard C. Tinney, Annotation, *Nature of Collateral Which Secured Party May Sell or Otherwise Dispose of Without Giving Notice to Defaulting Debtor Under UCC § 9-504(3),* 11 A.L.R.4th 1060, 1064 (1982).

under the suggested interpretation), such as securities and commodities, that also would not be sold on a recognized market.[261] The Drafting Committee presumably contemplated that some items of collateral not sold on a recognized market might be subject to widely distributed standard price quotations; otherwise, the latter exception is redundant. One possibility is an automobile for which a vehicle valuation (the so-called "blue book" value) is published by the National Automobile Dealers Association (NADA).[262] But because no two vehicles are identical in every respect, the stated price may be better viewed as a mere starting point for price negotiation,[263] a factor that reduces the likelihood that the published valuations are "widely distributed standard price quotations."[264] Other than motor vehicles, one is left to ponder whether

261. For evidence that significant overlap between the two exceptions may exist, see U.C.C. § 9-627 cmt. 4 (1999) (describing a "recognized market" as a market "in which there are standardized price quotations"). Notice the omission of "widely distributed." *Cf. id.* § 9-610(c)(2) (referring to "widely distributed standard price quotations").

262. *See generally* N.A.D.A., OFFICIAL USED CAR GUIDE (1998).

263. *See In re* Ruiz, 227 B.R. 264, 267 (Bankr. W.D. Tex. 1998) (observing that a "blue book" quote "is only a guide" and "is in no way definitive with regard to . . . the particular replacement value"); *In re* Younger, 216 B.R. 649, 655 (Bankr. W.D. Okla. 1998) (noting that NADA price quotes "do not purport to constitute definitive appraisals of particular vehicles"); Carter v. Ryburn Ford Sales, Inc., 451 S.W.2d 199, 202–03 (Ark. 1970) (stating that price quotes in NADA books are "merely a guide"); Jon Ann Giblin & Stephen P. Strohschein, *Current Issues and Recent Developments in Consumer Bankruptcy*, 52 CONSUMER FIN. L.Q. REP. 78, 79 (1998) (observing that NADA price quotes "may be inaccurate as regards particular vehicles"); Alvin C. Harrell, *Consumer Credit 1997*, 52 CONSUMER FIN. L.Q. REP. 104, 105 (1998) (contending that NADA price quotes "are notoriously inaccurate in the context of an individual transaction"); *see also In re* Brown, 221 B.R. 46, 48 (Bankr. S.D. Ga. 1998) (observing, in a case involving a foreclosure sale of two mobile homes, that "NADA values have no relevance unless some evidentiary connection is established with the actual mobile homes in question"); Northern Commercial Co. v. Cobb, 778 P.2d 205, 210–11 (Alaska 1989) (holding that market publications listing wholesale and retail prices did not mean Caterpillar tractor was subject to widely distributed standard price quotations); Hayes v. Ring Power Corp., 431 So. 2d 226, 228–29 (Fla. Dist. Ct. App. 1983) (ruling that auction value publications listing successful bids at public auctions did not create widely distributed standard price quotations for Caterpillar tractor). *But see* Mount Vernon Dodge, Inc. v. Seattle-First Nat'l Bank, 570 P.2d 702, 712 (Wash. Ct. App. 1977) (concluding, with no analysis, that new and used cars, trucks, and campers are not only sold on a recognized market but also subject to widely distributed standard price quotations). Courts have had little trouble concluding that other types of collateral are not subject to the exception. *See, e.g.,* Cooper Invs. v. Conger, 775 P.2d 76, 81 (Colo. Ct. App. 1989) (restaurant equipment and furniture); Hertz Commercial Leasing Corp. v. Dynatron, Inc., 427 A.2d 872, 876 (Conn. Super. Ct. 1980) (photocopier); M.P. Crum Co. v. First Southwest Sav. & Loan Ass'n, 704 S.W.2d 925, 927 (Tex. App.—Tyler 1986, no writ) (residential mortgages).

264. *M.P. Crum Co.*, 704 S.W.2d at 927.

any other collateral, not already sold on a recognized market, falls within the exception. For whatever reason (perhaps, in light of extensive revisions elsewhere, a desire to leave untouched language that has generated little controversy), the Drafting Committee declined to clarify the intended meaning of "widely distributed standard price quotations," and failed to offer any examples.[265] In the absence of any official pronouncement, creditors are well-advised to place little, if any, reliance on this exception as an excuse to purchase collateral at a private disposition.

Revised Article 9 expressly offers purchasers a benefit not provided by current Article 9—warranties. Under revised § 9-610, a creditor that disposes of collateral provides the purchaser with warranties relating to title, possession, quiet enjoyment, and the like if those warranties, as a matter of law, accompany a voluntary disposition of such collateral.[266] For example, if the creditor is selling collateral consisting of goods, then the creditor provides the purchaser with the title warranty of § 2-312(1),[267]

---

265. The author requested clarification by the Drafting Committee. *See* Zinnecker Memorandum, *supra* note 102, at 2.

266. *See* U.C.C. § 9-610(d) (1999); *see also* PEB STUDY GROUP REPORT, *supra* note 7, at 218–19 (recommending that a foreclosing creditor provide warranties that can be disclaimed or modified).

267. Under § 2-312, the foreclosing creditor does not warrant good title because foreclosure sales are "out of the ordinary commercial course." *See* U.C.C. § 2-312(2) & cmt. 5 (1995). The Drafting Committee has expressly rejected this assumption, setting up a conflict between Article 2 and Revised Article 9. *See id.* § 9-610 cmt. 10 (1999). To resolve the conflict, comment 5 to § 2-312 will be revised to read as follows:

> 5. Subsection (2) recognizes that sales by sheriffs, executors, ~~certain~~ foreclosing lienors and persons similarly situated ~~are~~ may be so out of the ordinary commercial course that their peculiar character is immediately apparent to the buyer and therefore no personal obligation is imposed upon the seller who is purporting to sell only an unknown or limited right. This subsection does not touch upon and leaves open all questions of restitution arising in such cases, when a unique article so sold is reclaimed by a third party as the rightful owner.
>
> Foreclosure sales under Article 9 are another matter. Section 9-610 provides that a disposition of collateral under that section includes warranties such as those imposed by this section on a voluntary disposition of property of the kind involved. Consequently, unless properly excluded under subsection (2) or under the special provisions for exclusion in Section 9-610, a disposition of collateral consisting of goods under Section 9-610 includes the warranties imposed by subsection (1) and, if applicable, subsection (3).

Id. § 2-312(2) cmt. 5 (1999).

For an article critical of this about-face, see Robyn L. Meadows, *Warranties of Title, Foreclosure Sales, and the Proposed Revision of U.C.C. § 9-504: Has the Pendulum Swung Too Far?*, 65 FORDHAM L. REV. 2419, 2433–41 (1997) (suggesting that a title warranty will increase the risks, complexity, and costs associated with secured lending).

the warranty of merchantability under § 2-314(1) (if the creditor is a merchant in this type of collateral), and, in applicable situations, the warranty of fitness for a particular purpose in § 2-315. And if the creditor opts to lease, rather than sell, any goods, then the creditor may trigger the warranty provisions of Article 2A concerning interference and infringement, merchantability, and fitness for a particular purpose.[268]

Most creditors will not be pleased that Revised Article 9 exposes them to potential liability for a warranty breach, especially when potential damages may exceed the disposition proceeds. That displeasure should be short-lived, as revised § 9-610 permits the creditor to disclaim the warranties by communicating to the purchaser: "There is no warranty relating to title, possession, quiet enjoyment, or the like in this disposition" (or words of similar import).[269] What remains to be resolved is whether the creditor may disclaim the warranties in all situations, or only in those situations where to do so is commercially reasonable. The statute does not expressly place any limits on the ability to disclaim the warranties, suggesting the creditor has unfettered discretion. If the warranty disclaimer is one of the "other terms" under revised § 9-610(b) that must be commercially reasonable, however, then a cautious creditor may hesitate to disclaim any warranties; to do so may invite the debtor to argue that the disclaimer depressed the sales price and, therefore, was commercially unreasonable.[270] Guidance

---

268. See U.C.C. §§ 2A-211, 2A-212, 2A-213 (1995) (respectively). Some of these warranties are made only if the creditor-lessor is a merchant. See id. §§ 2A-211(2), 2A-212; cf. Mercedes-Benz Credit Corp. v. Lotito, 703 A.2d 288, 292 (N.J. Super. Ct. App. Div. 1997) (permitting consumer lessee to assert breach of warranty against financing lessor having close relationship with seller and manufacturer).

269. See U.C.C. § 9-610(f) (1999). The communication may be in any form provided by applicable law or in the form of a "record" as defined in § 9-102(a)(69). See id. § 9-610(e)–(f) & cmt. 11.

270. See Meadows, supra note 267, at 2444–49; see also Rapson, supra note 4 ("[I]f the secured party is conducting a public foreclosure sale of new automobiles, would it be commercially reasonable for the automobiles to be sold without the customary manufacturer's warranties that usually accompany the sale of new cars?"). But see Weise Memorandum, supra note 198 ("I would think that it would be unlikely that it would not be commercially reasonable to do something (disclaim a warranty) that the statute expressly authorizes.").

on this issue from the Drafting Committee would have been most welcome.[271]

Three other foreseeable questions arise. First, is "as is," "with all faults," or other language "of similar import"?[272] If the law that creates the warranties makes such a disclaimer effective, then such a disclaimer is effective under revised § 9-610.[273] Second, may a creditor that adopts the recommended disclaimer but fails to expressly reference the warranties against merchantability (if a sale) or interference and infringement (if a lease) rely on the phrase "or the like" as an effective disclaimer of those warranties?[274] Probably not. Those warranties, if applicable, do not arise under revised § 9-610 and, therefore, must be disclaimed in the manner required by other governing law.[275] And third, must any disclaimer be conspicuous?[276] If warranties of title, possession, quiet enjoyment, and the like are disclaimed, the disclaimer need not be conspicuous. Whether disclaimers of other warranties must be conspicuous is governed by law other than Revised Article 9.[277] Prudence dictates that a creditor take steps to avoid these potential landmines.

---

271. The author requested guidance from the Drafting Committee. *See* Zinnecker Memorandum, *supra* note 102, at 2.

272. *See* U.C.C. § 2-316(3)(a) (1995) (permitting waiver of implied warranties through the use of "as is," "with all faults," or similar language); *id.* § 2A-214(3)(a) (same).

273. *Id.* § 9-610(e)(1) & cmt. 11 (1999).

274. *See id.* § 2-316(2) (1995) (indicating that a waiver must mention merchantability); *id.* § 2A-214(4) (requiring "specific" language in order to waive warranties against interference and infringement).

275. *Id.* § 9-610 cmt. 11 (1999).

276. *Id.* §§ 2-316(2), 2A-214(2), 2A-214(4) (1995) (requiring "conspicuous" language); *see also id.* § 1-201(10) (defining "conspicuous").

277. *Id.* § 9-610 cmt. 11 (1999).

REVISED § 9-611

NOTIFICATION BEFORE DISPOSITION OF COLLATERAL

Under current Article 9, a secured party that intends to dispose of collateral is almost always required to send notice of the intended disposition to the debtor.[278] Several reasons justify the notice requirement: (i) it informs the debtor how long it has to redeem the collateral; (ii) it permits the debtor to attend, and actively participate in, any public sale; (iii) it allows the debtor to contact other potential buyers; and (iv) it gives the debtor an opportunity to monitor the commercial reasonableness of the disposition.[279] Under current law, the creditor is excused from sending any notice in limited situations but is required to send notices to additional parties at other times.[280] This duty to send notice, together with some of the procedural aspects of that duty and the composition of the distribution list, are found in revised § 9-611.

A creditor that disposes of collateral under revised § 9-610 must send "a reasonable authenticated notification of disposition."[281] As under current law, notice is excused if the collateral

---

278. *See id.* § 9-504(3) (1995).

279. *See, e.g.,* Central W. Rental Co. v. Horizon Leasing, 967 F.2d 832, 839 (3d Cir. 1992); *In re* Excello Press, Inc., 890 F.2d 896, 902 (7th Cir. 1989); Travis v. Boulevard Bank N.A., 880 F. Supp. 1226, 1232 (N.D. Ill. 1995); Peoples Heritage Sav. Bank v. Theriault, 670 A.2d 1391, 1393 (Me. 1996); Robert M. Lloyd, *The Absolute Bar Rule in UCC Foreclosure Sales: A Prescription for Waste,* 40 UCLA L. REV. 695, 715–20 (1993). Professor Lloyd offers an additional and "perhaps the most important reason" why business debtors want notice: it tells them how fast to file a bankruptcy petition that will halt the proposed sale. *Id.* at 716.

280. *See* U.C.C. § 9-504(3).

281. *See id.* § 9-611(b) (1999). The contents of the notification are the subject of § 9-613 (transactions other than consumer-goods transactions), and § 9-614 (consumer-goods transactions). *See infra* notes 337–80 and accompanying text.

(i) is perishable, (ii) threatens to decline speedily in value, or (iii) is of a type customarily sold on a recognized market.[282] The reason for the first two exceptions is rather obvious: any benefit afforded by giving notice is more than offset by the harm resulting from a decrease in potential proceeds (and a corresponding increase in the size of the deficiency) if disposition is postponed until after notice is given and the debtor is given a commercially reasonable period of time to protect its interests.[283] Notice is excused when the collateral is sold on a recognized market for the same reason that permits a creditor to buy such collateral at a private sale; independent market forces dictate a uniform price against which the reasonableness of the price received by the creditor is easily measured. That same reason permits a creditor to buy at a private sale if the collateral is subject to widely distributed standard price quotations, so it remains a mystery why the statute does not similarly excuse notice when the creditor disposes of such collateral.[284] In

282. U.C.C. § 9-611(d) (1999); *id.* § 9-504(3) (1995).

283. Courts have refused to find these two exceptions applicable in most cases. *See, e.g.,* United States v. Mid-States Sales Co., 336 F. Supp. 1099, 1103 (D. Neb. 1971) (cattle); Hollander v. California Mfg. Enters., Inc., 51 Cal. Rptr. 2d 694, 698–99 (Ct. App. 1996) (business machines and equipment); Backes v. Village Corner, Inc., 242 Cal. Rptr. 716, 717–19 (Ct. App. 1987) (restaurant equipment); Rock Rapids State Bank v. Gray, 366 N.W.2d 570, 574 (Iowa 1985) (restaurant equipment); McKesson Corp. v. Colman's Grant Village, Inc., 938 S.W.2d 631, 632 (Mo. Ct. App. 1997) (pharmaceuticals, pharmacy records, and customer lists); Boatmen's Bank v. Dahmer, 716 S.W.2d 876, 879 (Mo. Ct. App. 1986) (cattle); Roberts v. First-Citizens Bank & Trust Co., 478 S.E.2d 809, 813 (N.C. Ct. App. 1996) (certificate of deposit); Chittenden Trust Co. v. Andre Noel Sports, 621 A.2d 215, 218 (Vt. 1992) (outdated, high-fashion ski and sports apparel). *But see* Diamond Bank v. Carter (*In re* Carter), 203 B.R. 697, 702 (Bankr. W.D. Mo. 1996) (stating that the exception applicable to collateral threatening to decline speedily in value "may well be applicable" to cattle); *In re* Umbles Drew-Hale Pharmacy, Inc., 80 B.R. 421, 425 (Bankr. N.D. Ohio 1987) (concluding that approaching expiration dates of pharmaceuticals made exceptions applicable); Moutray v. Perry State Bank, 748 S.W.2d 749, 752 (Mo. Ct. App. 1988) (holding that evidence of significant price declines and impending harvests of competing wheat and corn crops established collateral of milo threatened to decline speedily in value); American City Bank v. Western Auto Supply Co., 631 S.W.2d 410, 420–21 (Tenn. Ct. App. 1981) (holding that exceptions applied to the November sale of Christmas toys and other seasonal items); *cf.* City Bank & Trust Co. v. Van Andel, 368 N.W.2d 789, 794 (Neb. 1985) (noting that whether cattle were perishable was a question of fact).

284. No such exception exists under current Article 9 either. *See* U.C.C. § 9-504(3) (1995). *But see id.* § 9-504 cmt. 18 (Draft Nov. 15, 1995) ("[T]he presence of a recognized market provides an independent check on the price received upon disposition, thereby eliminating the need to notify the debtor of an intended disposition. Under this view, notification probably also should be excused if the collateral is 'of a type which is the subject of widely distributed standard price quotations.' "). The author requested an explanation by the Drafting Committee. *See* Zinnecker Memorandum, *supra* note 102, at 2.

any event, a creditor that fails to send notice should not place too much hope in the forgiveness offered by the narrow exceptions.

As before, the notice must be sent to the debtor.[285] A frequently litigated issue has been whether a guarantor is a "debtor" and thus entitled to notice.[286] That issue disappears under the revisions, which obligate the creditor to send notice to any "secondary obligor,"[287] a term that includes guarantors.[288]

Yet, while the revised statute expands the circle of recipients in some transactions, it contracts the circle elsewhere. For example, Bank makes a $10,000 loan to Borrower, who offers no collateral. At Borrower's encouragement (and Bank's insistence), however, Parent offers collateral to secure repayment of the loan. When Borrower defaults, Bank seizes and prepares to sell the collateral. Under current Article 9, Bank is required to send notice of the sale to Borrower and Parent, both of whom are "debtors."[289] Under the revisions, however, Bank is obligated to send notice only to Parent (the "debtor").[290] Borrower is not entitled to notice; it is not a "debtor" under revised § 9-102(a)(28), and its liability as the maker of the note is primary, so it is not a "secondary obligor" under revised § 9-102(a)(71). That this is

---

285. See id. § 9-611(c)(1) (1999); id. § 9-504(3) (1995).

286. See Annotation, *Construction of Term "Debtor" As Used In UCC § 9-504(3), Requiring Secured Party to Give Notice to Debtor of Sale of Collateral Securing Obligation*, 5 A.L.R.4th 1291 (1981) (listing cases); see also Harry C. Sigman, *Guarantors' Pre-Default Waivers of Article 9 Debtors' Rights to Notice and Commercially Reasonable Disposition Should Be Effective*, 29 IDAHO L. REV. 627, 636–37 (1992–1993) (suggesting that the drafters never intended for guarantors to fall within the definition of "debtor").

287. See U.C.C. § 9-611(c)(2) (1999).

288. See id. § 9-102(a)(59) (defining "obligor" in a manner that includes any party that "(i) owes payment or other performance of the obligation . . . or (iii) is otherwise accountable in whole or in part for payment or other performance of the obligation"); id. § 9-102(a)(71) (including within the definition of "secondary obligor" an obligor whose obligation is "secondary"); id. § 9-102 cmt. 2a (directing the reader to "consult the law of suretyship to determine whether an obligation is secondary"); RESTATEMENT (THIRD) OF SURETYSHIP AND GUARANTY § 15(a) (1996) ("[I]f the parties to a contract identify one party as a 'guarantor' or the contract as a 'guaranty,' the party so identified is a secondary obligor . . . ."); see also Willoughby v. Board of Trustees, 466 S.E.2d 285, 289 (N.C. Ct. App. 1996) (observing that "a guarantor . . . is only secondarily or derivatively liable"); Garner v. Corpus Christi Nat'l Bank, 944 S.W.2d 469, 475 (Tex. Ct. App.—Corpus Christi 1997, writ denied) (noting that "[a] guaranty creates a secondary obligation"), cert. denied, 119 S. Ct. 410 (1998).

289. See U.C.C. § 9-105(1)(d) (1995).

290. See id. § 9-611(c)(1) (1999).

the intended result is evidenced by the official comments.[291] And excluding Borrower from the notice provisions seems fair, as Borrower's ultimate liability either to Bank (on the promissory note) or to Parent (on Borrower's reimbursement obligation) remains the same, whether or not Borrower receives notice of the disposition.

If the collateral consists of consumer goods, then the creditor need not send notice to anyone other than the debtor and any secondary obligor.[292] This rule makes sense in most transactions because the value of the collateral makes it attractive as security only to the foreclosing creditor, usually holding a purchase-money security interest. It is conceivable, however, that a high-dollar consumer good that retains its value over a period of time (such as a grand piano) might simultaneously serve as collateral on multiple loans. Nevertheless, the statute does not require the foreclosing creditor to give notice to any other secured creditor.

Under current Article 9, a creditor disposing of collateral other than consumer goods is obligated to send notice to other secured parties from whom the creditor has timely received written notice of a competing interest in the collateral.[293] Under Revised Article 9, the secured party must send its notice to three additional parties. First, any other person claiming an interest (whether statutory, judicial, or consensual) in the collateral is entitled to notice if the creditor has received, before the "notification date,"[294] an authenticated notification of the competing interest.[295] Second, any other secured party or lienholder is entitled to notice if, ten days prior to the "notification date," its interest was perfected by a financing statement that identified the

291. See *id.* § 9-611 cmt. 3; *id.* § 9-102 cmt. 2a (example 3).
292. *Id.* § 9-611(c); *cf. id.* § 9-504(3) (1995) (requiring a secured party to send notice of a disposition of consumer goods only to a "debtor," a term often interpreted to include any guarantor). Both of these versions of Article 9 define "consumer goods" in the same manner. See *id.* § 9-102(a)(23) (1999); *id.* § 9-109(1) (1995).
293. See *id.* § 9-504(3) (1995).
294. As used in revised § 9-611, the "notification date" refers to the date when the creditor sends its disposition notice to the debtor and any secondary obligor, unless all of those parties have previously waived their right to notice in accordance with revised § 9-624(a), in which case the "notification date" is the date of the last waiver. See *id.* § 9-611(a) (1999).
295. See *id.* § 9-611(c)(3)(A).

collateral, was indexed under the debtor's then-existing name, and was filed in the then-proper place.[296] And third, any other secured party (regardless of priority) is entitled to notice if, ten days prior to the "notification date," it held a security interest perfected by compliance with any statute, regulation, or treaty referenced in revised § 9-311(a).[297]

As revised, Article 9 no longer allows the creditor to remain passive, sending notice only to those parties that have contacted it. Instead, in order to ensure that notice is sent to all required parties, the foreclosing creditor not only must order a U.C.C. search report listing financing statements filed against the debtor[298] but also must be familiar with other means of perfection, and order search reports from appropriate recording officers. This should not pose a problem for most parties that hold a

---

296. *See id.* § 9-611(c)(3)(B) & cmt. 4. For much of the drafting process, the statute required notice to other secured parties *but not to lienholders.* This created an unexplained inconsistency with statutory language requiring a secured party to send notice of a strict foreclosure to other secured parties *and lienholders. See id.* §§ 9-611(c)(3)(B), 9-621(a)(2) (Draft approved at NCCUSL Annual Meeting, July 30, 1998). The author questioned this inconsistency, and it was remedied in a subsequent draft. *See* Zinnecker Memorandum, *supra* note 102, at 4; *see also* U.C.C. § 9-611(c)(3)(B) (Draft Nov. 16, 1998) (inserting "or lienholder").

297. *See id.* § 9-611(c)(3)(C) (1999). For some unexplained reason, the provision does not protect lienholders, who also are excluded from the companion notice provision in the strict foreclosure statute. Perhaps the referenced statutes, regulations, and treaties do not allow for the recordation of judicial, statutory, and other nonconsensual liens, whereas applicable law may permit lienholders to evidence their property interest by filing a financing statement in the U.C.C. records.

298. Prior to the 1972 amendments to Article 9, § 9-504(3) obligated a creditor to send notice to any other person with a security interest in the collateral who had duly filed a financing statement indexed in the name of the debtor. *See id.* § 9-504(3), 3B U.L.A. 128 (1992) ("Text Prior to 1972 Amendment"). The 1972 amendments deleted this requirement because the drafters believed that the "burdens of searching the record . . . were greater than the circumstances called for because as a practical matter there would seldom be a junior secured party who really had an interest needing protection in the case of a foreclosure sale." *Id.* at 129 ("Official Reasons for 1972 Change"). Nevertheless, a few states that adopted the 1972 amendments retained this requirement. *See, e.g.,* Ariz. Rev. Stat. Ann. § 47-9504(c) (West 1997); Fla. Stat. Ann. § 679.504(3) (West Supp. 1998); Tex. Bus. & Com. Code Ann. § 9.504(c) (West 1992); Wash. Rev. Code Ann. § 62A.9-504(3) (West 1995); Wis. Stat. Ann. § 409.504(3) (West 1995); *see also* Clark, *supra* note 2, ¶ 4.06[3], at 4-99 (suggesting that the pre-1972 statutory requirement of sending notice to all secured parties of record was "better public policy"); *cf.* PEB Study Group Report, *supra* note 7, at 214–15 (encouraging the Drafting Committee to consider requiring a disposing creditor to notify other secured parties of record but revealing a preference by a "substantial majority" of the PEB Study Group to retain existing notice requirements).

perfected security interest, for it is not likely that any other competing interest is perfected in a manner or place different from the manner and place of its own perfection.[299] No doubt some delay will arise between ordering and receiving information from public recording officers. The statute acknowledges this delay and affords the creditor a safe harbor against challenges from non-notified parties if the creditor complies with two requirements. First, the creditor must request (in a commercially reasonable manner) the search report no later than twenty days, and no earlier than thirty days, before the notification date.[300] Second, if the creditor receives a response before the notification date, the creditor must send its notice before the notification date to each named secured party and lienholder whose financing statement covers the collateral.[301] Because the safe harbor requires the secured party to send notice only to parties "named in that response,"[302] the secured party need not worry that it has breached its duty by failing to notify a party erroneously omitted from the report. Placing the risk of non-notification on the non-notified parties rather than on the foreclosing creditor seems fair for two reasons. First, the non-notified parties are somewhat

---

299. This will be true in most, but certainly not all, situations. For example, Bank may perfect a security interest in Dealer's inventory of motor vehicles by filing a financing statement. Dealer's inventory may include a trade-in that is subject to a security interest perfected by the former owner's creditor under a certificate of title statute. The vehicle would be encumbered by two security interests perfected in different ways. Also, Lender may perfect a security interest in Dealer's inventory of musical instruments by filing a financing statement with the central filing office (e.g., the U.C.C. filing office of the Texas Secretary of State). Dealer's inventory may include a used piano acquired from a musician who used it as a consumer good. The used piano is subject to a non-purchase-money security interest perfected by the musician's creditor under a financing statement recorded with the local filing office (e.g., the U.C.C. filing office of Harris County, Texas). The piano would be encumbered by two security interests perfected by filing, but the filings would be recorded in different locations.

300. *See* U.C.C. § 9-611(e)(1) (1999). Conduct that may prevent the search from being commercially reasonable includes: submitting the request to the wrong public official; submitting the request in a manner not prescribed by the public official; failing to include the required fee with the request; and submitting a request against a trade name, misspelled name, or otherwise incorrect name of the debtor.

301. *See id.* § 9-611(e)(2). Subsection (e)(2) did not reference "lienholder" until very late in the drafting process. *Compare id.* § 9-611(e)(2)(B) (Draft Nov. 15, 1998) ("each secured party named in that response"), *with id.* (1999) ("each secured party or other lienholder named in that response").

302. *Id.* § 9-611(e)(2)(B) (1999).

protected through the foreclosing creditor's obligation to conduct a commercially reasonable disposition.[303] And second, any person with a competing property interest can obligate the foreclosing creditor to send a disposition notice to it merely by timely notifying the foreclosing creditor of its interests.[304]

An issue occasionally litigated under present law is whether oral notice is acceptable. Current Article 9 does not expressly require written notice,[305] and a few courts have concluded that the notice may be oral.[306] By requiring the creditor to send "authenticated notification,"[307] the revised statute stops short of requiring written notice, but it does effectively preclude oral notice.[308] Although oral notice can just as easily accomplish the underlying

303. *See id.* § 9-610(b).

304. *See id.* § 9-611(c)(3)(A). A holder of a subordinate property interest that does not receive notice of a disposition because the U.C.C. search report either is not timely received by the foreclosing creditor or provides incorrect or incomplete information does not have any remedy against the foreclosing creditor (notwithstanding the termination of the holder's subordinate property interest under revised § 9-617(a)(3)). *See id.* § 9-611 cmt. 4. A non-notified holder may have a remedy, however, if it timely notified the foreclosing creditor of its competing property interest under revised § 9-611(c)(3)(A). Therefore, the holder should take steps to inform the foreclosing creditor of its property interest and not rely solely on the notice provided by its financing statement that may not appear on a search report that may not be timely received by the foreclosing creditor.

305. *Cf. id.* § 9-504(3) (1995) (referencing the creditor's receipt of "written notice" from competing claimants); *id.* § 9-505(2) (requiring the creditor to send "[w]ritten notice" of its proposal to retain collateral in satisfaction of the unpaid obligation); *see also id.* § 1-201(38) (defining "send" in a manner strongly suggesting a written product).

306. *See, e.g., In re* Excello Press, Inc., 890 F.2d 896, 902–03 (7th Cir. 1989); BancFlorida v. De Pasquale (*In re* De Pasquale), 166 B.R. 663, 674 (Bankr. N.D. Ill. 1994) (applying Florida law); Hall v. Owen County State Bank, 370 N.E.2d 918, 925 (Ind. Ct. App. 1977); Crest Inv. Trust, Inc. v. Alatzas, 287 A.2d 261, 264 (Md. 1972); Schulke v. Gemar, 870 P.2d 1378, 1380 (Mont. 1994); Beltran v. Groos Bank, N.A., 755 S.W.2d 944, 945–46 (Tex. App.—San Antonio 1988, no writ). *But see* Executive Fin. Servs., Inc. v. Garrison, 722 F.2d 417, 418–19 (8th Cir. 1983) (concluding that Missouri law requires written notice); Jones v. First Nat'l Bank, 505 So. 2d 352, 355–56 (Ala. 1987) (holding that oral notice is not permitted by Tennessee law); Walker v. Grant County Sav. & Loan Ass'n, 803 S.W.2d 913, 916–17 (Ark. 1991) (ruling that notice must be written); Stoppi v. Wilmington Trust Co., 518 A.2d 82, 86 (Del. 1986) (requiring written notice); Van Ness v. First State Bank, 430 N.W.2d 109, 110–11 (Iowa 1988) (holding that oral notice is insufficient); McKee v. Mississippi Bank & Trust Co., 366 So. 2d 234, 238 (Miss. 1979) (requiring written notice); Lendal Leasing, Ltd. v. Farmer's Wayside Stores, Inc., 720 S.W.2d 376, 379 (Mo. Ct. App. 1986) (concluding that notice must be written); DeLay First Nat'l Bank & Trust Co. v. Jacobson Appliance Co., 243 N.W.2d 745, 749 (Neb. 1976) (holding that secured creditor must send written notice).

307. U.C.C. § 9-611(b) (1999).

308. *See id.* § 9-611 cmt. 5; *id.* § 9-102(a)(7) (defining "authenticate"); *id.* § 9-102 cmt. 9.

purposes of the notice requirement as a written notice, oral notice does expose the sender to proof problems not associated with written notice, such as whether notice was sent (and, if so, its contents). These proof problems are reduced, if not eliminated, by the statutory requirement that notification be authenticated.

As under the current statute, notice must be sent but need not be received.[309] Assuming that the creditor sends notice to the last known address with proper postage but discovers that a party has not received the notice, must the creditor resend the notice or attempt to contact the party by other means? Current Article 9 does not expressly address the issue,[310] so any guidance offered by the revisions would have been most welcome. Revised Article 9 acknowledges the issue but delegates it "to judicial resolution, based upon the facts of each case."[311] As the case law has been mixed,[312] prudence dictates that a creditor utilize all information

309. *See id.* § 9-611(b) (obligating the creditor to "send" notice to various parties); *id.* § 9-504(3) (1995) (stating that reasonable notification shall be "sent"); *see also id.* § 1-201(38) (defining "send"); *id.* § 1-201 cmt. 26 (contrasting "send" and "receive"); Commerce Bank v. Dooling, 875 S.W.2d 943, 946 (Mo. Ct. App. 1994) ("Bank correctly notes that the code requires only that a secured party send notice of a sale and not that the debtor actually receive it."); First Nat'l Bank v. Mork, 850 P.2d 954, 956 (Mont. 1993) ("However, [§ 9-504(3)] must be read in conjunction with [§ 1-201(26)], which does not require that the debtor receive actual notice of the sale; it only requires that the creditor take reasonable steps to assure that the debtor is notified.").

310. *But see* CAL. COM. CODE § 9504(3) (West Supp. 1998) (requiring notice to the debtor to be "delivered personally or be deposited in the United States mail" using the address from the financing statement, the security agreement, or "such other address as may have been furnished to the secured party in writing for this purpose," or, in the absence of any of the foregoing, to the "last known address"); MONT. CODE ANN. § 30-9-504(3)(b) (1997) (stating that notice is reasonable when sent by certified mail from the debtor's most recent address in the loan documents or in any other writing from the debtor and received by the creditor).

311. U.C.C. § 9-611 cmt. 6 (1999).

312. *See, e.g.,* Ford Motor Credit Co. v. Solway, 825 F.2d 1213, 1219 (7th Cir. 1987) (holding that creditor's notice sent to address in contract was commercially reasonable as creditor had no knowledge that debtor had moved); *In re* Marshall, 219 B.R. 687, 690–91 (Bankr. M.D.N.C. 1997) (concluding that notices sent via first class mail or certified mail, return receipt requested, to debtors' last known address were reasonable even though secured party knew debtors no longer resided at that address); Stone v. Cloverleaf Lincoln-Mercury, Inc., 546 So. 2d 388, 390 (Ala. 1989) (concluding that creditor who sold collateral one day before receiving "unclaimed" certified notice acted in commercially reasonable manner); Underwood v. First Alabama Bank, 453 So. 2d 742, 745 (Ala. Civ. App. 1983) (holding that notice sent to contract address was reasonable, even though notice was returned because contract address did not provide apartment number); Day v. Schenectady Discount Corp., 611 P.2d 568, 573 (Ariz. Ct. App. 1980) (concluding that a question of fact existed on reasonableness of notice sent to debtor's last known address that creditor knew was not current); Friendly Fin. Corp. v. Bovee, 702 A.2d 1225, 1228

readily available to it in an effort to notify the intended party. Otherwise, a court may conclude that the creditor has failed to take all steps necessary to provide "reasonable" notification,[313] a conclusion that could result in damages[314] and affect the amount of any deficiency.[315]

(Del. 1997) (determining that notice sent to an address with an incorrect zip code was not reasonable notice); Henson v. Foremost Ins. Co., 280 S.E.2d 848, 849–50 (Ga. Ct. App. 1981) (holding that a creditor who made unsuccessful efforts to discover debtor's forwarding address could rely on certified notice sent to debtor's last known address); La Grange Bank & Trust Co. v. Rodriguez, 485 N.E.2d 394, 398 (Ill. App. Ct. 1985) (concluding that creditor's decision to send notice to debtor at his wife's address rather than to debtor's last known address raised an issue of fact on the reasonableness of notice); Fidelity Fin. Servs., Inc. v. Stewart, 608 So. 2d 1111, 1112–14 (Miss. 1992) (imposing duty on creditor to make additional good faith effort to notify debtor after creditor received notice receipt signed by debtor's neighbor-relative); Commerce Bank, 875 S.W.2d at 947 (holding that the creditor failed to take reasonable steps to notify debtor where creditor, with knowledge that debtor had not received mailed notice, failed to utilize telephone numbers and work address on loan application); First Nat'l Bank & Trust Co., 850 P.2d at 956 (holding that the return of creditor's notice sent to last known address did not make notice unreasonable as creditor had no knowledge of debtor's new address and had contacted debtor's former wife who also had no knowledge of debtor's new address); First Nat'l Bank & Trust Co. v. Hermann, 286 N.W.2d 750, 751–53 (Neb. 1980) (concluding that the creditor could rely on certified notice, sent to correct address but returned unclaimed, even though creditor knew debtor's telephone number at place of employment and had previously contacted debtor at that number on other matters); Altman Tractor & Equip. Co. v. Weaver, 343 S.E.2d 444, 445 (S.C. 1986) (holding that the creditor was not required to take further action after sending registered mail to proper address and receiving acknowledgment signed by third person); NationsBank v. Clegg, 29 U.C.C. Rep. Serv. 2d (CBC) 1366, 1373 (Tenn. Ct. App. 1996) ("While absolute proof of receipt of notice may not be required in every instance, a creditor, who only makes one attempt to contact the debtor, and is left uncertain of receipt of the notice, has not fulfilled its obligation to the debtor when it proceeds with a disposition less than two weeks from mailing its first [certified] notice."); ITT Indus. Credit Co. v. Rector, 34 U.C.C. Rep. Serv. (Callaghan) 379, 380–81 (Tenn. Ct. App. 1982) (ruling that the creditor was required to attempt to contact debtor by known telephone number after properly-addressed notice was returned unclaimed); Commercial Credit Corp. v. Cutshall, 28 U.C.C. Rep. Serv. (Callaghan) 277, 279–82 (Tenn. Ct. App. 1979) (finding reasonable notification by creditor that unsuccessfully attempted to contact debtor through relatives and employer after registered notice sent to most recently known address of debtor was returned unclaimed); Mallicoat v. Volunteer Fin. & Loan Corp., 415 S.W.2d 347, 351 (Tenn. Ct. App. 1966) (ruling that the creditor's reliance on registered notice returned unclaimed was not commercially reasonable because creditor had knowledge of debtor's place of employment and parents' residence); First Virginia Bank-Mountain Empire v. Ruff, 17 U.C.C. Rep. Serv. 2d (CBC) 663, 664 (Va. Cir. Ct. 1992) (concluding that bank could not rely on notice sent to contract address because bank knew debtor had not received notice and bank knew of other possible addresses which it could use but did not).

313. See U.C.C. § 9-611(b) (1999) (obligating the secured party to send "reasonable authenticated notification") (emphasis added).

314. See id. § 9-625(b) (stating that "a person is liable for damages in the amount of any loss caused by a failure to comply with this article"). But see id. § 9-628(a) (excusing liability if a secured party does not know how to communicate with a debtor or obligor).

315. See id. § 9-626(a)(3)–(4).

REVISED § 9-612

TIMELINESS OF NOTIFICATION BEFORE DISPOSITION OF COLLATERAL

Current Article 9 does not expressly state how much "advance warning" a disposition notice must provide, but it does require "reasonable notification."[316] Current default provisions do not define "reasonable notification," but the comments indicate that "at a minimum [notice] must be sent in such time that persons entitled to receive it will have sufficient time to take appropriate steps to protect their interests" in the collateral.[317] Not surprisingly, the timeliness of the creditor's notice is occasionally litigated.[318] Many creditors confront the issue by including in the loan documents a variation of the following: "Notice sent not

---

316. *See id.* § 9-504(3) (1995).
317. *See id.* § 9-504 cmt. 5.
318. *See, e.g.,* City Nat'l Bank v. Unique Structures, Inc., 929 F.2d 1308, 1312–13 (8th Cir. 1991) (holding that two weeks' notice of date after which collateral could be sold at private sale was reasonable); Bagel Break Bakery, Inc. v. Bagelman's, Inc., 431 So. 2d 676, 676–77 (Fla. Dist. Ct. App. 1983) (holding that two days' notice was unreasonable); Wells v. Central Bank of Alabama, N.A., 347 So. 2d 114, 119 (Ala. Civ. App. 1977) (ruling that notice received by debtor on same day as sale was "clearly deficient"); Credithrift of Am., Inc. v. Smith, 308 S.E.2d 53, 53 (Ga. Ct. App. 1983) (concluding that notice sent 10 days prior to public sale was reasonable, but finding that other parts of notice were unreasonable); Ennis v. Atlas Fin. Co., 172 S.E.2d 482, 484 (Ga. Ct. App. 1969) (concluding that the reasonableness of a two-day notice of private sale was a jury issue); Chemlease Worldwide Inc. v. Brace, Inc., 338 N.W.2d 428, 436 (Minn. 1983) (holding that notice postmarked on date of sale was inadequate); Chadron Energy Corp. v. First Nat'l Bank, 459 N.W.2d 718, 729 (Neb. 1990) (observing that compliance with state's minimum requirement of three business days may not be commercially reasonable in all cases); Levers v. Rio King Land & Inv. Co., 560 P.2d 917, 919 (Nev. 1977) (holding that a creditor who sold collateral on June 2, after sending letter on May 25, did not give timely notice); Franklin State Bank v. Parker, 346 A.2d 632, 635 (N.J. Dist. Ct. 1975) (holding that three days' notice of private sale was not timely).

less than _____ calendar days prior to any disposition of collateral shall be commercially reasonable." So long as the number of days is not manifestly unreasonable,[319] most courts uphold the provision.[320]

Revised Article 9 speaks directly to the timeliness of notice through revised § 9-612, which states that the issue usually raises a question of fact, not law.[321] The question becomes one of law, however, and is resolved in the secured party's favor, if the secured party sends notice at least ten days prior to the earliest time of disposition stated in the notice.[322] To avail itself of this safe harbor, the creditor must satisfy three conditions.

First, the secured party must send notice after default;[323] it cannot send notice prior to default (but at least ten days before any scheduled disposition) and fall within the ambit of the statute.[324]

Second, the *manner* in which the notice is sent must be commercially reasonable.[325] As the definition of "send" permits a "deposit in the mail,"[326] notice deposited with the U.S. Postal Service should suffice, at least if the secured party and the recipient are both located in the same state or, perhaps excluding Alaska and Hawaii, different states. In other situations, notice sent by

319. *See* U.C.C. § 9-501(3) (1995) (permitting parties to agree on standards by which statutory rights and duties are to be fulfilled if standards are not manifestly unreasonable).

320. *See, e.g.,* Aetna Fin. Co. v. Culpepper, 320 S.E.2d 228, 232–33 (Ga. Ct. App. 1984) (upholding a 10-day notice provision); Mullins v. Horne, 587 P.2d 773, 776–77 (Ariz. Ct. App. 1978) (upholding a five-day notice provision); Liberty Bank v. Honolulu Providoring Inc., 650 P.2d 576, 579–80 (Haw. 1982) (upholding a five-day notice provision, but observing that the creditor failed to comply with it); Wippert v. Blackfeet Tribe, 695 P.2d 461, 464 (Mont. 1985) (upholding a five-day notice requirement); Byrd v. General Motors Acceptance Corp., 581 S.W.2d 198, 201 (Tex. Civ. App.—Waco 1979, no writ) (upholding a 10-day notice requirement).

321. *See* U.C.C. § 9-612(a) (1999); *cf.* BancFlorida v. De Pasquale (*In re* De Pasquale), 166 B.R. 663, 674 (Bankr. N.D. Ill. 1994) (holding that the *adequacy* of notice raised question of law, but that the issue did not concern the *timeliness* of notice); West Chicago State Bank v. Rogers, 515 N.E.2d 1261, 1268 (Ill. App. Ct. 1987) (same); First Nat'l Bank v. DiDomenico, 487 A.2d 646, 649 (Md. 1985) (same).

322. *See* U.C.C. § 9-612(a), (b) (1999); *see also* PEB STUDY GROUP REPORT, *supra* note 7, at 231 (recommending a 10-day safe harbor).

323. *See* U.C.C. § 9-612(b) (1999).

324. *See id.* § 9-612 cmt. 3.

325. *See id.*

326. *Id.* § 1-201(38) (1995).

"regular mail" may not be commercially reasonable if the time necessary to accomplish delivery leaves the recipient with little or no time in which to take steps to protect its interest in the collateral.[327] Prudence suggests that the few extra dollars spent to send notice by an expedited delivery service is money well spent if the creditor is concerned that the timeliness of notice sent by other means may be challenged.[328] Alternatively, the creditor may attempt to avoid those challenges by selecting a disposition date that is more than ten days after notice is sent.

And third, the transaction cannot be a consumer transaction.[329] During much of the drafting process, the Drafting Committee contemplated a twenty-one-day safe harbor in consumer secured transactions and a ten-day safe harbor in other transactions,[330] but this distinction disappeared by the summer of 1997.[331] What, then, is the rule in consumer transactions? During part of the drafting process, revised § 9-612 included a subsection (c), which stated:

> The limitation of the rule in subsection (b) to transactions other than consumer transactions is intended to leave to the court the determination of the proper rule in consumer transactions. The court may not infer from that limitation the nature of the proper rule in consumer transactions and may continue to apply established approaches.[332]

Subsection (c) was deleted late in the drafting process,[333] but the substance of the subsection was retained in an accompanying

327. *See id.* § 9-612 cmt. 3 (1999) (suggesting that a creditor may not invoke the statutory safe harbor by using surface mail to contact an overseas debtor).

328. The secured party may wish to include some variation of the following provision in the security agreement: "Notice sent by either party via [list of mutually acceptable delivery services] shall be deemed a commercially reasonable means of delivery."

329. *See* U.C.C. § 9-612(b); *see also id.* § 9-102(a)(26) (defining "consumer transaction").

330. *See, e.g., id.* § 9-612 (Draft Oct. 1996); *id.* § 9-504(j) (Draft July 28–Aug. 4, 1995).

331. *See, e.g., id.* § 9-612 (Draft July 25–Aug. 1, 1997) (providing a 10-day safe harbor in transactions other than consumer-goods secured transactions, but not providing any safe harbor for consumer-goods secured transactions). This draft offered no explanation for the change from the preceding February 1997 draft.

332. *Id.* § 9-612(c) (Draft July 24–31, 1998).

333. *Id.* § 9-612 (Draft approved at NCCUSL Annual Meeting, July 30, 1998).

comment.[334] This comment, however, did not survive the final editing process. It seems curious that the Drafting Committee chose not to offer any guidance, especially when some direction may have reduced the foreseeable problem of nonuniform results.

The statute does not obligate the creditor to give at least ten days notice; the creditor can give notice less timely. A creditor that does so, however, invites challenges on the timeliness of the notice. Such a challenge raises a fact question,[335] which will frustrate the creditor's ability to win a deficiency judgment on a motion for summary judgment. A creditor that desires more flexibility than that afforded by the ten-day safe harbor may wish to negotiate a shorter period into the security agreement. A creditor's compliance with the negotiated provision should survive scrutiny, absent a finding that the shorter period is manifestly unreasonable.[336]

---

334. *Id.* § 9-612 cmt. 4 (Draft Nov. 16, 1998).

335. *See id.* § 9-612(a), (b) (1999).

336. *See id.* § 9-603(a); *see also* Mullins v. Horne, 587 P.2d 773, 776–77 (Ariz. Ct. App. 1978) (upholding a five-day notice provision); Liberty Bank v. Honolulu Providoring Inc., 650 P.2d 576, 579–80 (Haw. 1982) (same); Wippert v. Blackfeet Tribe, 695 P.2d 461, 464 (Mont. 1985) (same). The same contractual option should be available in a consumer transaction, where any timeliness issue raises a question of fact. *See* U.C.C. § 9-612(a).

REVISED § 9-613

CONTENTS AND FORM OF NOTIFICATION BEFORE DISPOSITION OF COLLATERAL: GENERAL

Current Article 9 requires the creditor to send "reasonable notification" but provides little guidance on its contents. A notice of public disposition must give the time and place of disposition,[337] and a notice of private disposition must provide the time after which the disposition will occur.[338] Creditors that send notices with this minimum information, and then dispose of collateral accordingly, withstand content-based challenges on the reasonableness of the notice. But creditors who send a notice that does not provide the minimum information, or who dispose of collateral contrary to the notice, often find themselves litigating their compliance with § 9-504(3)—usually unsuccessfully.[339]

---

337. *See* U.C.C. § 9-504(3) (1995).

338. *See id.*

339. *See, e.g.,* Lavender v. AmSouth Bank, N.A., 539 So. 2d 193, 194–95 (Ala. 1988) (holding that notice stating collateral "will be sold at public auction or private sale" failed to notify debtor of subsequent public sale); Simmons Mach. Co. v. M & M Brokerage, Inc., 409 So. 2d 743, 749–50 (Ala. 1981) (concluding that a letter stating equipment would be "eligible" for resale after a specific date was defective); Connecticut Bank & Trust Co., N.A. v. Incendy, 540 A.2d 32, 34–37 (Conn. 1988) (ruling that the creditor's failure to give notice of subsequent private sale of unauctioned collateral violated § 9-504(3), even though the notice of earlier public sale was proper); Hertz Commercial Leasing Corp. v. Dynatron, Inc., 427 A.2d 872, 874–76 (Conn. Super. Ct. 1980) (concluding that proper notice of public sale in August 1977 did not give debtor reasonable notice of private sale held in May 1978); Staley Employee Credit Union v. Christie, 443 N.E.2d 731, 732–33 (Ill. App. Ct. 1982) (holding that notice of public sale to be held on June 17 at a particular time and place did not give notice of subsequent sales on June 29 and

The contents of reasonable notice are now prescribed with much more particularity by revised § 9-613, a section that does not apply to consumer-goods transactions.[340] Under this section, a notice of disposition is sufficient if it: (i) describes the debtor and the secured party; (ii) describes the collateral to be disposed; (iii) states the method of disposition (e.g., sale, lease, license, etc.); (iv) states that the debtor is entitled to an accounting of the unpaid debt for a stated fee; and (v) states the time and place of any public sale of the collateral or the time after which the collateral will be disposed by another manner.[341]

June 30); Peoples Heritage Sav. Bank v. Theriault, 670 A.2d 1391, 1392–94 (Me. 1996) (ruling that the creditor failed to comply with notice requirements by sending letter stating: "The purpose of this notice is to provide you with notice of the Bank's intent to dispose of the Collateral by private sale. Therefore, please be advised that the Collateral will be sold at public auction on August 20, 1993."); Society Bank, N.A. v. Cazeault, 613 N.E.2d 1103, 1105–06 (Ohio Ct. App. 1993) (holding that the creditor's failure to include state—which was different from debtor's residence, location of creditor's office, and place where collateral was seized—and full name of city in notice was fatal); Finova Capital Corp. v. Nicolette, 689 A.2d 924, 927–28 (Pa. Super. Ct. 1997) (concluding that a letter stating that the creditor "will proceed with reclaiming the equipment on or shortly after May 10, 1993," and will subsequently "proceed with the sale of the equipment" failed to comply with statutory requirements), *cert. denied sub nom.* Finova Capital Corp. v. Lifecare X-Ray, Inc., 118 S. Ct. 1185 (1998); General Motors Acceptance Corp. v. Carter, 349 S.E.2d 342, 343–44 (S.C. Ct. App. 1986) (ruling that a letter indicating vehicle "*may* be sold at any time" after a specific time was defective), *vacated*, 361 S.E.2d 620 (S.C. Ct. App. 1987); Knights of Columbus Credit Union v. Stock, 814 S.W.2d 427, 430–31 (Tex. App.—Dallas 1991, writ denied) (holding that a letter referring to "possible sale," without more information, was inadequate); Wright v. Interfirst Bank Tyler, N.A., 746 S.W.2d 874, 875–77 (Tex. App.—Tyler 1988, no writ) (concluding that a letter advising debtor of "public sale on April 13, 1984 at 12:00 Noon at the location of Interfirst Bank, Tyler, Texas" was inadequate to give notice of private sale on May 24, 1984); Scharf v. BMG Corp., 700 P.2d 1068, 1071 (Utah 1985) (holding that a letter stating equipment "will be sold *on September 30, 1980*" did not reasonably inform the debtor of private sales on October 1 and 9, 1980).

340. *See* U.C.C. § 9-613 (1999); *see also id.* § 9-102(a)(24) (defining "consumer-goods transaction"). The content and form of disposition notices in consumer-goods transactions are governed by revised § 9-614. *See infra* notes 361–80 and accompanying text. Although revised § 9-613 does not apply to consumer-goods transactions, the notice contents listed in revised § 9-613(1) are required to be included in a disposition notice in a consumer-goods transaction through revised § 9-614(1)(A). The rights and duties created by revised § 9-613 cannot be waived or varied. *See* U.C.C. § 9-602(7) (1999).

341. *See* U.C.C. § 9-613(1) (1999).

The statute offers the following model form:

NOTIFICATION OF DISPOSITION OF COLLATERAL

To: [*Name of debtor, obligor, or other person to which the notification is sent*]

From: [*Name, address, and telephone number of secured party*]

Name of Debtor(s): [*Include only if debtor(s) are not an addressee*]

[*For a public disposition:*]
We will sell [or lease or license, *as applicable*] the [*describe collateral*] [to the highest qualified bidder] in public as follows:
Day and Date:
Time:
Place:

[*For a private disposition:*]
We will sell [or lease or license, as applicable] the [*describe collateral*] privately sometime after [*day and date*].

You are entitled to an accounting of the unpaid indebtedness secured by the property that we intend to sell [or lease or license, *as applicable*] [for a charge of $_____]. You may request an accounting by calling us at [*telephone number*].[342]

The proposed form requires a collateral description but does not dictate how detailed the description must be. A description that is lifted from the security agreement or financing statement and otherwise "reasonably identifies what is described"[343] should be acceptable, but the failure of the statute to expressly require a description used in either document suggests that other descriptions may be sufficient.[344] Incorporating the description from either document by reference (i.e., "the 'Collateral' as defined in

342. *Id.* § 9-613(5).
343. *See id.* § 9-108(a); *cf. id.* § 9-110 (1995) (stating that a description is sufficient "if it reasonably identifies what is described").
344. *Cf.* N.C. GEN. STAT. § 25-9-602(c) (1995) (suggesting that a notice of public sale should describe the collateral "as it is described in the security agreement . . . and may add such further description as will acquaint bidders with the nature of the property").

the Security Agreement executed by Debtor and Secured Party and dated March 1, 1998," or "the 'Collateral' as described in financing statement no. 98-12345 filed with the Texas Secretary of State on March 1, 1998") may be permissible but is not a practice to be encouraged. The time and expense necessary to either accurately retype, or attach a photocopy of, the description pales in comparison to the time and expense that may be incurred in litigating the propriety of referencing a description in an ancillary document, a copy of which the recipient may not possess or readily obtain.

The model notice leaves to the creditor's discretion whether to charge a fee for the accounting and, if so, how much. A decision to charge a fee no greater than the amount in revised § 9-210(f)[345] should be safe from challenge. The reasonableness of a larger fee—which could appear to be intended to suppress the request, rather than to compensate the creditor for its reasonable expenses—may be scrutinized.

The creditor need not adopt the proposed form verbatim;[346] a notice that substantially complies with the five requirements of revised § 9-613(1) is sufficient.[347] By adopting a "substantial compliance" standard, the statute acknowledges that the slightest error may not necessarily destroy the reasonableness of the notification. Failure to rigidly adhere to the statutory requirements will not be fatal if the errors are "minor errors that are not seriously misleading."[348] Rephrased, non-fatal errors are both minor and not seriously misleading; all other errors destroy the effectiveness of the notice. By adopting a literal reading, however, a court is permitted to conclude that a major error cannot be excused even if the error is not seriously misleading. Yet, if evidence reveals that the fatally flawed notice accomplished its intended purpose of providing the recipient with an opportunity to protect its interest in the collateral, then perhaps a court should overlook the defect, notwithstanding

---

345. U.C.C. § 9-210(f) (1999) (providing the debtor with one free request for an accounting every six months, but permitting the creditor to charge $25 for each additional request); cf. id. § 9-208(3) (1995) (same, with a $10 maximum charge).

346. See id. § 9-613(4) (1999).

347. See id. § 9-613(1)–(3).

348. Id. § 9-613(3)(B).

the statutory language. A court might reach that result by concluding that an error not seriously misleading must be minor.

Although used in a different context, the phrase "minor errors that are not seriously misleading" has a home and a history under current Article 9,[349] spawning a legion of cases.[350] This suggests that whether a notice contains an error that is minor or seriously misleading is likely to be the subject of frequent debate with inconsistent results. Some courts may conclude that the complete omission of any of the five prescribed elements from the notice is a major error,[351] while others may hold that the failure to include any of the required information is not fatal if the notice accomplishes its intended purpose.[352] Examples of errors that may be minor but not seriously misleading include some typographical mistakes and digit transpositions, such as referring to the debtor as "XYZ Corp." instead of "XYZ, Inc."[353] or switching the last two numbers of the zip code of the debtor's address if the switch does not frustrate timely delivery.[354] Examples of errors that may not be minor include providing the required day and date of public sale but using inconsistent information (e.g., indicating that the sale will be held on Tuesday, July 20, when July 20 is a Monday) or selling

---

349. *See id.* § 9-402(8) (1995) (preserving the effectiveness of financing statements with minor errors that are not seriously misleading).

350. *See, e.g.,* 9 HAWKLAND ET AL., *supra* note 15, § 9-402:14; CLARK, *supra* note 2, ¶ 2.10.

351. *See, e.g.,* Guardian State Bank v. Lambert, 834 P.2d 605, 606–08 (Utah Ct. App. 1992) (holding that the creditor's failure to comply with statutory signature requirements rendered financing statement ineffective and could not be saved by the "minor errors" exception of § 9-402(8)).

352. *See, e.g.,* Riley v. Miller, 549 S.W.2d 314, 315–16 (Ky. Ct. App. 1977) (holding that the absence of statutorily mandated addresses of debtor and secured party from financing statement was not fatal error where lien creditor lived in same town as debtor and secured party, and lien creditor knew their respective addresses). Courts should be mindful that the sufficiency of a notice lacking any of the information in revised § 9-613(1) "is a question of fact." *See* U.C.C. § 9-613(2) (1999).

353. *See, e.g., In re* Reeco Elec. Co., 415 F. Supp. 238, 240–42 (D. Me. 1976) (concluding that financing statements identifying Reeco Electric Co., Inc., as "Reeco Electric" and Petersbuilt Incorporated as "Petersbuilt, Inc." were effective, and misidentifications were minor errors not seriously misleading).

354. *Cf.* Adams v. Nuffer, 550 P.2d 181, 182 (Utah 1976) (holding that the discrepancy between boat's serial number on financing statement—D.M.F.A. 0082 M-75L—and actual serial number—D.M.F.A. 0082 M-74L—was insufficient to invalidate effectiveness of financing statement).

collateral that is described in the security agreement and financing statement but not described in the notice.[355]

Creditors may supplement the model form with additional information—such as a reference to one or more of the loan documents, a description of the event of default, or a statement of acceptable payment methods—without necessarily removing the notice from the safe harbor.[356] If the additional information is erroneous and concerns any rights provided to the recipient by Revised Article 9, however, the notice may be defective.[357] For example, the notice might assert that the creditor is entitled to retain any surplus proceeds or advise the debtor that its right of redemption terminates on a specific date. Both declarations are incorrect statements of rights afforded to a debtor by Revised Article 9[358] and may destroy the effectiveness of an otherwise proper notice.

A creditor that departs from, negligently completes, or supplements the model form invites challenges to the propriety of its notice.[359] In some cases, the creditor may find a lifeline in the

355. *See, e.g.,* Rotta v. Early Indus. Corp., 733 P.2d 576, 577–78 (Wash. Ct. App. 1987) (holding that the creditor who used financing statement description of collateral in disposition notice failed to give reasonable notice of sale of collateral described in security agreement but not described in financing statement).

356. *See* U.C.C. § 9-613(3)(A) (1999).

357. Late in the drafting process, revised § 9-613 permitted erroneous information not otherwise required by the statute "unless the erroneous information is misleading with respect to rights and remedies arising under this article." *See id.* § 9-613(4)(B) (Draft Mar. 1998). The quoted language was deleted in the next draft. *See id.* § 9-613(3) (Draft Apr. 6, 1998). Most, if not all, erroneous information concerning a recipient's statutory rights would be seriously misleading, a major error, or both. The language may have been deleted as unnecessary or redundant in light of nearby language that overlooks an error only if the error is minor and not seriously misleading.

358. *See id.* § 9-615(d)(1) (1999) (requiring the secured party to remit surplus proceeds to the debtor); *id.* § 9-623(c)(2) (permitting a debtor to redeem collateral at any time before a secured party has disposed of the collateral or entered into a disposition contract). For a case in which the creditor's misstatement of the debtor's redemption rights destroyed the effectiveness of its notice under § 9-504(3), see *DiDomenico v. First Nat'l Bank*, 468 A.2d 1046, 1048 (Md. Ct. Spec. App. 1984), *aff'd*, 487 A.2d 646 (Md. 1985). For a case in which the creditor's overstatement of the redemption price destroyed the effectiveness of its notice under § 9-504(3), see *Fielder v. Credit Acceptance Corp.*, 19 F. Supp. 2d 966, 986 (W.D. Mo. 1998).

359. Does such a challenge raise a question of fact, or a question of law? If the challenge concerns the absence of information described in subsection (1), the challenge raises a question of fact. *See* U.C.C. § 9-613(2) (1999). However, the statute does not address whether any other type of error creates a legal or factual issue. The omission of statutory clarification may lead courts to apply inconsistent labels. The author requested clarification from the Drafting Committee. *See* Zinnecker Memorandum, *supra* note 102, at 3.

words of the statute. In other cases, however, the lifeline will be nothing more than a rope of sand. As failure to provide reasonable notice can have adverse consequences for the creditor,[360] prudence suggests that a creditor adhere to, and carefully complete, the model form. A creditor that does so will have no difficulty proving that its notice complies with revised § 9-613.

---

360. *See, e.g.,* U.C.C. § 9-625(b), (c) (1999); *id.* § 9-626(a)(3), (4).

REVISED § 9-614

Contents and Form of Notification before Disposition of Collateral; Consumer-Goods Transaction

This section prescribes the contents and form of notice for dispositions of collateral in transactions excluded from revised § 9-613—consumer-goods transactions.[361]

Unlike revised § 9-613, which states that a notice is "sufficient" if certain information is provided,[362] revised § 9-614 indicates that the notice in a consumer-goods transaction "must" include all of the following:[363] (i) a description of the debtor, the secured party, and the collateral that is being disposed; the method of disposition; a statement that the debtor is entitled to an accounting of the unpaid debt and the charge, if any, for the accounting; and "the time and place of a public sale or the time after which any other disposition is to be made";[364] (ii) a description of the recipient's liability for any deficiency;[365] (iii) a telephone number from which the recipient can obtain the redemption price of the collateral;[366] and (iv) a telephone number or

---

361. *See id.* § 9-614 ("In a consumer-goods transaction, the following rules apply . . . ."); *id.* § 9-613 ("Except in a consumer-goods transaction, the following rules apply . . . ."); *see also id.* § 9-102(a)(24) (defining "consumer-goods transaction"). The rights and duties created by § 9-614 cannot be waived or varied. *See id.* § 9-602(7).

362. *Id.* § 9-613(1).

363. *Id.* § 9-614(1).

364. *See id.* § 9-614(1)(A) (incorporating the information described in § 9-613(1)).

365. *See id.* § 9-614(1)(B); *cf.* NEB. REV. STAT. § 9-504(6) (1992) (requiring a disposition notice to include "a statement to the effect that the debtor may be liable for any deficiency existing after sale or disposition of collateral").

366. *See* U.C.C. § 9-614(1)(C) (1999).

mailing address from which the recipient can obtain additional information concerning the disposition and the obligation.[367]

The section suggests that the sender adopt the following model notice:

[Name and address of secured party]
[Date]

NOTICE OF OUR PLAN TO SELL PROPERTY

[Name and address of any obligor who is also a debtor]
Subject: *[Identification of Transaction]*

We have your *[describe collateral]* because you broke promises in our agreement.

[For a public disposition:]
We will sell *[describe collateral]* at public sale. A sale could include a lease or license. The sale will be held as follows:

    Date:
    Time:
    Place:

You may attend the sale and bring bidders if you want.

[For a private disposition:]
We will sell *[describe collateral]* at private sale sometime after *[date]*. A sale could include a lease or license.

The money that we get from the sale (after paying our costs) will reduce the amount you owe. If we get less money than you owe, you *[will or will not, as applicable]* still owe us the difference. If we get more money than you owe, you will get the extra money, unless we must pay it to someone else.

You can get the property back at any time before we sell it by paying us the full amount you owe (not just the past due payments), including our expenses. To learn the exact amount you must pay, call us at *[telephone number]*.

If you want us to explain to you in writing how we have figured the amount that you owe us, you may call us at *[telephone number]* [or write

---

367. *See id.* § 9-614(1)(D).

us at [*secured party's address*]] and request a written explanation. [We will charge you $_____ for the explanation if we sent you another written explanation of the amount you owe us within the last six months.]

If you need more information about the sale call us at [*telephone number*] [or write us at [*secured party's address*]].

We are sending this notice to the following other people who have an interest in [*describe collateral*] or who owe money under your agreement: [*Names of all other debtors and obligors, if any*][368]

The opening paragraph of the notice suggests that the creditor must possess the collateral that is being disposed. As a practical matter this is true. The disposition price will be adversely affected if the debtor possesses the collateral, a complication that most likely would prompt an interested party to challenge the commercial reasonableness of the disposition. Nevertheless, as a matter of law the creditor is permitted to dispose of collateral that remains on the debtor's premises.[369]

The third paragraph (which begins "The money that we get from the sale") informs the obligated party that it may remain liable for any deficiency and should dispel (albeit belatedly) the popular notion held by many consumers that surrendering the collateral, voluntarily or otherwise, effectively discharges the consumer's liability for any unpaid debt.[370] This warning will hopefully prompt the recipient to take steps to protect its interest in the collateral, rather than remain passive, believing that the debt has been forgiven.

The following paragraph (which begins "You can get the property back") prompts two comments. First, the notice informs the recipient that it can redeem the collateral "at any time before we sell it." The notice would be more precise if it informed the recipient that it may redeem the collateral "at any time before

---

368. *Id.* § 9-614(3).
369. *See id.* § 9-609(a)(2); *see also id.* § 9-610(a) (indicating that the only predicate to disposition is a default).
370. *See* Gail Hillebrand, *The Redrafting of UCC Articles 2 and 9: Model Codes or Model Dinosaurs?*, 28 Loy. L.A. L. Rev. 191, 207 (1994) ("Consumers who surrender vehicles on request from creditors often think that the surrender unwinds the transaction and that there will be no deficiency."); McGrady v. Nissan Motor Acceptance Corp., 40 F. Supp. 2d 1323, 1327 (M. D. Ala. 1998) (revealing debtor's "understanding was that upon repossession of the vehicle, the account was satisfied").

we sell it or enter into a contract for its disposition."[371] Second, the recipient may be surprised that the "full amount" of the redemption price may include future payments, not just past-due amounts. Mere surprise alone does not make the notice misleading, but the creditor is reminded that, when calculating the "full amount," it should not include future payments if either the loan documents do not include an acceleration clause or the creditor has failed to properly exercise the clause.

The subsequent paragraph (beginning "If you want") provides the creditor with discretion to charge a fee for providing the recipient with a written explanation of the amount owed to the creditor. A creditor probably should not charge more than $25.[372]

As under revised § 9-613, the creditor need not adopt the particular phrasing of the proposed form.[373] A creditor is cautioned that the degree to which erroneous information is tolerated by revised § 9-614 greatly differs from revised § 9-613. Under revised § 9-614, the absence of required information makes the notice insufficient as a matter of law.[374] Also, an error in supplemental information is acceptable "unless the error is misleading with respect to rights arising under this article."[375] And the effect of voluntary information provided in a non-model form is determined by law other than Article 9.[376] This deference

371. *See* U.C.C. § 9-623(c)(2) (1999).

372. *See id.* § 9-210(f).

373. *See id.* § 9-614(2); *id.* § 9-613(4).

374. *See id.* § 9-614(1) & cmt. 2 (stating that notice "must" provide certain information); *cf. id.* § 9-613(2) (permitting a trier of fact to conclude that the absence of specific information does not destroy the sufficiency of the notice).

375. *Id.* § 9-614(5); *cf. id.* § 9-613(3)(B) (allowing minor errors that are not *seriously* misleading).

376. *See id.* § 9-614(6); *cf. id.* § 9-613(3)(A) (permitting the inclusion of supplemental information). The numerous changes over the last several months of the drafting process to provisions ultimately codified at revised § 9-614 suggest that treatment of errors and supplemental information was the subject of much debate. *See, e.g., id.* § 9-613(b)(3) (Draft Jan. 1998) (allowing substantial compliance and permitting "minor errors that are not seriously misleading"); *id.* § 9-613A(3) (Draft Mar. 1998) (bracketing language permitting substantial compliance and prohibiting "erroneous information [that] is misleading with respect to rights and remedies arising under this article"); *id.* § 9-613A(a)(4) (Draft Apr. 6, 1998) (allowing the standard form to contain errors in supplemental information "unless the error is misleading with respect to rights arising under this article," and permitting a court "to apply established approaches" to determine "the proper rule for notifications in another form and for errors in information not required"); *id.* § 9-614(6) (Draft approved at NCCUSL Annual Meeting, July 30, 1998) ("If a notification under this section

to other law may result in inconsistent results, as courts grapple with what test to apply and whether the test raises questions of law or fact. Unpredictability should encourage a secured party to adhere to, and carefully complete, the model form. A legitimate threat of a class action for significant statutory damages also should motivate a secured party to be diligent and precise.[377]

Undoubtedly, creditors that transact business with both consumers and non-consumers will be unhappy that Revised Article 9 does not provide one generic, all-purpose notice and a single set of rules governing permitted errors. Those creditors may be concerned that Revised Article 9 forces them to correctly determine whether a transaction is a consumer-goods transaction before they can send notice. In many transactions the concern will be short-lived because the classification will be obvious.[378] Additionally, Revised Article 9 provides a safe harbor for the creditor that acts in reasonable reliance on the debtor's representations concerning the purpose for which the collateral has been used, acquired, or held.[379] Therefore, in order to protect itself against a challenge that the wrong form of notice was sent, a creditor should revise its loan documents—particularly those used in transactions with consumers—to include such a warranty.

By proposing a notice unique to consumer-goods transactions, adoption of which is strongly encouraged through adherence standards that are less predictable than those applied to notices sent under § 9-613, the Drafting Committee has acknowledged the proposition that consumers, in general, are less sophisticated in commercial matters than their business

---

is not in the form of paragraph (3), law other than this article determines the effect of including information not required by paragraph (1).").

377. *See* Rapson, *supra* note 4.

378. The mere presence of an individual debtor does not make the election obvious. For example, a music store may intend to sell a repossessed piano originally sold on credit to an individual. If the individual used the piano for personal enjoyment and relaxation, the instrument is a consumer good under revised § 9-102(a)(23), the transaction is a consumer-goods transaction under revised § 9-102(a)(24), and the form and content of the disposition notice is subject to revised § 9-614. If the individual is a professional musician who used the piano primarily in a studio, however, the instrument is equipment under revised § 9-102(a)(33), the transaction is not a consumer-goods transaction, and the form and content of the disposition notice is governed by revised § 9-613.

379. *See* U.C.C. § 9-628(c)(1) (1999).

counterparts, and, as a result, must rely on the law to protect their interests which they themselves cannot adequately protect. If that proposition reflects reality, then the desired purpose could have been better achieved if the circle of protection had been drawn in a manner that included all consumer debtors, not just those who incur a debt for a particular purpose or offer specific types of collateral.[380]

---

380. *See id.* § 9-102(a)(24) (defining "consumer-goods transaction" in a manner that requires an obligation incurred "primarily for personal, family, or household purposes" collateralized by "consumer goods").

REVISED § 9-615

APPLICATION OF PROCEEDS OF DISPOSITION; LIABILITY FOR DEFICIENCY AND RIGHT TO SURPLUS

Under current Article 9, a creditor applies proceeds received from a collateral disposition according to a four-step payment scheme.[381] Revised Article 9 prescribes a five-step payment scheme that resembles—but does not mirror—its predecessor. Revised § 9-615 codifies the new payment scheme.[382]

Like its predecessor, revised § 9-615 initially permits a creditor to recover its reasonable expenses incurred in retaking, holding, and disposing of the collateral,[383] such as out-of-pocket payments

---

381. *See* U.C.C. § 9-504(1), (2) (1995).

382. The payment scheme analyzed in this section is codified in revised U.C.C. § 9-615(a), which applies only to cash proceeds. A creditor that receives noncash proceeds, such as a promissory note, is under no obligation to apply the proceeds unless the failure to do so is commercially unreasonable; a creditor that applies noncash proceeds must do so in a commercially reasonable manner. *See id.* § 9-615(c) and cmt. 3 (1999). The duties imposed by revised § 9-615(c) cannot be waived or varied. *See id.* § 9-602(4). However, the creditor and the debtor may contractually agree on the application of noncash proceeds through terms that are not manifestly unreasonable. *See id.* § 9-615 cmt. 3; *see also supra* notes 159–67 and accompanying text.

A creditor's decision to forego applying noncash proceeds was not expressly subject to a commercial reasonableness test until late in the drafting process. *Compare* U.C.C. § 9-615(c) (Draft July 24–31, 1998) ("A secured party need not apply or pay over for application noncash proceeds of disposition under this section."), *with id.* § 9-615(c) (Draft approved at NCCUSL Annual Meeting, July 30, 1998) (adding "unless the failure to do so would be commercially unreasonable" to the end of the sentence).

383. *See* U.C.C. § 9-615(a)(1) (1999); *id.* § 9-504(1)(a) (1995); *see also* Contrail Leasing Partners, Ltd. v. Consolidated Airways, Inc., 742 F.2d 1095, 1098–99 (7th Cir. 1984) (concluding creditor was entitled to recover reasonable expenses of $26,143.77

made to a repossession company, a storage facility, or an auctioneer. Additionally, a creditor can reimburse itself for reasonable attorneys' fees and legal expenses, but only to the extent provided for by agreement and not prohibited by law.[384] A secured party should revise its loan documents accordingly.

Like current § 9-504, revised § 9-615 next permits the creditor to apply the proceeds against the debt secured by the disposed collateral.[385] This permits a creditor to apply proceeds to multiple debts if those debts are secured by the disposed collateral; otherwise, the creditor cannot apply the proceeds to other obligations of the debtor.[386]

---

incurred in rebuilding aircraft propellers); CIT Corp. v. Nielson Logging Co., 706 P.2d 967, 969–70 (Or. Ct. App. 1985) (holding creditor can recover commercially reasonable costs even if the sale itself is not commercially reasonable). *But see* Ford & Vlahos v. ITT Commercial Fin. Corp., 23 Cal. Rptr. 2d 175, 184–87 (Ct. App. 1993) (affirming trial court's decision to disallow all but $82,743 of over $400,000 spent to repossess and refurbish repossessed aircraft where creditor failed to provide adequate documentation of costs); West Des Moines State Bank v. Ralph's Distrib. Co., 516 N.W.2d 801, 802 (Iowa 1994) (reducing bank's judgment against debtor by excessive liquidation expenses of $137,000); Imperial Discount Corp. v. Aiken, 238 N.Y.S.2d 269, 270–71 (Civ. Ct. 1963) (concluding unpaid debt of $11.75 made creditor's fees and expenses of $128.80 oppressive, confiscatory, and unconscionable); Hall v. Crocker Equip. Leasing, Inc., 737 S.W.2d 1, 2–4 (Tex. App. 1987, writ denied) (holding proof that expenditures were *necessary* to transport, repair, store, and insure repossessed helicopter did not necessarily mean that charges of $132,344.79 were *reasonable*).

384. *See* U.C.C. § 9-615(a)(1) (1999); *id.* § 9-504(1)(a) (1995); *see also* Continental Grain Co. v. Brandenburg, 587 N.W.2d 196, 204–05 (S.D. 1998) (permitting creditor to recover reasonable attorneys' fees in light of U.C.C. § 9-504(1)(a) and contract provision); Wilson Leasing Co. v. Seaway Pharmacal Corp., 220 N.W.2d 83, 87–88 (Mich. Ct. App. 1974) (same). *But see* White v. Associates Commercial Corp., 725 S.W.2d 7, 9–10 (Ark. Ct. App. 1987) (holding contractual provision permitting recovery of attorneys' fees was not enforceable under Arkansas statute prohibiting recovery of attorneys' fees except in lawsuits on promissory notes); First Nat'l Bank v. Schroeder, 355 N.W.2d 780, 782–83 (Neb. 1984) (concluding contract provision requiring debtor to pay attorneys' fees was contrary to public policy, void, and unenforceable); First Bank v. Haberer Dairy & Farm Equip., Inc., 412 N.W.2d 866, 874–75 (S.D. 1987) (ruling state statute permitting attorneys' fees in cases only if "specifically provided by statute" did not authorize award under U.C.C. § 9-504(1)(a)); *cf.* Kan. Stat. Ann. § 16a-2-507 (1995) (limiting enforceability of attorneys' fee clauses in consumer credit transactions).

385. U.C.C. § 9-615(a)(2) (1999); *id.* § 9-504(1)(b) (1995).

386. *See, e.g., In re* Russell, 165 B.R. 262, 263 (Bankr. E.D. Ark. 1994) (concluding bank's failure to properly cross-collateralize truck loan and camper loan prevented bank from applying surplus proceeds from sale of camper against deficiency resulting from sale of truck); *Wilson Leasing,* 220 N.W.2d at 89–90 (concluding proceeds from dispositions of distinct collateral items pledged pursuant to distinct security agreements were to be applied separately; creditor had no discretion in applying proceeds to debts as each security interest secured but one debt).

In many cases the proceeds will not completely extinguish the unpaid debt, leaving the creditor with a deficiency claim against the debtor.[387] Occasionally, however, some proceeds remain. Under current law, these excess proceeds are applied to reduce debt of other parties, subject to several requirements. First, the debt must be encumbered by a security interest in the collateral;[388] unsecured debts, and debts secured by an encumbrance other than a security interest, such as a judgment lien, are ineligible.[389] Second, the security interest must be subordinate to the interest under which the disposition is made; interests that enjoy priority or share equal rank do not qualify.[390] And third, the creditor that disposes of the collateral must receive a written demand for excess proceeds from the junior creditor before the proceeds are completely distributed.[391]

Revised § 9-615 has adopted current § 9-504(1)(c), with some modifications. The debt to be paid with excess proceeds still must be secured by an interest in the disposed collateral,

---

387. Generally the debtor is liable for any deficiency if the creditor has disposed of the collateral in accordance with the rules of Article 9. *See* U.C.C. § 9-504(2)(1995); *id.* § 9-615(d)(2) (1999). An exception exists when the underlying transaction involved the sale of certain assets to the secured party. *See id.* § 9-504(2) (1995); *id.* § 9-615(e)(2) (1999).

388. *See id.* § 9-504(1)(c) (1995).

389. *But see* CLARK, *supra* note 2, ¶ 4.06[3], at 4-99 ("It is unfortunate that [§ 9-504(1)(c)] gives junior judgment creditors no protection."); 2 GILMORE, *supra* note 2, § 44.8, at 1250 (suggesting that "the reference [to 'security interests'] should be read broadly to include . . . liens"); C. Edward Dobbs, *Enforcement of Article 9 Security Interests—Why So Much Deference to the Junior Secured Party?*, 28 LOY. L.A. L. REV. 131, 138 (1994) (contending that the payment scheme of § 9-504(1) triggers a "palpably unfair" result for the holder of a lien that is subordinate to the security interest of the foreclosing creditor but senior to a junior security interest). *Cf.* U.C.C. § 9-504(4) (1995) (indicating that disposition terminates "any security interest *or lien* subordinate thereto") (emphasis added).

390. *See* U.C.C. § 9-504(1)(c) (1995). Debts secured by subordinate security interests are eligible for payment because the disposition terminates those interests; non-junior interests survive disposition, so holders of those interests have no need of monetary protection. *See id.* § 9-504(4). This statutory protection may ring hollow if the senior creditor cannot locate either the purchaser or the collateral—a distinct possibility if the creditor does not receive notice of the disposition. *See* Dobbs, *supra* note 389, at 140. Under current law, a senior creditor is entitled to notice only if the foreclosing creditor has received timely written notice of the senior interest. *See* U.C.C. § 9-504(3) (1995).

391. *See* U.C.C. § 9-504(1)(c) (1995). The creditor may ignore the written demand for excess proceeds if the junior creditor fails to timely furnish the creditor with reasonable proof of the subordinate interest. *Id.*

but that interest can be either a security interest or a lien.[392] The competing property interest must be subordinate to the security interest under which the disposition is made,[393] but the subordinate property interest must enjoy priority over the competing interest of any consignor.[394] Although the creditor may have knowledge of the subordinate property interest and may have sent notice of the disposition to the holder of that interest,[395] the foreclosing creditor need not disgorge excess proceeds to the holder of the subordinate property interest

---

392. *See id.* § 9-615(a)(3) (1999); *see also* PEB STUDY GROUP REPORT, *supra* note 7, at 215 (recommending that any holder of a subordinate property interest should be entitled to receive excess proceeds if the holder has given the foreclosing creditor a timely written demand).

393. *See* U.C.C. § 9-615(a)(3) (1999).

394. *See id.* § 9-615(a)(3)(B). If a consignor has an interest in the disposed collateral that is not junior to the subordinate interests of secured creditors or lienholders, then the consignor is entitled to the excess proceeds (regardless of the priority of its interest against the security interest held by the foreclosing creditor) if the foreclosing creditor has timely received an authenticated demand from the consignor. *See id.* § 9-615(a)(4). The statute does not require the consignor to comply with a request by the foreclosing creditor for reasonable proof of the consignor's interest unless the consignor's interest is subordinate to the interest of the foreclosing creditor. *See id.* § 9-615(b). This may be a drafting oversight. Fairness to all concerned parties dictates that the foreclosing creditor should be entitled to demand proof of a consignor's interest (regardless of its priority) in the foreclosing collateral before disbursing excess funds to that person. Nor does the statute expressly state how excess proceeds should be applied if all of the following conditions are present: (i) a consignor has an interest in the disposed collateral that is subordinate to the interest of the foreclosing creditor (or, alternatively, the consignor's interest is not subordinate but the foreclosing creditor never timely receives the consignor's authenticated demand for payment), (ii) a secured party (or lienholder) has a security interest (lien) in the disposed collateral that is subordinate to the interest of the foreclosing creditor, (iii) the consignor's interest is senior to the interest of the subordinate secured party (lienholder), and (iv) if the consignor's interest is subordinate to the interest of the foreclosing creditor, the consignor fails to timely comply with the foreclosing creditor's request for reasonable proof of the consignor's interest. The foreclosing creditor can avoid paying excess proceeds to the subordinate secured party (lienholder) under revised § 9-615(a)(3)(B), the consignor with an interest not subordinate to the foreclosing creditor's interest under revised § 9-615(a)(4), and the consignor with an interest subordinate to the foreclosing creditor's interest under revised § 9-615(b). Following the payment scheme, the foreclosing creditor should remit excess proceeds to the debtor under revised § 9-615(d)(1). Because the interests of the subordinate security interests and liens are terminated by the disposition, see revised § 9-617(a)(3), a more equitable payment scheme would permit the foreclosing creditor to remit excess proceeds to the holders of those subordinate security interests and liens if a consignor has an interest in the disposed collateral but fails to satisfy the conditions of revised §§ 9-615(a)(4) or 9-615(b).

395. *See id.* § 9-611(c)(3).

unless the foreclosing creditor has timely received an authenticated demand for the excess proceeds from the holder of that property interest.[396] As a general rule under both current and Revised Article 9, the debtor is entitled to any surplus proceeds.[397] Under current law, the debtor is not entitled to surplus proceeds resulting from the creditor's disposition of accounts or chattel paper that the creditor has purchased from the debtor unless their security agreement so provides.[398] Revised § 9-615 continues this exception in modified form. As revised, the creditor need not remit to the debtor any surplus proceeds resulting from the disposition of accounts or chattel paper or—as the result of the expanded scope of Revised Article 9[399]—payment intangibles or promissory notes sold by the debtor to the creditor.[400] Unlike current § 9-502(2), which permits the parties to contractually override the exception, revised § 9-615 does not specifically permit contrary agreement. However, revised § 9-615(e) (the statutory address for this exception) is not referenced among the numerous statutes listed in revised § 9-602 (the

396. *See id.* § 9-615(a)(3)(A); *see also id.* § 9-102(a)(7) (defining "authenticate"). The foreclosing creditor is entitled to request reasonable proof of the subordinate security interest or lien. Failure by the holder of that interest or lien to timely comply with the request relieves the creditor from honoring the holder's demand for proceeds. *See id.* § 9-615(b).

397. *Id.* § 9-615(d)(1); *id.* § 9-504(2) (1995); *see also* Bill Fitts Auto Sales, Inc. v. Daniels, 922 S.W.2d 718, 720–21 (Ark. 1996) (affirming trial court's judgment awarding surplus proceeds to debtor). This duty to account for surplus proceeds is (under current Article 9) and remains (under Revised Article 9) a duty that cannot be waived or varied. *See* U.C.C. § 9-501(3)(a) (1995); *id.* § 9-602(5) (1999).

Under current Article 9, if the creditor knows that a party other than the debtor owned the collateral, then the owner—rather than the debtor—is entitled to the surplus proceeds. *See id.* §§ 9-112, 9-504 cmt. 2 (1995). This provision is necessary because current § 9-105(1)(d) defines "debtor" in a manner that includes parties without a property interest in the collateral. As revised § 9-102(a)(28) defines "debtor" in a more restrictive manner, Revised Article 9 has no provision comparable to current § 9-112.

In many transactions, the proceeds will not satisfy the foreclosing creditor's expenses and debt, leaving the creditor with a deficiency. Under current Article 9, the "debtor" remains liable for any deficiency. *See id.* § 9-504(2) (1995). Under Revised Article 9, the liability falls on any "obligor" (who may not be a "debtor"). *See id.* § 9-615(d)(2) (1998); *see also id.* § 9-102(a)(28) & (59) (defining "debtor" and "obligor," respectively).

398. *See id.* § 9-504(2) (1995); *see also id.* § 9-102(1)(b) (including within the scope of current Article 9 the sale of accounts and chattel paper).

399. *See id.* § 9-109(a)(3) (1999); *see also* Donald J. Rapson, *"Receivables" Financing Under Revised Article 9*, 73 AM. BANKR. L.J. 133, 136–40 (1999) (discussing expansion).

400. *See* U.C.C. § 9-615(e)(1) (1999).

"anti-waiver" provision).[401] Therefore, language expressly permitting parties to contract around the exception is not necessary and, in light of revised § 9-602, would be redundant.

In those instances where proceeds remain after the foreclosing creditor has paid its reasonable expenses and its debt, the payment scheme may raise questions for the foreclosing creditor that are not easily answered. How does the creditor determine whether a security interest or lien is junior to its own interest? How does it resolve the priority of multiple (but allegedly subordinate) security interests or liens? And what if the debtor disputes the amount owed to the other secured creditors or lienholders or the validity of the security interest or lien? Revised § 9-615 offers no guidance.[402] Presumably a creditor would not violate its disbursement obligations by depositing the excess proceeds into court and bringing an interpleader action against all interested parties.[403]

Noticeably excluded from the current and revised payment schemes as a potential recipient is any creditor whose interest in the collateral is not junior to the interest of the foreclosing creditor.[404] There is a reason that the payment scheme makes a priority-based distinction: the interest of a junior creditor is terminated

401. *Cf.* § 9-602(4) (referencing revised § 9-615(c)); *id.* § 9-602(5) (referencing revised § 9-615(d)); *id.* § 9-602(8) (referencing revised § 9-615(f)).

402. *Cf.* PEB STUDY GROUP REPORT, *supra* note 7, at 216 (recommending that the official comments provide a safe harbor for a secured party that disburses disposition proceeds in good faith).

403. *Cf.* N.C. GEN. STAT. §§ 25-9-504.1, -504.2(1997) (permitting a secured party to tender any surplus to a court clerk who may institute a special proceeding to determine ownership).

404. An early draft of Article 9 expressly provided for payment of proceeds to holders of senior security interests and liens before all other interests, including the interest under which the disposition occurred, but the provision never became part of the official text. *See* Steve H. Nickles, *Rights and Remedies Between U.C.C. Article 9 Secured Parties with Conflicting Security Interests in Goods*, 68 IOWA L. REV. 217, 242–44 (1983) (discussing drafting history of § 9-504).

405. *See* U.C.C. § 9-617(a)(3) (1999); *id.* § 9-504(4) (1995). This statutory protection offers little solace if the non-junior creditor is not informed of the disposition or cannot locate either the purchaser or the collateral. Revised Article 9 reduces this likelihood by expanding the list of parties to whom the foreclosing creditor must send its disposition notice. *Compare id.* § 9-611(c) (1999) (requiring notice to certain creditors that have either provided the foreclosing creditor with written notice of a competing interest or perfected the competing interest by filing a financing statement or complying with other

when the collateral is disposed, but the interest of a non-junior creditor survives the disposition.[405] Nevertheless, this point has eluded courts in the past.[406] Revised § 9-615 should reduce, if not eliminate, this confusion.[407] Under subsection (g), a foreclosing creditor can retain cash proceeds free of non-junior property interests (whether in the form of a security interest or a lien), is not obligated to apply the proceeds to the debt secured by those property interests, and is not required to pay any surplus proceeds to any holder of such property interest.[408] However, the foreclosing creditor cannot invoke subsection (g) unless it receives the cash proceeds "in good faith and without knowledge that the receipt violates the rights of the holder" of the property interest.[409]

---

law), *with id.* § 9-504(3) (1995) (requiring notice to certain creditors that have provided the foreclosing creditor with written notice of a competing interest).

406. *See, e.g.,* Stotts v. Johnson, 791 S.W.2d 351, 352–53 (Ark. 1990) (relying on priority provisions of current Article 9 to conclude that a senior secured creditor has a claim to proceeds of a sale conducted by a junior secured creditor); Delaware Truck Sales, Inc. v. Wilson, 618 A.2d 303, 308 (N.J. 1993) (relying on U.C.C. § 9-306(2) to hold that absent countervailing considerations a senior secured creditor could require a junior secured creditor to disgorge proceeds from collection of accounts receivable); Roemer & Zeller, Inc. v. Ace Transmission Center, Inc., 454 N.Y.S.2d 377, 378 (1982) (noting that although junior creditor had right to replevy and sell inventory, senior creditor would enjoy priority in any sale proceeds); Consolidated Equip. Sales, Inc. v. First State Bank & Trust Co., 627 P.2d 432, 438 (Okla. 1981) (relying on U.C.C. §§ 9-312(5) and 9-306(2) to hold that junior secured creditor had obligation to tender sales proceeds to senior secured creditor and that failure to do so amounted to conversion). *But see* Continental Bank, N.A. v. Krebs, 540 N.E.2d 1023, 1026 (Ill. App. Ct. 1989) (holding senior creditor was not entitled to proceeds of disposition conducted by junior creditor); Chadron Energy Corp. v. First Nat'l Bank, 459 N.W.2d 718, 731–32 (Neb. 1990) (concluding junior secured creditor was not guilty of conversion for retaining proceeds from disposition without first applying them to debt secured by senior security interests); 4 WHITE & SUMMERS, *supra* note 36, § 34-10, at 433–34 (observing that the "drafters plainly knew the difference between senior and junior claimants" and expressing disbelief that failure to reference a senior claimant's rights to proceeds in the distribution scheme was "inadvertent"); Cynthia Starnes, *U.C.C. § 9-504 Sales By Junior Secured Parties: Is A Senior Party Entitled To Notice And Proceeds?,* 52 U. PITT. L. REV. 563, 583–88 (1991) (criticizing court decisions permitting senior creditors to share in sale proceeds received by junior creditor). *See generally* Nickles, *supra* note 404, at 241–56 (analyzing the propriety of a senior secured creditor's claim to proceeds).

407. The PEB Study Group recognized this confusion and recommended that § 9-504 explicitly permit a junior secured party to dispose of collateral and retain and apply proceeds without regard for any senior security interests. *See* PEB STUDY GROUP REPORT, *supra* note 7, at 218–19.

408. *See* U.C.C. § 9-615(g) (1999).

409. *Id.; see also id.* § 9-102(a)(43) (defining "good faith"); *id.* § 1-201(24) (1995) (stating when a person "knows" or has "knowledge" of a fact).

Hopefully, courts will not conclude that the foreclosing creditor has acquired the adverse knowledge merely because evidence reveals that the creditor knew that the competing property interest existed (e.g., through the discovery of a financing statement); that conclusion is erroneous.[410]

A related issue not expressly addressed by revised § 9-615 is whether a secured creditor, holding a security interest that is not subordinate to the security interest held by the foreclosing secured creditor, can claim that its security interest attaches to any surplus proceeds that are remitted to the debtor. A secured creditor retains a security interest in identifiable proceeds "[e]xcept as otherwise provided" by Revised Article 9 (and § 2-403(2)).[411] Assuming that the proceeds remain identifiable, the secured creditor may argue that its security interest extends to the surplus in the debtor's hands because revised § 9-615 does not, in clear language, "otherwise provide."[412] However, that

---

410. One need only look to the definition, and rights, of a "buyer in ordinary course of business," to recognize the distinction between knowledge of the competing property interest and knowledge of a violation of the rights of the holder of that property interest. *See id.* § 1-201(9) (1999) (defining "buyer in ordinary course of business" as a person "without knowledge that the sale violates the rights of another person"); *id.* § 9-320(a) (indicating that a buyer in the ordinary course of business acquires the goods free of a security interest even if the buyer knows that the security interest exists); *id.* § 9-320 cmt. 3 (clarifying the distinction between knowledge of a security interest and knowledge of a violation of third-party rights; *see also id.* § 9-307 cmt. 2 (1995) (making same distinction); *id.* § 9-402 cmt. 2 (indicating that a financing statement "indicates merely that the secured party who has filed *may* have a security interest") (emphasis added). Query whether a senior secured party could provide the requisite adverse knowledge by filing a financing statement that states "SECURITY INTERESTS GRANTED IN FAVOR OF, AND RETENTION OF PROCEEDS IN ANY FORM BY, ANY OTHER PARTY VIOLATE THE RIGHTS OF THE SECURED PARTY IDENTIFIED HEREIN." *See* Rapson, *supra* note 4 (discussing use of so-called "bulletin board" financing statements).

411. *See* U.C.C. § 9-315(a)(2) (1999); *cf. id.* § 9-306(2) (1995) (extending a secured party's interest to identifiable proceeds "[e]xcept where this Article otherwise provides").

412. There is judicial and scholarly precedent for this proposition under current Article 9. *See, e.g.,* Chadron Energy Corp. v. First Nat'l Bank, 459 N.W.2d 718, 733 (Neb. 1990) ("[I]f the disposition of the collateral by a junior secured party produces a surplus which the debtor is entitled to receive pursuant to § 9-504(2), such proceeds are subject to the continuing security interest of the senior secured party."); Nickles, *supra* note 404, at 241–42 n.86, 245 n.103, and 254; Starnes, *supra* note 406, at 586 n.110 and 587. *Cf.* 9 HAWKLAND ET AL., *supra* note 15, § 9-306:03, at 37 (indicating, under the "except" clause of U.C.C. § 9-306(2), that a secured party's interest in proceeds may be subject to the interest of other parties under specific list of sections that does not include U.C.C. § 9-504).

result would seem to violate the spirit of the payment scheme of revised § 9-615, which excludes those very creditors from the list of potential recipients. It makes little sense to expressly exclude a party from a payment scheme if that same party can recover the payment via another statutory avenue. Nevertheless, a provision or comment on this issue would have been welcome.[413]

Normally a foreclosing creditor has every incentive to maximize disposition proceeds. As Judge Easterbrook observed:

> [W]hy shouldn't they maximize? Even if the secured party could be assured of a judgment for the full deficiency, why would it forgo a dollar today for the chance to enforce a deficiency judgment tomorrow? . . . [T]he secured party will expend every cost-justified effort because it prefers money now to judgment later. . . . Add the uncertainty of recovery in litigation and this preference for cash grows stronger. That the debtor has defaulted is an indication that it is unlikely to be good for all of any judgment the creditor is able to get.[414]

What the foregoing passage fails to acknowledge is that a secured party may, after conducting a disposition that satisfies the procedural requirements of commercial reasonableness, calculate its

---

413. Guidance on this issue was requested in the Zinnecker Memorandum, *supra* note 102. Louisiana has addressed the issue by defining "proceeds" in a manner that excludes "receipts that are derived from the disposition of collateral by a secured party by way of public or private sale under R.S. 10:9-504 or by judicial sale pursuant to applicable law." LA. REV. STAT. ANN. § 9-306(1) (West Supp. 1997).

414. *In re* Excello Press, Inc., 890 F.2d 896, 901 (7th Cir. 1989); *see also* Huntington Nat'l Bank v. Elkins, 559 N.E.2d 456, 459 (Ohio 1990) ("Given the economic realities of the lending industry, a secured creditor will generally attempt to obtain the highest possible price for the collateral since the recovery of a deficiency judgment against a defaulted debtor is usually dubious."); Edward J. Heiser, Jr. & Robert J. Flemma, Jr., *Consumer Issues in the Article 9 Revision Project: The Perspective of Consumer Lenders*, 48 CONSUMER FIN. L.Q. REP. 488, 495 (1994) (contending that a secured creditor has every incentive to maximize disposition proceeds "because every dollar sacrificed on the sale of collateral becomes an unsecured claim against a debtor who is necessarily a bad risk by virtue of his default"); Richard B. Wagner, *Commentary: Proposed Consumer Changes to Article 9 of the Uniform Commercial Code Would Adversely Affect Consumer Credit*, 50 CONSUMER FIN. L.Q. REP. 92, 93 (1996) (noting "the powerful incentives that creditors have to maximize recovery from the sale of collateral given the uncertainty of collection of deficiencies").

deficiency claim by using an unreasonable sales price. For example, Seller repossesses equipment following Debtor's default on a $100,000 debt. Seller paints and cleans the equipment and advertises the disposition in all of the appropriate newspapers and trade journals. Seller has the equipment appraised at $75,000, but because the equipment will be sold at foreclosure, Seller realistically expects a successful bid somewhere between $55,000 and $65,000. Seller conducts a public sale at a convenient time and place. Although all procedural aspects of the sale are commercially reasonable, no serious buyers attend the public sale other than Seller, who bids $10,000. Two weeks later, Seller sells the equipment to a dealer for $60,000. Soon thereafter, Seller sues Debtor for a $90,000 deficiency ($100,000 debt minus a $10,000 credit from the foreclosure sale[415]). If all procedural aspects of the foreclosure sale were commercially reasonable, must Debtor accept Seller's calculation of a $90,000 deficiency claim?

The answer is found in revised § 9-615(f), which permits a debtor (or obligor) to challenge the amount of the deficiency claim.[416] Revised § 9-615(f) provides a special formula for calculating a surplus or deficiency resulting from selected collateral dispositions.[417] The special formula does not subject a secured party's *disposition* to judicial scrutiny if the *procedures* are commercially reasonable. But it does place the spotlight on the *amount of proceeds* used by the secured party to calculate its deficiency claim. And if the spotlight reveals that the secured party calculated its deficiency claim by using an unreasonably

---

415. "When the secured party 'bids in' the collateral it does not pay money; rather it just allows a credit against the outstanding debt. That is called a credit bid." Donald J. Rapson, *Deficient Treatment of Deficiency Claims: Gilmore Would Have Repented*, 75 WASH. U. L.Q. 491, 497 n.22 (1997); *see also* 2 GILMORE, *supra* note 2, § 43.2, at 1188–89 (noting that "the person who buys at the sale today, nine times out of ten, is not our hero, the good faith purchaser for value, but the holder of the security interest who pays not in cash but by a credit against the debt").

416. *See* U.C.C. § 9-615(f) (1999). This statutory provision cannot be waived or varied. *See id.* § 9-602(8).

417. *See id.* § 9-615 cmt. 6.

low amount of proceeds, the deficiency is recalculated by using the amount of proceeds that would have been realized in a commercially reasonable disposition to a party other than the secured party, a party related to the secured party, or a secondary obligor.[418]

Focusing attention on any aspect of a collateral disposition may displease a foreclosing creditor, but several reasons should mitigate a creditor's expected disfavor with revised § 9-615(f). First, the provision applies only if a secured party disposes of collateral to itself, a "person related to" the secured party,[419] or a secondary obligor;[420] it does not apply to all dispositions.[421] Second, the provision applies only if the secured party's calculation utilizes an amount of proceeds that falls *significantly*[422] below the *range* of proceeds that would have been realized from a disposition to a party outside the three classes; it does not apply merely because the disposition failed to yield a credit that approximates an amount that the debtor perceives is the

---

418. *See id.* § 9-615(f). Mr. Rapson, a member of the Drafting Committee, is most responsible for the formula that is codified at subsection (f). He recounts his efforts to persuade the Drafting Committee to adopt the formula in Rapson, *supra* note 415, at 512–36. Already subsection (f) is being referred to as "the Rapson Rule." *See* Barkley Clark & Barbara Clark, *Special Report: New Article 9*, 31 UCC L.J. 243, 257 (1999).

419. *See* U.C.C. § 9-102(a)(62) (1999) (defining "person related to" an individual); *id.* § 9-102(a)(63) (defining "person related to" an organization). The definitions are patterned after UNIF. CONSUMER CREDIT CODE 1974 § 1.301(32), 7A U.L.A. 48–49 (1985) (defining "person related to").

420. What appears to be a disposition to a secondary obligor may not be treated as a "disposition." *See* U.C.C. § 9-618 (1999), discussed *infra* notes 479–512 and accompanying text.

421. *See id.* § 9-615(f)(1).

422. As noted by Professor Braucher, "[t]he cute litigation game here will be how low is significantly below the range of foreclosure sale prices to others." Jean Braucher, *Deadlock: Consumer Transactions Under Revised Article 9*, 73 AM. BANKR. L.J. 83, 105 (1999). History suggests that such an imprecise term encourages litigation that may not produce consistent results. For example, current § 9-302(1)(e) provides a secured party with automatic perfection of an assignment of accounts that does not constitute "a significant part" of the debtor's outstanding accounts. Courts have used various tests to craft the contours of the nebulous phrase. *See, e.g.*, 9 HAWKLAND ET AL., *supra* note 15, § 9-302:10, at 9-1336 to 9-1339 (1997); *id.* § 9-302:10, at 9-113 (Supp. 1998) (summarizing tests and citing cases); Kristine Cordier Karnezis, Annotation, *When Is Filing Of Financing Statement Necessary To Perfect An Assignment Of Accounts Under UCC § 9-302(1)(e)*, 85 A.L.R.3d 1050 (1978); *id.* at 73 (Supp. 1998) (collecting and analyzing cases).

approximate fair market value of the collateral.[423] Third, the burden of proof under revised § 9-615(f) rests not on the secured party but on the party challenging the deficiency calculation.[424] And fourth, a similar rule already exists under real estate law.[425]

---

423. *See* U.C.C. § 9-615(f)(2) (1999).

424. *See id.* § 9-626(a)(5). Mr. Rapson suggests that the party challenging the deficiency calculation may satisfy its burden of proof by introducing the following evidence: (i) the actual condition of the collateral; (ii) collateral appraisals, evaluations, surveys, and the like; (iii) guidebooks with values of the kind or type of collateral at the time of disposition; (iv) any estimates of value or ranges of value made or obtained by the secured party in establishing the minimum acceptable purchase price from an unrelated purchaser; (v) prices paid at any subsequent dispositions of the collateral by the purchaser, taking into consideration the proximity of the time of such dispositions to the initial disposition and any costs incurred by the purchaser in protecting, marketing, repairing, or improving the collateral; (vi) prices paid at comparable dispositions of the kind or type of collateral; (vii) whether the purchaser regularly sells the kind or type of collateral; and (viii) market practices and conditions for dispositions of the kind or type of collateral at the time and place of the disposition. Rapson, *supra* note 415, at 522–23.

425. *See* RESTATEMENT (THIRD) OF PROPERTY (MORTGAGES) § 8.4 (1997).

REVISED § 9-616

Explanation of Calculation of Surplus or Deficiency

Sometime after it has disposed of the collateral, the secured creditor will return any surplus to, or, more likely, demand payment of any deficiency from, the appropriate party. Revised § 9-616, which has no predecessor under current Article 9, imposes a duty on a secured creditor to provide that party, in selected situations, with certain information.[426]

Revised § 9-616 requires the secured party in a consumer-goods transaction to send an "explanation" to each consumer obligor liable for any deficiency or, if applicable, a debtor entitled to any surplus.[427] The "explanation" must be sent no later than when the secured party initially demands, in writing, payment of the deficiency by the consumer obligor or, if applicable, remits the surplus to the debtor.[428] The secured party also must send an "explanation" within fourteen days after it receives from a debtor or consumer obligor an authenticated record requesting the creditor to provide an "explanation."[429]

---

426. This duty cannot be waived or varied. *See* U.C.C. § 9-602(9) (1999).

427. *See id.* § 9-616(b).

428. *See id.* § 9-616(b)(1)(A). A secured party's oral demand for payment of a deficiency need not be accompanied (or preceded) by an "explanation."

429. *See id.* § 9-616(b)(1)(B) (referencing a "request"); *id.* § 9-616(a)(2) (defining "request"). Alternatively, the secured party may, within 14 days after receiving the consumer obligor's request, send to the consumer obligor a record in which the secured party waives its right to any deficiency. *Id.* § 9-616(b)(2).

A secured party is entitled to charge the recipient up to $25 for sending an explanation in response to the recipient's request if the secured party has already sent an explanation to the recipient during the previous six months. *See id.* § 9-616(e).

What is an "explanation"? It is a writing[430] that provides four pieces of information. First, the writing must state the amount of the deficiency or surplus.[431] Second, it must explain how the creditor calculated the deficiency or surplus,[432] using the following formula:

A. aggregate debt secured by security interest in
   disposed collateral, calculated as of (date)[433] $_____

B. proceeds from disposition[434] $_____

C. "A" minus "B"[435] $_____

D. disposition expenses, and attorneys' fees
   secured by the disposed collateral[436] $_____

---

430. *See id.* § 9-616(a)(1). As the statute elsewhere refers to an authenticated record, see *id.* § 9-616(a)(2), it is obvious that the reference to "writing" is intentional. What is not so obvious is why the "explanation" must be a writing, rather than an authenticated record. Perhaps consumer representatives expressed concern that consumers might fail to timely review e-mail correspondence. *See* Weise Memorandum, *supra* note 198.

431. *See* U.C.C. § 9-616(a)(1)(A) (1999).

432. *See id.* § 9-616(a)(1)(B).

433. *See id.* § 9-616(c)(1). If the secured party took possession of the collateral after default, the secured debt cannot be calculated as of a date more than 35 days before the possession date. *See id.* § 9-616(c)(1)(A). For example, if the creditor repossessed collateral on July 20 (a post-default date), then the secured debt set forth in the "explanation" can be calculated as of any date after June 14 (including any date after July 20). If, however, the secured party either took possession of the collateral before default or never took possession, then the secured debt cannot be calculated as of a date more than 35 days before the date of disposition. *See id.* § 9-616(c)(1)(B). For example, if a default occurred on May 1, the creditor never took possession of the collateral (or, alternatively, took possession before May 1), and the collateral was sold on October 15, then the secured debt set forth in the "explanation" can be calculated as of any date after September 9 (including any date after October 15).

Presumably the purpose for requiring a creditor to select a calculation date no earlier than 35 days before a particular date is a desire to arrive at an amount of secured debt that more closely approximates the actual figure (which may change daily). If so, then one must wonder why the statute adopts a bifurcated approach in which the counting date turns on when (or if) the creditor takes possession of the collateral, rather than a single rule that applies in all situations and that measures the 35-day period from the disposition date—a date more current than the possession date (which may pre-date the disposition date by weeks or months). For a while, the statute provided a uniform rule pegged to the disposition date (*see* U.C.C. § 9-616(b)(2)(A) (Draft July 25–Aug. 1, 1997)), but late in the drafting process (and without explanation) the statute created two possession-sensitive rules (*see* U.C.C. § 9-616(c)(1) (Draft Apr. 6, 1998)). An explanation of the bifurcated approach was requested in the Zinnecker Memorandum, *supra* note 102, at 3.

434. *See* U.C.C. § 9-616(c)(2) (1999).

435. *See id.* § 9-616(c)(3).

436. *See id.* § 9-616(c)(4). The expenses may be reflected by type or in the aggregate. *See id.* To avoid double-counting, one would think that these expenses should be a separate line item only if they are not part of the aggregate debt mentioned in "A." *Cf. id.* § 9-616(c)(5) (referencing credits "which are not reflected in the amount in ['A']"). For a

E. credits not included in "A"[437] $_____

F. deficiency or surplus[438] $_____

Third, the explanation must state, if applicable, that the surplus or deficiency may be affected by future debits, credits, charges, rebates, and expenses.[439] And fourth, the writing must include a telephone number or mailing address that can be used by the recipient to obtain additional information about the transaction.[440] The section neither proposes a model form of explanation nor mandates that an explanation include any particular language.[441] An explanation is sufficient if it substantially complies with the content requirements of revised § 9-616(a) even if the explanation has minor errors that are not seriously misleading.[442] Rather than rely on the nebulous flexibility afforded by the statute,[443] a creditor should exercise care in preparing the explanation and adhere to the content requirements. Otherwise, the creditor may be liable for damages equal to any loss caused by its noncompliance[444] plus (in some instances) $500.[445]

Revised § 9-616, which applies only in consumer-goods transactions,[446] "reflects the view that, in every consumer-goods transaction, the debtor or obligor is entitled to know the amount

while, language similar to that quoted from revised § 9-616(c)(5) appeared in revised § 9-616(c)(4). See, e.g., id. § 9-616(c)(4) (Draft July 24–31, 1998). The language was deleted in a subsequent draft. See, e.g., id. § 9-616(c)(4) (Draft approved at NCCUSL Annual Meeting, July 30, 1998). An explanation for this late revision was requested in the Zinnecker Memorandum, supra note 102, at 3.

437. See U.C.C. § 9-616(c)(5) (1999).

438. See id. § 9-616(c)(6).

439. See id. § 9-616(a)(1)(C).

440. See id. § 9-616(a)(1)(D).

441. See id. § 9-616(d).

442. See id. Although revised §§ 9-616 and 9-614 both describe notices to be sent in consumer-goods transactions, the two sections do not treat errors in a uniform manner. See id. § 9-614(4)–(6). Why a uniform standard does not apply to all notices sent in consumer-goods transactions is unclear. Clarification was requested in the Zinnecker Memorandum, supra note 102, at 3.

443. Several questions come to mind: What is "substantial compliance"? When is an error "minor"? Can a monetary error ever be "minor"? When is an error "seriously" misleading? Should an error not "minor" be tolerated if it is not "seriously misleading"?

444. See U.C.C. § 9-625(b) (1999). The secured party's noncompliance will not trigger liability for minimum statutory damages calculated under revised § 9-625(c)(2). See id. § 9-625(c) ("Except as otherwise provided in Section 9-628 . . . ."); id. § 9-628(d).

445. See id. § 9-625(e)(5), (6).

446. See id. § 9-616(b).

of a surplus or deficiency and the basis upon which the surplus or deficiency was calculated."[447] The reason for imposing a duty on the creditor to send the required notice makes sense, and imposing a statutory duty on a foreclosing creditor to provide that basic information (which perhaps may indirectly encourage the foreclosing creditor to more carefully monitor its disposition-related conduct) makes revised § 9-616 a welcome addition to the default provisions. However, all obligors and debtors have an interest in knowing the amount of any deficiency or surplus and how the creditor calculated that amount, and the usefulness and importance of that information justifies a provision requiring the secured party to send an explanation in all transactions, not just consumer-goods transactions.

447. *Id.* § 9-616 cmt. 2.

REVISED § 9-617

RIGHTS OF TRANSFEREE OF COLLATERAL

Current Article 9, through § 9-504(4), sets forth the property rights of a purchaser that acquires collateral at foreclosure. With some change, these rights are codified in Revised Article 9 at § 9-617.

Current Article 9 refers to the acquiring party as a "purchaser."[448] Under Revised Article 9 the acquiring party is known as a "transferee."[449] Revised Article 9 does not define "transferee," but a "purchaser" is a party that takes by "purchase,"[450] a term that "includes taking by sale, discount, negotiation, mortgage, pledge, lien, security interest, issue or re-issue, gift, or any other voluntary transaction creating an interest in property."[451] By acquiring an interest in the foreclosed property by sale or other voluntary transaction, the successful bidder at a public or private disposition appears to be a "purchaser." The official comments expressly refute that idea by indicating that a "a buyer at a foreclosure sale does not meet the definition of 'purchaser' in § 1-201."[452] The reason is that a foreclosure disposition is not a "voluntary transaction" when viewed through the eyes of the debtor, the party that created the property interest being foreclosed.[453]

---

448. *See id.* § 9-504(4) (1995).

449. *See id.* § 9-617 (1999).

450. *See id.* § 1-201(33).

451. *Id.* 1-201(32). The definition of "purchase" has been revised by inserting "security interest," after "lien," and a comma after "gift." *Id.*

452. *Id.* § 9-617 cmt. 2.

453. *See id.* One could argue that if the debtor contractually acknowledges that the secured party, upon default, enjoys all rights and remedies afforded by law (including U.C.C. Article 9), then the debtor has indeed consented to the disposition, making the disposition a "voluntary transaction."

As before, the transferee acquires all of the debtor's rights in the collateral.[454] Additionally, the transferee acquires the collateral free of the foreclosing creditor's security interest.[455] Furthermore, the transferee takes the collateral free of any security interest or lien in the collateral that is subordinate to the security interest of the foreclosing creditor.[456] By providing the transferee with immunity from the foregoing title claims, it is hoped that the disposition will attract additional prospective transferees and result in higher prices. In this manner the statute benefits not only the transferee but also the foreclosing creditor and the debtor.[457]

Under current Article 9, a secured party's noncompliance with the default provisions (or, if applicable, any judicial proceeding[458]) does not affect the rights of a purchaser at a public sale if the purchaser did not know of any sale defects and did

---

454. *See id.* § 9-617(a)(1); *id.* § 9-504(4) (1995); *see also* Thomas v. Price, 975 F.2d 231, 240 (5th Cir. 1992) (holding transferee acquired debtor's rights in collateral at time of sale); Krueger v. Saiki, 820 F. Supp. 467, 473 (W.D. Mo. 1993) (same); Leasing Serv. Corp. v. Graham, 646 F. Supp. 1410, 1419 (S.D.N.Y. 1986) (same); Commercial Discount Corp. v. King, 515 F. Supp. 988, 992 (N.D. Ill. 1981) (same); Sloves Assocs. v. Boudouris, 592 N.Y.S.2d 236, 237 (Civ. Ct. 1992) (same); Auton's Fine Jewelry & Bridal Center, Inc. v. Beckners, Inc., 707 S.W.2d 539, 540 (Tenn. Ct. App. 1986) (same).

455. *See* U.C.C. § 9-617(a)(2) (1999); *id.* § 9-504(4) (1995); *see also* Wachovia Bank & Trust Co. v. McCoy, 270 S.E.2d 164, 166 (W. Va. 1980) (concluding purchaser acquires property free of seller's security interest).

456. *See* U.C.C. § 9-617(a)(3) (1999); *id.* § 9-504(4) (1995); *see also* Mastro v. Witt, 39 F.3d 238, 243 (9th Cir. 1994) (holding foreclosure sale discharged subordinate security interest); Hope v. Performance Automotive Inc., 710 So. 2d 1235, 1239–41 (Ala. 1998) (same); Food City, Inc. v. Fleming Cos., 590 S.W.2d 754, 758 (Tex. App. 1979, no writ) (same); David Frisch, *The Implicit Takings Jurisprudence of Article 9 of the Uniform Commercial Code*, 64 FORDHAM L. REV. 11, 23 (1995) ("As a general rule, a person who buys property at a foreclosure sale acquires the debtor's equity plus the equity created by the absence of the lien being foreclosed and all subordinate liens and interests."). Notwithstanding revised § 9-617(a)(3), the secured party and any prospective transferee should consult a lawyer familiar with the provisions of the Internal Revenue Code (particularly 26 U.S.C. § 7425 (1994)) to determine whether the disposition will terminate a subordinate federal tax lien.

457. *See* Robyn L. Meadows, *A Potential Pitfall for the Unsuspecting Purchaser of Repossessed Collateral: The Overlooked Interaction Between Sections 9-504(4) and 2-312(2) of the Uniform Commercial Code*, 44 AM. U. L. REV. 167, 177–78 (1994).

458. This reference to "any judicial proceeding" has left more than one scholar befuddled. *See, e.g.,* 2 GILMORE, *supra* note 2, § 44.7, at 1248 (describing the reference as "mystifying"); 9 HAWKLAND ET AL., *supra* note 15, § 9-504:11, at 841 ("Exactly what is meant by 'any judicial proceeding' is not known.").

not collude with the secured party.[459] If the disposition is not by public sale, the purchaser must merely act in good faith.[460] Revised § 9-617 changes the law in two respects.[461] First, it offers protection to a transferee when the secured party fails to comply with any requirement of Article 9, not just a default provision.[462] Second, the statute eliminates the "knowledge" and "collusion" tests and requires the transferee, in every type of disposition, to act in good faith.[463] This revision is welcome, for it

459. *See* U.C.C. § 9-504(4)(a) (1995); *see also id.* § 9-504 cmt. 4 (indicating that a purchaser has no duty to inquire into the circumstances of a public sale and is protected "so long as he is not actively in bad faith"); PWS, Inc. v. Ban, 285 Cal. Rptr. 598, 600–01 (Ct. App. 1991) (holding creditor that sold collateral to itself could not rely on U.C.C. § 9-504(4) as defense if debtor had sued to set aside sale when creditor-purchaser had to have knowledge of defect in sale held on July 22 where notice had indicated sale would occur on July 23); Sheffield Progressive, Inc. v. Kingston Tool Co., 405 N.E.2d 985, 988 (Mass. App. Ct. 1980) (concluding purchaser could not invoke protection of U.C.C. § 9-504(4) where evidence indicated purchaser colluded with foreclosing creditor in manner that violated the Uniform Fraudulent Transfer Act). However, although the foreclosing creditor's failure to conduct a proper disposition may not prevent a transferee from acquiring the collateral free of selected property interests, the foreclosing creditor may be liable to the debtor and other interested parties under revised § 9-625 for its misconduct (which, under revised § 9-626, may adversely affect the creditor's ability to recover any deficiency).

460. *See* U.C.C. § 9-504(4)(b) (1995); *see also* Duffy v. Big Al's Autorama, Inc. (*In re* Duffy), 186 B.R. 503, 505 (Bankr. D. Colo. 1995) (holding debtor's rights in repossessed vehicle were extinguished by sale to purchaser, even if creditor-seller failed to comply with statutory notice requirements); Pippin Way, Inc. v. Four Star Music Co. (*In re* Four Star Music Co.), 2 B.R. 454, 464–65 (Bankr. M.D. Tenn. 1979) (concluding buyer at private sale was not good-faith purchaser for value as terms of sale were so highly unusual and beneficial to buyer that buyer, as merchant—and thus chargeable with knowledge and skill of merchant—could not in good faith have believed that the terms were commercially reasonable); Lichty v. Federal Land Bank, 467 N.W.2d 657, 660 (Neb. 1991) (holding good-faith purchaser at private sale acquired collateral free of debtor's interest even if secured party failed to send, to debtor, reasonable notice of time after which private sale would occur).

461. Additionally, what was implied under current § 9-504(4) is now expressly stated: A transferee that does not satisfy the statutory requirements takes the collateral subject to the property interests of the debtor, the foreclosing creditor, and other secured creditors and lienholders. *See* U.C.C. § 9-617(c) (1999).

462. *See id.* § 9-617(b) (referencing noncompliance "with this article").

463. *See id.* § 9-617(b); *see also id.* § 9-102(a)(43) (defining "good faith"). This change occurred late in the revision process. During most of the process, the statute protected a transferee in a public sale only if the transferee (i) had no knowledge of any defects in the sale, (ii) did not collude with the secured party, other bidders, or the person conducting the sale, and (iii) acted in good faith. *See, e.g., id.* § 9-504(n) (Draft July 28–Aug. 4, 1995); *id.* § 9-617(b) (Draft July 24–31, 1998). *Cf. id.* § 9-617(b) (Draft approved at NCCUSL Annual Meeting, July 30, 1998) (deleting all requirements other than good faith). According to the official comments, no substantive change from current § 9-504(4) is intended, as a transferee's knowledge of sale defects, or its collusion with various parties, were merely "specific examples of the absence of good faith." *Id.* § 9-617 cmt. 3 (1999).

eliminates the distinction between acting in good faith and not acting in bad faith, a distinction that "has long troubled the law."[464]

When will a transferee fail to exercise good faith? The facts and circumstances surrounding the disposition will dictate the answer to that question.[465] However, as knowledge of existing security interests is generally irrelevant when resolving priority disputes, a transferee should not violate the good-faith requirement merely because it knows of a competing, but subordinate, property interest.[466] A contrary rule only discourages interested parties from searching the public records for property interests that might survive the transfer and, in effect, shrinks the pool of potential transferees to the detriment of both the foreclosing creditor and the debtor with no corresponding benefit to the holder of the subordinate interest.

By negative implication, the transferee obtains the collateral subject to any security interests or liens that are not junior to the security interest under which the disposition occurred.[467] Therefore, before participating in a public or private disposition

---

464. *See* Hogan, *supra* note 1, at 233 (1962); *see also* 2 GILMORE, *supra* note 2, § 44.7, at 1249 ("The distinction between the affirmative presence of good faith and the negative absence of bad faith . . . has never been a workable one.").

465. Note, however, that the transferee's good faith only becomes an issue if the foreclosing creditor has conducted an improper disposition. The transferee's good faith, or lack thereof, is irrelevant if the disposition is proper. *See* Thomas v. Price, 975 F.2d 231, 238–40 (5th Cir. 1992).

466. *See* Mastro v. Witt, 39 F.3d 238, 243 (9th Cir. 1994) (holding that good-faith requirement of U.C.C. § 9-504(4)(b) does not require purchaser of collateral to lack knowledge of any pre-existing subordinate claims against the collateral); Northwest Equip. Sales Co. v. Western Packers, Inc., 623 F.2d 92, 95–96 (9th Cir. 1980) (same); Landmark Land Co. v. Sprague, 529 F. Supp. 971, 981 (S.D.N.Y. 1981) (same), *rev'd on other grounds*, 701 F.2d 1065 (2d Cir. 1983); *cf.* Young v. Golden State Bank, 560 P.2d 855, 860 (Colo. Ct. App. 1977) (stating, in dicta, that purchaser's knowledge that the holder of a subordinate security interest had not been given notice of private disposition *might* be evidence of lack of good faith).

467. *See* Continental Bank v. Krebs, 540 N.E.2d 1023, 1026 (Ill. App. Ct. 1989); Utility Trailers v. Citizens Nat'l Bank & Trust Co., 726 P.2d 282, 285 (Kan. Ct. App. 1986); Chadron Energy Corp. v. First Nat'l Bank, 459 N.W.2d 718, 732–33 (Neb. 1990); Nickles, *supra* note 404, at 253 ("Upon the sale of the original collateral, the junior creditor's interest and any security interest or lien subordinate to his own are terminated, along with the debtor's rights in the property. Any senior security interest survives, however."); Luize E. Zubrow, *Rethinking Article 9 Remedies: Economic and Fiduciary Perspectives,*

of the collateral an interested party should review the public records to determine whether the collateral is encumbered by any security interests or liens that may survive the disposition, determine (if it can) the amount of debt secured by those security interests or liens, and factor that amount (together with the fair market value of the collateral) into its price deliberations. The transferee also should contact the holder of any security

42 UCLA L. Rev. 445, 457 (1994) ("Under Article 9 priority rules, the [senior] foreclosing creditor's claim would be superior to the ownership rights of . . . a [junior creditor's] purchaser."); *see also* 4 White & Summers, *supra* note 36, § 34-10, at 432 ("One thing is clear from [U.C.C. § 9-504(4)], namely, a senior secured party's interest in the collateral is not discharged by a junior's foreclosure sale, and continues to attach to the goods in the hands of the purchaser at the sale."). During most of the drafting process, Revised Article 9 included a statement making this point somewhat less implied and little more express. *See* U.C.C. § 9-504(o) (Draft July 28–Aug. 4, 1995) ("Except as otherwise provided in this subsection or elsewhere in this article, the disposition does not discharge any security interest or other lien."). *But see id.* § 9-615(d) (Draft Apr. 6, 1998) (deleting sentence).

Unless a secured party has authorized a disposition of collateral free and clear of its interest, the interest generally continues after the disposition "[e]xcept as otherwise provided in this article and in Section 2-403(2)." *Id.* § 9-315(a) (1999); *cf. id.* § 9-306(2) (1995) (continuing a security interest in collateral after disposition absent consent and "[e]xcept where this Article otherwise provides"). One of the exceptions "otherwise provided" is the "buyer in ordinary course of business" exception codified in revised § 9-320(a), the successor to current § 9-307(1). As Revised Article 9 rejects the notion that commercially reasonable dispositions are "out of the ordinary commercial course" or "peculiar," *see id.* § 9-610 cmt. 11 (1999), a transferee of collateral consisting of the debtor's inventory may, relying on the foregoing comment, invoke the "buyer in ordinary course of business" exception and argue that security interests that survive the disposition under revised § 9-617 are nevertheless terminated by revised § 9-320(a). One response is that the transferee is not a "buyer in ordinary course of business" as defined in revised § 1-201(9) because a party excluded from the broad definition of "purchaser" cannot be a "buyer." *But see id.* § 9-617 cmt. 2 (referring to a "*buyer* at a foreclosure sale") (emphasis added). Another response is that the transferee is not a "buyer in ordinary course of business" because a foreclosure sale does not "comport[] with the usual or customary practices in the kind of business in which the seller is engaged or with the seller's own usual or customary practices." *Cf.* Nickles, *supra* note 404, at 254 n.146 ("Is such a buyer [at a foreclosure sale] one not in the ordinary course . . . ?"); *id.* at 254 n.148 (stating that a buyer at a foreclosure sale is "probably a buyer *not* in the ordinary course"); Zubrow, *supra*, at 837 n.30 ("In a battle between the original secured creditor and the purchaser, the secured creditor wins because the purchaser at a foreclosure sale is not a buyer in the ordinary course of business."). However, comment 11 to revised § 9-610 somewhat undercuts that response. Perhaps a better response is that the transferee is not a "buyer in ordinary course of business" because the definition requires the transferee to buy goods from a person "in the business of selling goods of that kind." U.C.C. § 1-201(9) (1999). But this requirement only disqualifies a transferee when the foreclosing creditor is a bank, finance company, or other party that is not in the business of selling goods like the collateral. The goods may have been sold on credit to the debtor by the foreclosing creditor, interest that survives the disposition in order to terminate the priority afforded to post-disposition advances funded by that holder.[468] The transferee should be prepared to either pay off the debt secured by the surviving interest or surrender possession of the collateral. If the transferee is unable or unwilling to do so, it may be liable for conversion.[469] The transferee's recourse will be against the foreclosing creditor for breaching any title warranty given under revised § 9-610(d).[470] If the foreclosing creditor disclaimed any title warranty and did not otherwise agree to indemnify the transferee against title claimants, the transferee may find itself without a legal remedy under Revised Article 9.[471]

in which case the foreclosing creditor would indeed be "in the business of selling goods of that kind." (Query whether a finance company that is closely affiliated with a merchant also could be held to be "in the business of selling goods of that kind." *See* Mercedes-Benz Credit Corp. v. Lotito, 703 A.2d 288, 292–95 (N.J. Super. Ct. App. Div. 1997) (permitting consumer lessee to assert breach of warranty against financing lessor having close relationship with seller and manufacturer); U.C.C. § 2A-103(g) (1995) (defining "finance lease"); *id.* § 2A-103 cmt. g (stating that Article 2A "creates no special rule where the lessor is an affiliate of the supplier").) Perhaps the best response is that even if the transferee is a "buyer in ordinary course of business," revised § 9-320(a) offers no protection to the transferee because the statute allows a transferee to acquire collateral free of a security interest only if the security interest was "created by the buyer's seller." The transferee's seller at a disposition is the foreclosing creditor, but the security interest referenced in revised § 9-320(a) was created by someone else: the debtor.

468. *See* U.C.C. § 9-323(d) (1999) (permitting selected buyers to acquire goods free of a security interest to the extent that the interest secures repayment of advances made after the earlier of (i) the time when the secured creditor acquires knowledge of the buyer's purchase and (ii) the 45th day after the date of purchase); *id.* § 9-323(e) (protecting advances made pursuant to a commitment entered into by a secured party without knowledge of the buyer's purchase and entered into no later than the 45th day after the purchase); *id.* § 9-102(a)(68) (defining "pursuant to commitment"). Current Article 9 offers similar protection. *See id.* §§ 9-307(3), 9-105(k) (1995).

469. *See id.* § 9-306 cmt. 3 (1999) ("[S]ince the transferee takes subject to the security interest, the secured party may repossess the collateral from him or in an appropriate case maintain an action for conversion."); Steve H. Nickles, *Enforcing Article 9 Security Interests Against Subordinate Buyers of Collateral,* 50 Geo. Wash. L. Rev. 511, 520–36 (1982).

470. *See* U.C.C. § 9-610(d) (1999).

471. A sympathetic court might invoke equitable principles and permit the transferee to recover the purchase price from the seller. *See id.* § 1-103 (1995) (allowing principles of equity to supplement U.C.C. provisions). However, because the giving (and waiving) of title warranties are expressly addressed in revised § 9-610(d), and as revised § 9-617 contemplates the post-disposition survival of certain security interests and liens, equitable principles would seem to be "displaced by the particular provisions" of Revised Article 9. *Id.*

Revised § 9-617 applies only to post-default dispositions.[472] What rights are acquired by a transferee if the debtor was not in default at the time of disposition? Under pre-U.C.C. law, the transferee (if a good-faith purchaser for value) acquired the property free of the debtor's interest, even if the foreclosing creditor was liable to the debtor for conversion.[473] By introducing a post-default requirement, Article 9 departs from pre-U.C.C. law and no longer provides the good-faith transferee with any rights in property acquired at a pre-default disposition.[474] What property

472. See id. § 9-617(a) (1999) ("A secured party's disposition of collateral *after default* . . . .") (emphasis added); see also id. § 9-504(4) (1995) ("When collateral is disposed of . . . *after default* . . . .") (emphasis added).
473. See 2 GILMORE, *supra* note 2, § 44.7, at 1247 (discussing Uniform Trust Receipts Act § 6(3)(c), the forerunner of U.C.C. § 9-504(4)); see also U.C.C. § 9-504 cmt. 4 (1995) (referring to the Uniform Trust Receipts Act as its genesis).
474. The transferee may argue that revised § 9-617 and its predecessor do provide the transferee with rights in collateral acquired at a pre-default disposition. By disposing of collateral in the absence of a default, the foreclosing creditor has failed to comply with Article 9. See U.C.C. § 9-610(a) (1999) ("*After default*, a secured party may sell, lease, license, or otherwise dispose of any or all of the collateral . . . .") (emphasis added); id. § 9-504(1) (1995) ("A secured party *after default* may sell, lease, or otherwise dispose of any or all of the collateral . . . .") (emphasis added). Nevertheless, current and Revised Article 9 both permit the transferee to acquire the property free of the debtor's interest, the interest being foreclosed, and all subordinate property interests, even if the foreclosing creditor "fails to comply with . . . the requirements" of Article 9, as long as the transferee has acted in good faith (and, in a public disposition under current Article 9, without knowledge of any defect and not in collusion with other parties). See id. § 9-617(b) (1999); id. § 9-504(4) (1995). As attractive as that argument may be, its acceptance requires one to overlook the organization and language of the statute and accompanying comments, all of which suggest that the reference to non-compliance was included to address a secured party's post-default noncompliance, such as breaching the peace while repossessing the collateral, failing to send a disposition notice to all required parties, or disposing of collateral in a commercially unreasonable manner. See id. § 9-504 cmt. 4 ("Subsection (4) provides that a purchaser for value from a secured party *after default* takes free of any rights of the debtor and of the holders of junior security interests and liens, even though the secured party has not complied with the requirements of this Part or of any judicial proceedings.") (emphasis added); 2 GILMORE, *supra* note 2, § 44.7, at 1248 (noting that U.C.C. § 9-504(4) "distinguish[es] between wrongful pre-default and wrongful post-default transfers" and "covers only disposition[s] by a secured party 'after default' "); id. § 42.14, at 1175–76 (observing that no section of the U.C.C. deals with the status of a transferee who acquires collateral at a pre-default disposition); Meadows, *supra* note 457, at 180–81; cf. U.C.C. § 9-617 cmt. 2 (1999) (making no distinction between pre- and post-default noncompliance in its statement that a disposition "has the effect specified in subsection (a), even if the secured party fails to comply with this Article").

rights, if any, are held by the transferee are determined by other law.[475] So, too, are any rights that the transferee may have against the debtor (who may demand return of the collateral) and, if the title warranty under revised § 9-610 has been disclaimed, the foreclosing creditor.[476] Acknowledgment, if not closure, of this gap[477] in the default provisions would have been welcome.[478]

---

475. Even if the transferee of goods has acted in good faith and given value, it cannot claim the protection afforded by U.C.C. § 2-403, which states: "A person with voidable title has power to transfer a good title to a good faith purchaser for value." The foreclosing creditor that makes an unauthorized disposition of collateral has void, rather than voidable, title. *See* Meadows, *supra* note 457, at 182–90. Furthermore, the transferee is not a "purchaser." *See* U.C.C. § 9-617 cmt. 2 (1999).

476. Unlike the transferee, the debtor enjoys certain rights under Revised Article 9. For example, because a pre-default disposition is not sanctioned by revised § 9-610, the debtor's right of redemption under revised § 9-623 has not been terminated. Additionally, the debtor may collect damages under revised § 9-625. Furthermore, the debtor's liability for any deficiency may be reduced under revised § 9-626.

477. The "gap" may be more of a slight indentation than a chasm, as the issue may be more academic than practical. It is hoped that a debtor would promptly bring to the foreclosing creditor's attention its concern that a default has not yet occurred and that the creditor would only proceed with any scheduled disposition after addressing that concern.

478. For an excellent article that analyzes the problem and proposes a statutory solution, see Meadows, *supra* note 457, at 167.

REVISED § 9-618

RIGHTS AND DUTIES OF CERTAIN SECONDARY OBLIGORS

Consider the following typical transaction. Dealer sells a boat to Consumer pursuant to a retail installment sales contract that creates a security interest in the boat in favor of Dealer. Dealer then discounts the contract (chattel paper[479]) to Finance Company, with recourse. Consumer defaults on its payment obligations and Finance Company repossesses the boat. Dealer honors its recourse obligations by paying to Finance Company an amount equal to Consumer's unpaid debt. In return, Finance Company returns the contract (and the boat) to Dealer. Dealer then sells the boat to Purchaser and thereafter sues Consumer for a deficiency.

In the foregoing transaction, Dealer has sold the boat to Purchaser. But prior to that sale, had Finance Company "sold" the boat to Dealer when Dealer honored its recourse obligations? If so, several questions may arise. Which sale terminates Consumer's right of redemption[480] and Consumer's interest in the collateral?[481] Which sale requires the seller to send a sales notice to Consumer?[482] Which sale can be scrutinized for commercial reasonableness?[483] Which sales price is used in calculating a deficiency or surplus? *Which sale is a "disposition" under the default provisions of Article 9?*

---

479. *See* U.C.C. § 9-102(a)(11) (1999) (defining "chattel paper"); *id.* § 9-105(1)(b) (1995) (same). The sale of chattel paper is a transaction that falls within the scope of Article 9. *See id.* § 9-109(a)(3) (1999); *id.* § 9-102(1)(b) (1995).
480. *See id.* § 9-506 (1995); *id.* § 9-623(a), (c)(2) (1999).
481. *See id.* § 9-504(4) (1995); *id.* § 9-617(a)(1) (1999).
482. *See id.* § 9-504(3) (1995); *id.* § 9-611(b), (c)(1) (1999).
483. *See id.* § 9-504(3) (1995); *id.* § 9-610(b) (1999).

Current Article 9 states that collateral is not sold or otherwise disposed when a person honoring its obligations "under a guaranty, indorsement, repurchase agreement or the like" receives a transfer of collateral from, or is subrogated to the rights of, a secured party.[484] Revised Article 9 retains this concept, but not the language. Revised § 9-618 excludes from revised § 9-610[485] (and, therefore, any other disposition-related provision) (i) any "assignment of a secured obligation" from a secured party to a secondary obligor,[486] (ii) any "transfer of collateral" from a secured party to a secondary obligor that "agrees to accept the rights and assume the duties of the secured party,"[487] and (iii) any subrogation by a secondary obligor "to the rights of a secured party with respect to collateral."[488] The reason for treating transactions described in current § 9-504(5) and revised § 9-618 as non-dispositions "is to insure that the value of repossessed collateral is measured by a bona fide sale in the market place, and not by an artificial value, usually the balance due on the debtor's contract, set by a repurchase or guaranty agreement between a seller and a finance company."[489]

Revised § 9-618 is an improvement over its predecessor. The reference in current § 9-504(5) to "guaranty, indorsement, repurchase agreement or the like" suggests that its authors had sureties in mind.[490] Rather than continue to indirectly acknowledge suretyship concepts through a reference to the types of agreements that may create surety status, revised § 9-618 focuses

484. *See id.* § 9-504(5) (1995).
485. *See id.* § 9-618(b)(1) (1999).
486. *See id.* § 9-618(a)(1).
487. *See id.* § 9-618(a)(2).
488. *See id.* § 9-618(a)(3).
489. *See* Reeves v. Associates Fin. Servs. Co., 247 N.W.2d 434, 439 (Neb. 1976); *see also* Shields v. Bobby Murray Chevrolet, Inc., 261 S.E.2d 238, 240 (N.C. Ct. App.), *affirmed without precedential value*, 266 S.E.2d 658 (N.C. 1980) (indicating that the provision attempts to achieve a sales price "measured by a bona fide market value, and not by an artificial value"); 3 HOWARD RUDA, ASSET-BASED FINANCING § 28.04[3], at 28-10 to 28-11 (1993) (stating that a lender's sale of dealer's inventory to the manufacturer pursuant to the manufacturer's repurchase agreement "does not constitute a commercially reasonable sale because the price the manufacturer pays is tied to the indebtedness due the lender, not the market value of the collateral").
490. *See* Donald J. Rapson, *Repurchase (of Collateral) Agreements and the Larger Issue of Deficiency Actions: What Does Section 9-504(5) Mean?*, 29 IDAHO L. REV. 649, 651–54 (1992–1993).

attention on the surety status itself through its use of "secondary obligor."[491] Hopefully, the replacement of agreement-based language with a status-based term will reduce some of the confusion that has surrounded current § 9-504(5), particularly the meaning of "repurchase agreement."[492]

Another source of confusion has been the meaning of "transfer of collateral."[493] The phrase, isolated in current § 9-504(5), remains in revised § 9-618, but is accompanied by language requiring the transferee to "accept the rights and assume the duties of the secured party."[494] Additionally, new language in revised § 9-618 excludes from the disposition-relation provisions of Revised Article 9 any "assignment of a secured obligation" from a secured party to a secondary obligor.[495] Together, these changes clarify which "transfers of collateral" are intended to be treated as non-dispositions. Unless the secured party has assigned the secured debt to the secondary obligor, or achieved the functional equivalent of an assignment through the secondary obligor's agreement to step into the shoes of the secured party, the transaction between the secured party and the secondary obligor should be viewed as a sale of collateral, triggering application of all disposition-related provisions.[496] However, when evidence reveals that either the secured party has assigned its position to the

---

491. *Cf.* RESTATEMENT (THIRD) OF SURETYSHIP AND GUARANTY § 1(1)(a) (1996) (eschewing "surety" in favor of "secondary obligor"); Homer Kripke, *Practice Commentary to Section 9-504,* N.Y. U.C.C. LAW § 9-504, at 611–12 (McKinney 1964), *cited in* Rapson, *supra* note 490, at 653 (using the following caption in his description of § 9-504(5): Sale of Collateral Back to *Secondary Obligor*) (emphasis added). Mr. Rapson describes Professor Kripke as "one of the leading architects of Article 9, past and present, and probably the most knowledgeable secured transactions lawyer in the country." *See* Rapson, *supra* note 490, at 653.

492. *See, e.g.,* CLARK, *supra* note 2, ¶ 10.05[5], at 10-67 to 10-71; Rapson, *supra* note 490, at 660–66.

493. *See, e.g.,* CLARK, *supra* note 2, ¶ 4.08[8][c], at 4-171 to 4-172; Rapson, *supra* note 490, at 666–73.

494. U.C.C. § 9-618(a)(2) (1999).

495. *Id.* § 9-618(a)(1).

496. If revised § 9-618(a)(2) did not include language requiring the secondary obligor to agree "to accept the rights and assume the duties of the secured party," a statutory conflict would exist between revised § 9-618(a)(2) (which would treat any "transfer of collateral" from a secured party to a secondary obligor as a non-disposition) and revised § 9-615(f) (which acknowledges that a secondary obligor can be the transferee in a collateral disposition).

secondary obligor or the secondary obligor has agreed to assume that position, then the transaction should be viewed as a purchase of the secured debt, accompanied by the underlying security interest, rather than a purchase of the collateral.

Another clarification concerns subrogation rights. Under current § 9-504(5), collateral is not disposed when a guarantor or similar party becomes "subrogated to [the secured party's] rights."[497] That statement is narrowed by revised § 9-618, which indicates collateral is not disposed when a secondary obligor "is subrogated to the rights of a secured party *with respect to collateral.*"[498] In some transactions the secondary obligor's payment may be applied to unsecured debt.[499] In such a case, the secondary obligor is subrogated to certain rights of the creditor, but, as a result of the emphasized language, revised § 9-618 is implicated only to the extent that those subrogated rights are collateral-related.[500]

Although current § 9-504(5) states that the guarantor or similar party will, by honoring its contractual obligations, acquire the rights and duties of the secured party, the statute does not indicate whether the secured party remains liable for any prior breach of its duties or may be held liable for any subsequent breach of a duty by the guarantor or similar party.[501] Nor does the statute expressly state whether the guarantor or similar party can be held liable for the secured party's prior behavior. Revised § 9-618 clarifies the status of both parties. The statute provides that an

497. U.C.C. § 9-504(5) (1995).

498. *Id.* § 9-618(a)(3) (1999) (emphasis added).

499. In other transactions the secondary obligor may make a payment not in satisfaction of its secondary obligation but as the successful bidder at a public or private disposition. Revised Article 9 acknowledges that a secondary obligor can be the transferee in a collateral disposition. *See id.* § 9-615(f). If a party makes a payment with the intent to buy the collateral, rather than discharge its secondary obligation, the party is not subrogated to any of the secured party's rights and revised § 9-618 is inapplicable. To avoid any confusion concerning the capacity in which the payment is made, the secured party and the secondary obligor should document the nature and circumstances of the payment accordingly. *See id.* § 9-618 cmt. 2.

500. *See id.* § 9-618 cmt. 2; *cf. id.* § 9-618(a)(1), (b)(1) (stating that collateral is not disposed when a secondary obligor "receives an assignment of a *secured* obligation") (emphasis added).

501. *Cf.* PEB Study Group Report, *supra* note 7, at 237 (recommending that § 9-504 "should be revised to specify the circumstances under which a secured party continues to be responsible to the debtor," notwithstanding the secured party's assignment or transfer to a recourse party under § 9-504(5)).

assignment, transfer, or subrogation to which revised § 9-618 applies "relieves the secured party of further duties."[502] Therefore, while the secured party may not be held liable for the secondary obligor's subsequent noncompliance (e.g., failing to send notice of a disposition to the debtor as required by revised § 9-611(b)), the secured party does remain liable for its own prior misbehavior (e.g., repossessing collateral under revised § 9-609 in a manner that breaches the peace). And because the statute states that a secondary obligor "becomes obligated to perform the duties of the secured party *after* the secondary obligor" has received an assignment, transfer, or subrogation to which revised § 9-618 applies,[503] the secondary obligor should not inherit any liability arising from the secured party's earlier misconduct.[504]

Assuming that the Finance Company-Dealer transaction qualifies as an assignment, transfer, or subrogation governed by revised § 9-618,[505] it is the Dealer-Purchaser transaction, rather than the Finance Company-Dealer transaction, to which the disposition provisions of Revised Article 9 apply.[506] As a result,

502. U.C.C. § 9-618(b)(2).

503. *Id.* § 9-618(a) (emphasis added).

504. *See id.* § 9-618 cmt. 4.

505. Of course a court must examine the true nature of the relationship between Dealer and Finance Company, and the facts and circumstances surrounding their transaction, before concluding whether revised § 9-618 applies. *See, e.g.,* Reeves v. Associates Fin. Servs. Co., 247 N.W.2d 434, 439–40 (Neb. 1976) (concluding trial court's reliance on U.C.C. § 9-504(5) to grant summary judgment was premature where evidence raised conflicting inferences on whether parties enjoyed principal-agent relationship or had acted pursuant to a guaranty or repurchase agreement).

506. *See* Stoppi v. Wilmington Trust Co., 518 A.2d 82, 85 (Del. 1986) (concluding under § 9-504(5) that reassignment of collateral from bank to seller pursuant to repurchase agreement was not a collateral disposition); Weast v. Arnold, 474 A.2d 904, 912 (Md. 1984) (holding under § 9-504(5) that transfer of collateral from secured party to guarantor upon guarantor's payment of secured debt was not a "sale" of collateral); *Reeves,* 247 N.W.2d at 439 (citing § 9-504(5) for the proposition that a transfer of collateral from a finance company to a dealer that has honored its obligations under a repurchase agreement or guaranty is not a sale or disposition of collateral); Bexar County Nat'l Bank v. Hernandez, 716 S.W.2d 938, 938–39 (Tex. 1986) (relying on § 9-504(5) to conclude that bank's transfer of collateral to guarantor was not a disposition that required notice under § 9-504(3); instead, guarantor's subsequent transfer triggered the notice requirement); *cf.* Shields v. Bobby Murray Chevrolet, Inc., 261 S.E.2d 238, 241 (N.C. Ct. App.), *affirmed without precedential value,* 266 S.E.2d 658 (N.C. 1980) (concluding § 9-504(5) did not apply to public sale conducted by finance company that treated non-present dealer, under terms of repurchase agreement, as successful bidder in absence of any other bids at public sale); CLARK, *supra* note 2, ¶ 10.05[5], at 10-67 to 10-71 (arguing that certain repurchases by a manufacturer from a floor plan financer should be treated as Article 9 dispositions).

Dealer inherits all of the rights afforded to, and must perform all of the obligations thereafter placed on, a secured party.[507] Among these obligations are the duty to exercise reasonable care with respect to collateral in its possession,[508] the duty to send to Consumer a disposition notice,[509] the duty to conduct the disposition in a commercially reasonable manner,[510] and the duty to remit any surplus proceeds to Consumer.[511] Dealer's noncompliance may trigger statutory penalties and may adversely affect its ability to recover any deficiency from Consumer.[512]

---

507. *See* U.C.C. § 9-618(a) (1999) (stating that the secondary obligor "acquires the rights and becomes obligated to perform the duties of the secured party"); *cf. id.* § 9-504(5) (1995) (indicating that the transferee has "the rights and duties of the secured party").

508. *See id.* § 9-207(a) (1999); *id.* § 9-207(1) (1995); *see also* Murray v. Payne, 437 So. 2d 47, 53–54 (Miss. 1983) (concluding guarantor that succeeded to creditor's security interest in aircraft had duty to apply profits from operating aircraft against secured debt in accordance with U.C.C. § 9-207(2)(c)).

509. *See* U.C.C. § 9-611(b) (1999); *id.* § 9-504(3) (1995); *see also Stoppi*, 518 A.2d at 85–86 (ruling that transfer of collateral from bank to dealer under repurchase agreement placed duty on dealer to notify debtor of sale; dealer breached duty and could not rely on notice sent by bank as bank's transfer of collateral to dealer was not a sale); Papas v. Speizman, 511 N.E.2d 768, 769–70 (Ill. App. Ct. 1987) (holding that guarantors who paid secured debt and received assignment of creditor's security interest breached duty to give notice of subsequent disposition); Joyce v. Cloverleaf Homes, Inc., 344 S.E.2d 58, 60 (N.C. Ct. App. 1986) (concluding mobile home dealer that repurchased collateral from finance company breached its duty to send notice of subsequent sale); *Bexar County Nat'l Bank*, 716 S.W.2d at 938–39 (noting guarantor failed to give notice of disposition following transfer of collateral from bank to guarantor); Multi-Moto Corp. v. ITT Commercial Fin. Corp., 806 S.W.2d 560, 564–66 (Tex. App. 1990, writ denied) (holding finance company's transfer of dealer's repossessed inventory to seller was not a disposition that required prior notice).

510. *See* U.C.C. § 9-610(b) (1999); *id.* § 9-504(3) (1995); *see also* Erickson v. Marshall, 771 P.2d 68, 69–70 (Idaho Ct. App. 1989) (concluding trial court's grant of summary judgment motion was premature where behavior of guarantor that became subrogated to secured party's rights in collateral raised questions on commercial reasonableness of guarantor's disposition).

511. *See* U.C.C. § 9-615(d)(1) (1999); *id.* § 9-504(2) (1995); *see also Reeves*, 247 N.W.2d at 439 (stating that a debtor is entitled to recover surplus proceeds from a dealer, not a finance company, if the finance company has transferred its interest in the collateral to the dealer under a repurchase agreement or guaranty).

512. *See* U.C.C. § 9-625(b), (c) (1999) (stating noncompliance may trigger liability for actual damages and, in appropriate circumstances, statutory minimum damages); *id.* § 9-626(a)(3) (indicating noncompliance may reduce deficiency); *cf. id.* § 9-507(1) (1995) (imposing liability on secured party for "any loss caused" by noncompliance and, in appropriate circumstances, statutory minimum damages).

REVISED § 9-619

TRANSFER OF RECORD OR LEGAL TITLE

In most dispositions the transferee acquires all of the debtor's rights in the collateral.[513] Occasionally the debtor's ownership interest in the collateral has been recorded on a certificate of title (e.g., a motor vehicle[514]) or otherwise registered (e.g., an airplane[515] or copyright[516]). The transferee may demand that the certificate or registry reflect its ownership immediately following the foreclosure. That may be difficult if a new certificate cannot be issued, or the registry cannot be revised, without the debtor's consent or cooperation, which may not be forthcoming after

---

513. *See id.* § 9-617(a)(1) (1999); *id.* § 9-504(4) (1995).

514. *See, e.g.,* TEX. TRANSP. CODE ANN. § 501.022(a) (West 1997) ("The owner of a motor vehicle registered in this state may not operate or permit the operation of the vehicle on a public highway until the owner obtains a certificate of title for the vehicle."); *id.* § 502.002(a) (requiring the owner of a motor vehicle to "apply for the registration of the vehicle for: (1) each registration year in which the vehicle is used or to be used on a public highway"); *id.* § 502.152(a) (indicating that the Texas Department of Transportation will not register a motor vehicle unless the owner has obtained a certificate of title for the vehicle).

515. *See* 49 U.S.C. § 44101(a) (1994) (providing generally that "a person may operate an aircraft only when the aircraft is registered under section 44103 of this title"); § 44103(a) (indicating that, on application by the owner, the Administrator of the Federal Aviation Administration shall "register the aircraft" and "issue a certificate of registration to its owner").

516. *See* 17 U.S.C. § 410(a) (stating that the Register of Copyrights "shall register the claim and issue to the applicant a certificate of registration" for copyrightable subject matter).

default.[517] Unlike current Article 9, Revised Article 9 acknowledges this predicament and provides a mechanism for obtaining record or legal title. The mechanism is codified in revised § 9-619. The section contemplates use of a "transfer statement," a record that has been authenticated by the secured party[518] and which states the following:

- the debtor has defaulted on an obligation secured by specific collateral;[519]
- the secured party has exercised its post-default remedies with respect to the specific collateral;[520]
- the transferee has acquired the debtor's rights in the collateral as a result of the secured party's exercise of its post-default remedies;[521] and
- the name and mailing address of the secured party, the debtor, and the transferee.[522]

Upon receipt of the transfer statement and any applicable fee, revised § 9-619 directs the official to accept the statement, revise its records accordingly, and, if applicable, issue a new title certificate in the name of the transferee.[523]

Revised § 9-619 does not prescribe a model form,[524] perhaps because the recipient most likely will be a public official

---

517. The debtor's obstinance may not go unpunished. Title concerns may discourage potential buyers from attending the disposition or participating in the bidding process, and attendance and participation are factors that have a direct bearing on the ultimate disposition price and the amount of any deficiency for which the debtor may be liable or any surplus to which the debtor may be entitled.

Many creditors, cognizant that a debtor's post-default cooperation is unlikely, address the problem by including some variation of the following clause in the loan documents: "Debtor appoints Secured Party as its attorney-in-fact, effective upon the occurrence of a Default, with power to take such action (including the execution of documents) as Secured Party deems necessary or desirable. Debtor acknowledges that this power of attorney granted to Secured Party is irrevocable and coupled with an interest."

518. *See* U.C.C. § 9-619(a) (1999); *see also id.* § 9-102(a)(7) (defining "authenticate"); *id.* § 9-102(a)(69) (defining "record").

519. *See id.* § 9-619(a)(1).

520. *See id.* § 9-619(a)(2).

521. *See id.* § 9-619(a)(3).

522. *See id.* § 9-619(a)(4).

523. *See id.* § 9-619(b).

524. *Cf. id.* § 9-613(5) (providing form of notice of collateral dispositions in transactions other than consumer-goods transactions); *id.* § 9-614(3) (providing form of notice of collateral dispositions in consumer-goods transactions); *id.* § 9-616 (not providing form of explanation of calculation of surplus or deficiency).

with the authority to require the secured party to submit the information on (or attach it to) an "official" form.[525] Nor does revised § 9-619 address the treatment of major or minor errors that may or may not make the transfer statement seriously misleading.[526] This may not be an oversight. If the transfer statement is accepted and the records are revised to reflect the change in title, then the only error surviving the revision that could cause concern would be a typographical error in the name or mailing address of the transferee. Presumably the transferee will timely discover and report any such error to the public official, who then can take prompt remedial action to correct the certificate or registry.

If no official form is required,[527] the following proposed form (modified as necessary to fit a particular transaction) may be a useful guide:

---

525. See id. § 9-619(b) (contemplating a standard "request form").

526. Cf. id. § 9-613(3) (permitting minor errors that are not seriously misleading); id. § 9-614(5) (prohibiting misleading errors concerning statutory rights and deferring to non-U.C.C. law for treatment of some errors); id. § 9-616(d) (permitting minor errors that are not seriously misleading).

527. Applicable law may recognize the title-clearing problem addressed by revised § 9-619 without offering specific and exhaustive guidelines for its resolution. For example, the Texas Transportation Code provides: "If a lien [on a motor vehicle] is foreclosed by nonjudicial means, the department may issue a new certificate of title in the name of the purchaser at the foreclosure sale on receiving the affidavit of the lienholder of the fact of the nonjudicial foreclosure." TEX. TRANSP. CODE ANN. § 501.074(b) (West 1997). Because the statute does not state with particularity the contents of the affidavit, the secured party may find the proposed transfer statement a useful form of "affidavit" in Texas and other jurisdictions with a similar law. Cf. IDAHO CODE § 49-514 (1994 & Supp. 1998) (requiring "satisfactory proof" in the form of an "affidavit" by a person "setting forth facts entitling him to possession and ownership," together with a copy of the "instrument upon which the claim of possession and ownership is founded"); 625 ILL. COMP. STAT. ANN. 5/3-114(a) (West Supp. 1998) (requiring "proof of the transfer"); IOWA CODE ANN. § 321.47 (West 1997) (requiring "presentation of satisfactory proof . . . of ownership and right of possession to the vehicle"); OHIO REV. CODE ANN. § 4505.10(A) (Anderson 1997) (requiring "satisfactory proof . . . of ownership and rights of possession" in the form of an "affidavit" by a person "setting forth the facts entitling the person to the possession and ownership," accompanied by a copy of the "instrument upon which the claim of possession and ownership is founded"); WYO. STAT. ANN. § 31-2-104(c) (Michie 1997) (requiring a "verified or certified statement of the transfer of the interest" that sets forth "[t]he reason for the involuntary transfer, the interest transferred, the name of the transferee, the process or procedure effecting the transfer and other information requested by the county clerk").

TRANSFER FORM

Dear Public Official:

This letter is submitted as a "transfer form" as defined in Texas Business & Commerce Code § 9-619.

Under a security agreement dated _____, executed by [name/address of debtor] ("Debtor"), and [name/address of secured party] ("Secured Party"), Debtor granted a security interest in "Collateral" (as defined in the security agreement) to secure payment and performance of certain obligations owed to Secured Party. The "Collateral" includes a 1996 Ford Taurus (the "Vehicle"). Debtor's ownership of the Vehicle is evidenced by Texas Certificate of Title no. _____ issued on _____.

Debtor has defaulted in its obligations owed to Secured Party. Secured Party has exercised its post-default remedies, including disposing of the Vehicle as permitted by Texas Business and Commerce Code § 9-610. As a result of the disposition and pursuant to Texas Business and Commerce Code § 9-615, all of Debtor's rights in the Vehicle have been transferred to [name/address of transferee] (the "Purchaser").

Please promptly amend your records to reflect that Debtor's interest in the Vehicle has been transferred to Purchaser and mail a new certificate of title, issued in the name of Purchaser, to Purchaser at its address in the preceding paragraph.

Please contact me if you have questions on this matter or need additional information.

In an effort to expedite registration in the name of the successful purchaser, a secured party may attempt to obtain record or legal title prior to the foreclosure (which should improve the marketability of the collateral and, therefore, facilitate a sale). A transfer statement that is processed prior to foreclosure and transfers title from the debtor to the secured party does not of itself trigger either a "disposition"[528] under Article 9 or an accep-

---

528. *Cf.* U.C.C. § 9-619(c) (1999).

tance of the collateral in satisfaction of the debt.[529] The secured party remains obligated to perform its statutory duties,[530] such as the duty to send notice of the disposition,[531] and the debtor still enjoys its statutory rights, including the right to timely redeem the collateral.[532]

As the Official Comments acknowledge, revised § 9-619 is not intended to replace non-U.C.C. law that provides a means by which title records can be revised to reflect changes in ownership resulting from post-default dispositions under Article 9.[533] Therefore a secured party and its counsel should consult other federal and state law governing title to, and registration of, the collateral being disposed before concluding that revised § 9-619 applies. But to the extent that federal and state law fail to provide a title-clearing mechanism, revised § 9-619 affords welcome relief.

---

529. *See id.* § 9-620(b) (stating that a purported or apparent acceptance of collateral is ineffective unless certain conditions have been satisfied). *But see* Comer v. Green Tree Acceptance, Inc., 858 P.2d 560, 565 (Wyo. 1993) (holding that a strict foreclosure occurred when a creditor acquired title to a repossessed mobile home in its own name after default and before selling it). *Cf.* WYO. STAT. ANN. § 31-2-504(c) (stating that a transfer, by operation of law, of an interest in a mobile home to a creditor "shall not be considered a strict foreclosure or an election to retain the collateral in satisfaction of an obligation" under U.C.C. § 9-505 "and does not affect the debtor's right to redeem the collateral" under U.C.C. § 9-506).

530. *See* U.C.C. § 9-619(c) (1999).

531. *See id.* § 9-611(b).

532. *See id.* § 9-623(a), (c).

533. *See id.* § 9-619 cmt. 3.

REVISED § 9-620

ACCEPTANCE OF COLLATERAL IN FULL OR PARTIAL SATISFACTION OF OBLIGATION; COMPULSORY DISPOSITION OF COLLATERAL

Instead of disposing of collateral, a secured party may be willing to retain the collateral and forgive the unpaid secured debt. A secured party may find this option attractive for a variety of reasons. The creditor may have no desire to collect a deficiency for economic, social, or other reasons. The creditor may be worried that, despite its best efforts, it will trip over one or more of the procedural hurdles placed in its path by the disposition-related provisions and expose itself to potential liability for its noncompliance. The creditor may wish to avoid having its conduct scrutinized under a judicial microscope when the debtor alleges that the disposition was not commercially reasonable. And certainly the secured party may find the option attractive if it believes that the value of the collateral exceeds the unpaid debt. The debtor, too, may welcome such an offer, especially if it has no realistic hope of satisfying any deficiency or believes that a commercially reasonable disposition is not likely to produce any surplus proceeds. Recognizing that the debtor and secured party "are frequently better off without a resale of the collateral,"[534] current Article 9, through § 9-505, provides an alternative arrangement whereby the secured party may retain the collateral and forego

---

534. *See id.* § 9-505 cmt. 1 (1995); *see also* 2 GILMORE, *supra* note 2, § 44.3, at 1220 ("The best and simplest way of liquidating any secured transaction . . . is for the secured party to keep the collateral as his own free of the debtor's equity, waiving any clam to a deficiency judgment.").

any claim to a deficiency.[535] Revised Article 9, through § 9-620, continues to provide the secured party with this option, known as "strict foreclosure."[536]

Under current Article 9, a secured party may propose to keep the collateral "in satisfaction of the obligation."[537] Whether the statute permits partial strict foreclosure—a process by which the creditor retains the collateral, forgives *part* of the debt, and sues the debtor for an agreed-upon deficiency—has been the subject of debate.[538] Some interpret § 9-505(2) as an all-or-nothing proposition that requires a creditor to forgive the entire unpaid

---

535. *See* U.C.C. § 9-505(2).

536. *See, e.g., id.* § 9-620 cmt. 2 (1999) (stating that revised §§ 9-620, 9-621, and 9-622 "deal with strict foreclosure, a procedure by which the secured party acquires the debtor's interest in the collateral without the need for a sale or other disposition under Section 9-610"); LaRoche v. Amoskeag Bank, 969 F.2d 1299, 1303 (1st Cir. 1992) (referring to the " 'strict foreclosure' option available under U.C.C. § 9-505(2)"); LeRoy Adventures, Inc. v. Cafritz Harbour Group, Inc., 660 A.2d 908, 912 (D.C. 1995) (referring to the "remedy of strict foreclosure" under the local version of § 9-505); Patrick v. Wix Auto Co., 681 N.E.2d 98, 101 (Ill. App. Ct. 1997) (stating that § 9-505(2) "contains specific requirements for a strict foreclosure"); General Elec. Capital Corp. v. Vashi, 480 N.W.2d 880, 882 (Iowa 1992) (observing that the procedure of § 9-505(2) "is sometimes called 'strict foreclosure'"); Alvin C. Harrell, *1994 Meetings Refine Proposed Article 9 Revisions*, 48 CONSUMER FIN. L.Q. REP. 326, 329 (1994) ("Current section 9-505 permits a secured party to retain the collateral in satisfaction of the debt, subject to certain qualifications. This is called 'strict foreclosure.'"); Lloyd, *supra* note 279, at 695, 726 ("Article 9 expressly provides for strict foreclosure, but only under the very limited circumstances of [U.C.C. § 9-505]."); Steve H. Nickles & Edward S. Adams, *Tracing Proceeds to Attorneys' Pockets (and the Dilemma of Paying for Bankruptcy)*, 78 MINN. L. REV. 1079, 1160 (1994) (referencing "the strict foreclosure remedy of section 9-505").

Except as provided by revised § 9-624, the rights and duties under revised § 9-620 cannot be waived or varied. *See* U.C.C. § 9-602(10) (1999); *id.* § 9-624(b) (discussed *infra* notes 693–99, 705–07, and accompanying text).

537. *See* U.C.C. § 9-505(2) (1995). Under current Article 9, a creditor may propose strict foreclosure "after default." *Id.* § 9-505(2). Revised § 9-620 does not expressly require a default as a condition precedent to strict foreclosure, which might suggest that the creditor may propose strict foreclosure at any time during the transaction. However, revised § 9-601 discourages any such suggestion by stating: "*After default*, a secured party has the rights provided in this part . . . ." *Id.* § 9-601(a) (1999) (emphasis added).

538. The phrase "partial strict foreclosure" also could refer to the creditor's retention of part of the collateral in satisfaction of all of the unpaid debt. The creditor's ability to do so has not been challenged. *See* Weiss v. Alterman, 577 N.Y.S.2d 768, 771–72 (1991) (finding "no reason" to hold that U.C.C. § 9-505(2) does not permit a creditor to retain part of the collateral in full satisfaction of the debt, but refusing to apply that interpretation in a case where the creditor's notices did not clearly manifest that intent); 2 GILMORE, *supra* note 2, § 44.3, at 1223 n.2 (construing the statutory reference to "the collateral" as "all or part of the collateral"); 9 HAWKLAND ET AL., *supra* note 15, § 9-505:08, at 865–66 (suggesting that a creditor's proposal to keep some collateral and forgive the entire unpaid debt "would seem to create little problem").

debt and forego any deficiency if the collateral is kept, rather than disposed.[539] Others have concluded that § 9-505(2) permits (or should permit) partial strict foreclosure.[540] Revised Article 9 resolves the debate by permitting the creditor to accept collateral "in full or partial satisfaction" of the unpaid secured debt.[541] This clarification, which comports with pre-U.C.C. law,[542] benefits both parties by providing additional flexibility in a variety of situations, including when the creditor's unsecured position makes retention in full satisfaction of the debt impractical and any disposition is unlikely to result in net proceeds satisfactory to the

539. *See* U.C.C. § 9-505 cmt. 1 (1995) (indicating that a creditor may keep the collateral, "thus discharging the obligation and abandoning *any* claim for a deficiency") (emphasis added); *LaRoche*, 969 F.2d at 1303 (indicating that U.C.C. § 9-505(2) "permits the secured creditor to notify the debtor that it intends to retain the collateral in *complete satisfaction* of the indebtedness"); *Patrick*, 681 N.E.2d at 101 (stating that under U.C.C. § 9-505 "a creditor elects to retain the collateral as *full* satisfaction of the debtor's obligations") (emphasis added); 2 GILMORE, *supra* note 2, § 44.3, at 1223 n.2 (concluding that the statutory reference to "the obligation" requires discharge of "the entire obligation"); Clark & Clark, *supra* note 418, at 257 (suggesting that acceptance of collateral in partial satisfaction of the debt is "something that probably cannot be done under current law"); Edwin E. Smith, *Overview of Revised Article 9*, 73 AM. BANKR. L.J. 1, 51 (1999) (stating a secured party may not retain collateral in partial satisfaction of secured debt under current law); Neil B. Cohen, *Credit Enhancement in Domestic Transactions: Conceptualizing the Devices and Reinventing the Law*, 22 BROOK. J. INT'L L. 21, 52 (1996) ("Under current law, a secured party may propose retaining the collateral only in total satisfaction of the secured debt."); Wendell H. Holmes, *"Involuntary Strict Foreclosure" Under Section 9-505(2) of the Uniform Commercial Code: Tarpit for the Tardy Creditor*, 26 WAKE FOREST L. REV. 289, 298–99 n.50 (1991) ("The Code's language does not expressly foreclose [the creditor from proposing to retain all of the collateral as satisfaction of only part of the obligation], but surely it is beyond the policy of the statute."); Rapson, *supra* note 4 ("Present Article 9 makes no provision for acceptance of the collateral in partial satisfaction of the obligation.").

540. *See* Peter F. Coogan, *The New UCC Article 9*, 86 HARV. L. REV. 477, 520–24 (1973) (arguing that the "rights" which can be modified by a debtor under § 9-505 include the right to agree to a partial strict foreclosure); Alysse Kaplan, *Partial Satisfaction Under the UCC*, 61 FORDHAM L. REV. 221, 227–34 (1992) (offering statutory and policy reasons for permitting partial satisfaction under U.C.C. § 9-505(2)); WHITE & SUMMERS, *supra* note 36, § 34-9, at 428 ("All judges appear to agree that if the debtor has expressly agreed after default that the secured creditor may take the collateral at an agreed valuation in *partial* satisfaction of the debt, the secured creditor may still recover the balance owing."); *see also* Oraka v. Jaraysi, 486 S.E.2d 69, 71 (Ga. Ct. App. 1997) ("After default, a creditor cannot, absent express agreement of the debtor, take the collateral at a specific valuation and only give such credit against the deficiency."); S. M. Flickinger Co. v. 18 Genesee Corp., 423 N.Y.S.2d 73, 77 (App. Div. 1979) (Moule, J., dissenting) (citing Professor Coogan's article for the proposition that a debtor can agree to a partial strict foreclosure).

541. *See* U.C.C. § 9-620(a) (1999). Louisiana, through a non-uniform amendment to U.C.C. § 9-505, already expressly permits a creditor to retain collateral in partial satisfaction of the unpaid debt. *See* LA. REV. STAT. ANN. § 10:9-505(5) (West 1993).

542. *See* RESTATEMENT OF SECURITY § 55 cmt. a (1941) ("The pledgor and pledgee should not be prevented from making a bargain by which the pledged chattel can be taken in whole or in part satisfaction of the pledgee's claim.").

parties.[543] It also recognizes that a secured party already can achieve the functional equivalent of a partial strict foreclosure by buying collateral at public and, in limited situations, private dispositions[544] and then suing the debtor for a deficiency.[545]

Whether Revised Article 9 should permit partial strict foreclosure in consumer transactions was the subject of much debate during the revision process. Early drafts prohibited partial strict foreclosure in all consumer secured transactions.[546] Later, the blanket prohibition was deleted.[547] It subsequently reappeared as part of a compromise between representatives of consumer creditors and advocates of consumer interests.[548] As passed, Revised

543. *See* PEB STUDY GROUP REPORT, *supra* note 7, at 243–44.

544. *See* U.C.C. § 9-610(c) (1999); *id.* § 9-504(3) (1995); *see also* Zubrow, *supra* note 467, at 539 n.381 ("There is virtually no difference between strict foreclosure and the purchase of collateral by a creditor for its own account at a purportedly 'public' sale with only a few bidders.").

545. *See* U.C.C. § 9-615(d)(2) (1999); *id.* § 9-504(2) (1995). However, the amount of the deficiency might not be the same in both situations. One reason for a potential difference is that the debtor can attempt to negotiate the amount of the deficiency in a partial strict foreclosure before agreeing to the foreclosure. The debtor has much less control over the amount of the deficiency in a traditional disposition. A difference also could result from the presence or absence of disposition-related expenses (such as storage charges) and reasonable attorneys' fees and legal expenses.

546. *See id.* § 9-505(l) (Draft July 28–Aug. 4, 1995) ("In a consumer secured transaction, a secured party may accept collateral only in full satisfaction, and not in partial satisfaction, of the obligation it secures.").

547. *See id.* § 9-618 (Draft July 25–Aug. 1, 1997).

548. *See id.* § 9-618(h) (Draft Mar. 1998) ("In a consumer transaction, a secured party may not accept collateral in partial satisfaction of the obligation it secures."). The following excerpt reflects the "consumer compromise":

During the February, 1998, meeting of the Drafting Committee in Rosemont, Illinois, the Drafting Committee approved in principle, and asked the Reporters to incorporate in this draft, a list of proposed revisions relating to consumer transactions. Most of the proposals, but not all, relate to Part 6, Default. The chair of the Drafting Committee presented the proposals as a compromise, explaining that if the package of proposals were accepted by the Drafting Committee and its sponsors, representatives of consumer creditors involved in the process would actively support, and advocates of consumer interests involved in the process would not oppose, enactment of revised Article 9. The chair explained further that the alternative would be widespread opposition, with pitched battles in the various legislatures during the enactment process. This controversy could delay or inhibit enactment of the revisions. The compromise grew out of discussions among creditor and consumer representatives, a special consumer subcommittee organized by the NCCUSL leadership, and the chair of the Drafting Committee.

Under the proposal, several provisions of the prior draft would be deleted: Sections . . . 9-613(b)(3) (notice of disposition containing minor errors not seriously misleading is sufficient); 9-622 (reinstatement rights of consumer debtor or secondary obligor); 9-624(d) and (e) (reduction of secured party's liability for statutory damages by amount of loss of deficiency or actual damages awarded to

Article 9 prohibits partial strict foreclosure in a consumer trans-action.[549] The reason for prohibiting partial strict foreclosures in consumer transactions may have been in response to a concern that a consumer might not understand the creditor's proposal and accept it without realizing all of the ramifications.[550] Rather than address the concern through a blanket prohibition, the statute could have mandated the insertion of conspicuous language in the creditor's notice aimed at fully apprising the consumer of its rights and potential liability. In this manner, revised § 9-620 could have addressed the need to improve consumer awareness while concurrently preserving a remedy that both parties might find mutually beneficial.

consumer); 9-625, Alternative A (absolute bar rule alternative for consumer trans-actions); 9-627(d) (bona-fide error defense to statutory damages); 9-627(e) (limitation on recoveries in class actions); 9-628 (reciprocal attorney's fees in consumer transactions).

The proposal also calls for revision of several other provisions. Sections 9-104(f) and (g) (approving "dual status" rule and setting burden of proof) would be applicable only to non-consumer transactions, as would § 9-625, Alternative B (rebuttable presumption rule). . . . § 9-614A (post-disposition notice) would be revised to provide for a somewhat more general statement of how a deficiency or surplus was calculated. The comments to § 9-614 would be modified to delete any statement that "price" is not a term of a disposition that is required to be commercially reasonable, and an explanatory comment would be added to the effect that a low price mandates enhanced judicial scrutiny of the terms of a disposition. Finally, § 9-618 would be revised to prohibit partial strict foreclosure for consumer goods. Revised Article 9, Reporters' Prefatory Note, cmt. 2 (Draft Mar. 1998).

The debate over whether (and to what extent) Article 9 should govern consumer transactions has raged since original Article 9 was drafted. *See* 1 GILMORE, *supra* note 2, § 9.2, at 293 (contending that "[t]he controversy over the consumer question was one of the most violent in the history of the Code's drafting"); Grant Gilmore, *The Secured Transaction Article of the Commercial Code*, 16 LAW & CONTEMP. PROBS. 27, 44 (1951) (observing that "how much or how little Article 9 should do for the consumer, or about the special problems arising in the consumer field, has caused more debate than any other single matter that has been considered in the course of drafting"). William Burke, the chair of the Drafting Committee, has referred to the treatment of consumer issues as "the most difficult problem" confronted by the Drafting Committee. *See* Julian B. McDonnell, *Securing Consumer Credit Card Accounts With Goods Purchased: Celebration of Freedom or Exercise in Bondage?*, 31 UCC L.J. 332, 343 (1999).

549. *See* U.C.C. § 9-620(g) (1999); *see also id.* § 9-102(a)(26) (defining "consumer transaction"). A secured party may not contract around the prohibition. *See id.* § 9-602(10).

550. *See* Braucher, *supra* note 422, at 94–95 (noting that consumer advocates opposed partial strict foreclosure because "consumers might be misled and might not understand that they still owed money" after surrendering collateral and "might not read or understand form documents" proposing partial strict foreclosure); Michael M. Greenfield, *The Role of Assent in Article 2 and Article 9*, 75 WASH. U. L.Q. 289, 301 (1997) (stating that the Drafting Committee elected to prohibit partial strict foreclosure in consumer transactions in recognition of "the high risk of ineffective communication in the consumer context").

A creditor may accept collateral in full or partial satisfaction of the unpaid secured debt only if four conditions are satisfied. First, the debtor must consent to the creditor's proposal.[551] If the creditor proposes partial strict foreclosure, the debtor consents by agreeing to the proposal in a record authenticated after default.[552] If the creditor proposes full strict foreclosure, the debtor's consent can be express or implied. The debtor can expressly consent in a record authenticated after default.[553] Alternatively, the debtor's consent is implied if (i) the creditor's proposal is unconditional (or subject only to the condition that collateral not in the creditor's possession be preserved and maintained),[554] (ii) the creditor's proposal expresses an intent to accept collateral in full satisfaction of the unpaid secured debt,[555] (iii) the creditor fails to receive, within twenty days after sending its proposal to the debtor, the debtor's authenticated notification of objection,[556] and (iv) the creditor's proposal is made in good faith.[557]

Two observations on this first requirement are worth stating. First, the debtor's consent to a proposal of partial satisfaction must be express; it cannot be implied. The prohibition against implied consent to a partial strict foreclosure presumably results from a heightened concern that through mere silence a debtor should not lose its property *and* also remain liable for an amount of debt calculated by the creditor in its sole discretion. And second, unless

---

551. *See* U.C.C. § 9-620(a)(1) (1999).
552. *See id.* § 9-620(c)(1); *see also id.* § 9-102(a)(7) (defining "authenticate"); *id.* § 9-102(a)(69) (defining "record"); *cf. id.* § 9-505(2) (1995) (referencing the secured party's receipt of an "objection in writing").
553. *See id.* § 9-620(c)(2) (1999).
554. *See id.* § 9-620(c)(2)(A).
555. *See id.* § 9-620(c)(2)(B).
556. *See id.* § 9-620(c)(2)(C); *see also id.* § 9-102 cmt. 9b (indicating that an authenticated notification refers to an authenticated record that contains a notification). Under current Article 9, the debtor has a 21-day objection period that starts on the date when the creditor sends its notice. *See id.* § 9-505(2) (1995). Early drafts of Revised Article 9 continued the 21-day objection period. *See id.* § 9-505(d)(2)(iii) (Draft July 28–Aug. 4, 1995). The objection period lost a day in subsequent drafts for no apparent reason. *See id.* § 9-505(d)(2)(iii) (Draft July 12–19, 1996). Even so, the objection period remains more liberal than that currently adopted by the Kansas legislature. *See* KAN. STAT. ANN. § 84-9-505(2) (1996) (providing an objection period of 15 days).
557. *See* U.C.C § 9-620 cmt. 11 (1999).

the debtor receives the proposal on the date when it is sent by the creditor, the debtor does not have a full twenty days in which to object. The objection period begins running from the date when the creditor sends the notice, not the date when the debtor receives the notice.[558] Furthermore, the debtor's objection must be received within that twenty-day period; an objection sent within that period but received by the creditor thereafter is not timely. Therefore, a debtor should send the notice in a manner that provides objective evidence of the date of the creditor's receipt.

The second condition to an effective strict foreclosure is that the secured party must not timely receive an authenticated notification of objection from either (i) a party to whom the secured party is required to send its proposal or (ii) a lienholder or other secured party with a subordinate property interest in the collateral subject to the proposal.[559] To be timely, an objection from a party to whom the secured party is required to send its proposal must be received by the secured party within twenty days after the date when the secured party sent its proposal to that person.[560] An objection from any other party is timely if the secured party receives it within twenty days after the date when it last sent its proposal to any required recipient, unless the only party to whom the secured party is required to send its notice is the debtor, in which case an objection must be received before the debtor consents to the proposal.[561]

As mentioned before, the usual twenty-day objection period[562] begins running on the date when the creditor sends the notice, not the date when the objecting party receives the notice. Also observe that a non-recipient normally has a comparable

---

558. Prior to its amendment in 1972, U.C.C. § 9-505(2) provided the debtor with a 30-day objection period that commenced on the date of the debtor's receipt of the creditor's notice. *See id.* § 9-505 ("Text Prior to 1972 Amendment"). Through a non-uniform amendment to § 9-505(2), Wisconsin presently provides a debtor with a 21-day objection period that runs from the date of its receipt of the notice. *See* WIS. STAT. ANN. § 409.505(2) (West 1995).

559. *See* U.C.C. § 9-620(a)(2) (1999).

560. *See id.* § 9-620(d)(1).

561. *See id.* § 9-620(d)(2).

562. *Cf. id.* § 9-505(2) (1995) (providing a 21-day objection period); *id.* § 9-505(e) (Draft July 28–Aug. 4, 1995) (continuing the 21-day objection period); *id.* § 9-505(e) (Draft July 12–19, 1996) (shortening the period to 20 days).

objection period, but in those situations where the debtor is the only party to whom the secured party must send its proposal, the debtor's acceptance terminates a non-recipient's right to object or the effectiveness of any objection sent but not yet received by the secured party. Therefore, a non-recipient should expedite the creditor's receipt of any objection and not assume that it enjoys the normal objection period.

The third condition applies only if the collateral consists of consumer goods. A strict foreclosure of consumer goods is not effective if the debtor possesses the consumer goods when it consents to the strict foreclosure.[563] Presumably this limitation is included to address the concern that a consumer debtor may believe that as long as it exercises physical control of the item, the creditor cannot exercise strict foreclosure. In reliance on that erroneous belief the consumer may fail to timely object to a creditor's proposal, not realizing that silence may create implied consent.[564] To protect the consumer against the harsh results of its own inaction the statute renders ineffective any consent by a debtor that possesses the consumer goods.

But the condition extends too far and may have unintended consequences for the party it seeks to protect, the consumer debtor. Knowing that the consumer's consent, express or implied, to an offer of strict foreclosure is not effective if the consumer possesses the collateral, a creditor may repossess the collateral before sending its proposal. After adding the costs of repossession to the unpaid debt, the creditor may rethink its options. If the creditor foregoes strict foreclosure and decides to dispose of the collateral, the debtor not only loses its interest in the collateral but also is likely to be sued for a deficiency. The statute would better protect consumers against such litigation if it permitted debtors, in possession of consumer goods, to expressly consent to the creditor's proposal to take the collateral in satisfaction of the unpaid debt.

The fourth condition also applies only if the collateral consists of consumer goods. A creditor cannot exercise the remedy

---

563. *See id.* § 9-620(a)(3) (1999).
564. *See id.* § 9-620(c)(2).

of strict foreclosure if it possesses consumer goods and at least sixty percent of the cash price has been paid (if the security interest is a purchase-money security interest) or at least sixty percent of the principal amount has been paid (in non-purchase-money cases).[565] Instead, the creditor must timely dispose of the collateral.[566] Theoretically, a consumer debtor should benefit from this provision because a forced disposition of collateral in which the

565. *See id.* § 9-620(a)(4), (e); *see also id.* § 9-103 (discussing purchase-money concepts). Current Article 9 also prescribes a "60 percent" test. *See id.* § 9-505(1) (1995). Under pre-U.C.C. law, a creditor in a transaction governed by the Uniform Conditional Sales Act was required to dispose of repossessed collateral if the buyer had paid "at least fifty per cent of the purchase price at the time of the retaking." *See* UNIF. COND. SALES ACT § 19, 3B U.L.A. 585 (1992).

Notice that in a purchase-money transaction the test is 60% of the *cash price*, which may be different from the amount financed. For example, if a debtor buys a $30,000 car by making a $3000 down payment and financing the balance of $27,000, the test is satisfied (and strict foreclosure is not an option) when the debtor has paid $18,000 (60% of $30,000), not $16,200 (60% of $27,000).

566. *See* U.C.C. § 9-620(e), (f) (1999). The creditor must dispose of the collateral within 90 days after taking possession unless the debtor and all secondary obligors agree, after default and in an authenticated agreement, to a longer period. *See id.* § 9-620(f). The statute imposes a relatively short disposition period in an effort to avoid loss of value due to excessive depreciation, a trait common to most consumer goods. 9 HAWKLAND ET AL., *supra* note 15, § 9-505:02, at 854; Holmes, *supra* note 539, at 298.

Current Article 9 does not expressly permit the parties to extend the 90-day period. *See* U.C.C. § 9-505(1) (1995); *cf.* CAL. COM. CODE § 9505(1) (West 1990) (requiring the secured party to dispose of the collateral "within 90 days after he takes possession or within a reasonable time after such 90-day period"); OR. REV. STAT. § 79.5050(1) (1988) (providing a 180-day period). U.C.C. § 9-505(1) does permit a consumer, however, after default, to execute a statement "renouncing or modifying his rights." One court has construed this language as permitting a debtor to agree to extend the 90-day period. *See* Kelley v. Commercial Nat'l Bank, 678 P.2d 620, 622–24 (Kan. 1984) (concluding creditor that possessed collateral on November 4, 1981, and sold it on August 16, 1982, did not violate § 9-505(1) where evidence revealed debtor had agreed to extension of 90-day disposition period). *But see* 2 GILMORE, *supra* note 2, § 44.3, at 1222 ("What was meant was that the debtor could waive his right to a compulsory resale and agree to let the secured party keep the collateral as his own provided the debtor was discharged from his obligation."). The express flexibility provided by revised § 9-620(f) should benefit debtors when the market for collateral is seasonal. For example, a creditor may repossess a snowmobile from a Vermont resident in February. If the optimum market for snowmobile purchases does not fall in the 90-day period following repossession, the debtor can agree to extend the period into the fall or winter months, when the demand for snowmobiles may bring a sales price both higher than an off-season disposition and sufficient to compensate for any depreciation during the extension.

Under current Article 9, a creditor that fails to timely dispose of the collateral may be liable for conversion or other damages. *See* U.C.C. § 9-505(1). Under Revised Article 9, the creditor remains liable for damages. *See id.* § 9-625(b), (c) (1999). Accompanying comments reveal an intent to continue to allow an aggrieved party to recover a different measure of damages in tort. *See id.* § 9-625 cmt. 3.

debtor has significant equity should produce surplus proceeds.[567] But what should happen and what will happen may not mirror each other. The vagaries of market prices for used consumer goods, combined with the off-the-top payment of the creditor's costs of repossession and other disposition-related expenses,[568] may make the *possible* benefits afforded by revised § 9-620(e) less attractive to a risk-averse debtor than the *certain* advantages provided by an offer of strict foreclosure.[569] Recognizing that a consumer debtor may be better off accepting the creditor's offer of a strict foreclosure, current Article 9 permits a consumer debtor who satisfies the "60% test" to waive his right to a forced sale.[570] Revised Article 9 retains the same flexibility.[571]

Under current § 9-505, a secured creditor cannot propose to accept collateral in satisfaction of the debt unless it possesses the collateral.[572] This prevents strict foreclosure not only if the debtor

567. *See* 2 GILMORE, *supra* note 2, § 44.3, at 1222; 4 WHITE & SUMMERS, *supra* note 36, § 34–9, at 427; James P. Nehf, *Effective Regulation of Rent-to-Own Contracts,* 52 OHIO ST. L.J. 751, 803 (1991); *see also* Kelley, 678 P.2d at 623.

568. *See* U.C.C. § 9-615(a)(1) (1999); *id.* § 9-504(1)(a) (1995).

569. *See* Nehf, *supra* note 567, at 803 (concluding that, in the absence of "extraordinary circumstances," the possibility of a consumer receiving any surplus proceeds under U.C.C. § 9-505(1) is "remote"); *see also* Holmes, *supra* note 539, at 317–18 n.150 (suggesting that the rule is "probably perverse" because a forced sale of consumer goods that have rapidly depreciated "simply guarantee[s] a deficiency judgment").

570. *See* U.C.C. § 9-505(1) (1995).

571. *See id.* § 9-620(a)(4) (1999); *id.* § 9-624(b) (discussed *infra* notes 693–99, 705–07, and accompanying text). Not until very late in the drafting process did Revised Article 9 permit this waiver. *Compare id.* § 9-620(a)(4) (Draft approved at NCCUSL Annual Meeting, July 30, 1998) ("subsection (e) does not require the secured party to dispose of the collateral"), *with id.* §§ 9-620(a), 9-624 (Draft Nov. 15, 1998) (adding "or the debtor waives the requirement pursuant to Section 9-624" to end of revised § 9-620(a)(4) and adding new revised § 9-624(b) that allows the debtor to waive its right to require a disposition under revised § 9-620(e)).

572. *See id.* § 9-505(2) (1995); *see also* Bischoff v. Thomasson, 400 So. 2d 359, 368–69 (Ala. 1981) (holding that creditor could exercise strict foreclosure of ring in its possession); Sprangers v. Fundamental Bus. Tech., Inc., 412 N.W.2d 47, 48–50 (Minn. Ct. App. 1987) (concluding creditor could not exercise strict foreclosure of securities held by escrow agent where creditor was not party to escrow agreement, and holding unenforceable a provision in security agreement waiving possession requirement). *But see* Martin-Musumeci v. Law Offices of Herbert Hafif Pension & Profit Sharing Plan, 19 F.3d 28 (9th Cir.) (unpublished opinion), *cert. denied,* 115 S. Ct. 79 (1994) (concluding, for limited purpose of U.C.C. § 9-505(2), that creditor had possession of equity interest in a trust, a general intangible); CLARK, *supra* note 2, ¶ 4.10[2], at S4-73 ("There is no policy reason why that remedy should not be available for all types of collateral. Although U.C.C. § 9-505(2) refers to strict foreclosure as the remedy of a secured party 'in possession' of the collateral, it does not seem unreasonable to read that phrase as 'in possession, where possession is possible.' "); 2

possesses the collateral but also when the collateral is intangible, such as accounts and intellectual property. With the exception of consumer goods,[573] revised § 9-620 no longer requires a secured party to possess the collateral,[574] making this remedy an option in more post-default situations.[575]

An issue that exists under current Article 9 is whether a secured party that possesses collateral for an unreasonable period of time without attempting to dispose of it can be deemed, as a matter of law, to have elected to keep the collateral, forgive the debt, and waive any right to a deficiency, even though the creditor has never sent notice of that intent to the debtor and other interested parties. Courts have taken three different approaches. Some courts refuse to find that a creditor has involuntarily elected a strict foreclosure in the absence of any notice of that intent.[576]

GILMORE, *supra* note 2, § 44.3, at 1223 ("No satisfactory reason suggests itself why the formality of taking possession must be accomplished before the secured party can make a proposal under § 9-505(2) and set the time periods running."). *Cf.* PEB STUDY GROUP REPORT, *supra* note 7, at 239–41 (indicating that the PEB Study Group could not reach consensus on whether the possession requirement should be retained when collateral is tangible, but recommending elimination of the possession requirement when collateral is intangible).

573. *See* U.C.C. § 9-620(a)(3) (1999).

574. *See id.* § 9-620 cmt. 7.

575. If all parties agree to a strict foreclosure of accounts, payment intangibles, promissory notes, or chattel paper, then the secured party's acceptance of that collateral is treated as a "sale" by the debtor to the secured party, whose interest in the collateral will be considered a "security interest" under Revised Article 9. *See id.* § 9-109(a)(3). The secured party and the debtor need not execute a new security agreement to evidence the security interest, nor will the secured party need to file a new financing statement (assuming that any financing statement previously filed by the secured party perfected its security interest in the collateral prior to the strict foreclosure) or take any other action to perfect its interest. *See id.* § 9-620 cmt. 10.

576. *See, e.g.,* Warnaco, Inc. v. Farkas, 872 F.2d 539, 544–45 (2d Cir. 1989); Solfanelli v. Meridian Bank, 230 B.R. 54, 64–65 (M.D. Pa. 1999); Forbes v. Four Queens Enters., Inc., 210 B.R. 905, 910 (D.R.I. 1997); *In re* Nardone, 70 B.R. 1010, 1016–17 (Bankr. D. Mass. 1987); Bank of Boston Int'l v. Tefel, 644 F. Supp. 1423, 1428 (E.D.N.Y. 1986); *In re* Emergency Beacon Corp., 48 B.R. 341, 347 (S.D.N.Y. 1985); Hanam, B.V. v. Kittay, 589 F. Supp. 1042, 1048 (S.D.N.Y. 1984); Alamosa Nat'l Bank v. San Luis Valley Grain Growers, Inc., 756 P.2d 1022, 1026 (Colo. Ct. App. 1988); Allen v. Coates, 661 So. 2d 879, 887 (Fla. Dist. Ct. App. 1995); Munao v. Lagattuta, 691 N.E.2d 818, 822 (Ill. App. Ct. 1998); Stensel v. Stensel, 380 N.E.2d 526, 528–29 (Ill. App. Ct. 1978); Priggen Steel Bldgs. Co. v. Parsons, 213 N.E.2d 252, 253 (Mass. 1966); Jones v. Morgan, 228 N.W.2d 419, 423 (Mich. Ct. App. 1975); American Parts Sys., Inc. v. T & T Automotive, Inc., 358 N.W.2d 674, 677 (Minn. Ct. App. 1984); Clark Leasing Corp. v. White Sands Forest Products, Inc., 535 P.2d 1077, 1078 (N.M. 1975); Chrysler Credit Corp. v. Mitchell, 464 N.Y.S.2d 96, 97 (1983); S. M. Flickinger Co. v. 18 Genessee Corp., 423 N.Y.S.2d 73, 76 (App. Div. 1979); First Bank v. Haberer Dairy & Farm Equip., Inc., 412 N.W.2d 866, 870–71 (S.D. 1987). *Cf.* IFG Leasing Co. v. Gordon, 776 P.2d 607, 614 (Utah 1989) (declining to "address the various views regarding the issue, except to reiterate that section 9-501 expressly states that the requirement of actual written notice under section 9-505(2) cannot be varied or waived").

They reason that current § 9-505(2)'s notice requirement discourages an implied election and that a debtor can protect its interests under current § 9-507(1) by compelling a disposition or seeking damages.[577] Other courts have concluded that a creditor's retention of collateral for an unreasonable period of time can trigger a strict foreclosure.[578] These courts are concerned that a creditor may hold the collateral an unreasonable period of time and then sue on the underlying obligation with unfair consequences for the debtor.[579] And a third group has found a strict foreclosure if the creditor's behavior (or misbehavior) manifested an intent to accept the collateral in satisfaction of the unpaid

577. *See, e.g., Warnaco*, 872 F.2d at 544–45; *Jones*, 228 N.W.2d at 423; *S. M. Flickinger Co.*, 423 N.Y.S.2d at 76; *see also* U.C.C. § 9-504(2) (1995) (imposing liability on a debtor for a deficiency "unless otherwise agreed"). *But see* Moran v. Holman, 514 P.2d 817, 820 (Alaska 1973) (noting that the debtor's possible remedies under U.C.C. § 9-507 are "illusory in most cases" because of the debtor's "poor financial position" and the small amount involved); Haufler v. Ardinger, 28 U.C.C. Rep. Serv. (Callaghan) 893, 897 (Mass. Dist. Ct. 1979) ("In our opinion, a secured party should not be permitted to profit by his own failure to furnish requisite notice by both retaining the property for his own use and then seeking additional recovery from the debtor."); Schmode's, Inc. v. Wilkinson, 361 N.W.2d 557, 558 (Neb. 1985) ("We reject this view on the ground that a secured party ought not be allowed to penalize a debtor by asserting the secured party's own failure to give the notice contemplated by § 9-505(2).").

578. *See, e.g.,* Schultz v. Delaware Trust Co., 360 A.2d 576, 578 (Del. Super. Ct. 1976) ("There must be a reasonable limit to the length of time a secured party is permitted to hold collateral before it is deemed to have exercised its right to retain that collateral in satisfaction of the obligation."); Millican v. Turner, 503 So. 2d 289, 291 (Miss. 1987) (remanding for factual determination whether creditor had elected strict foreclosure by holding vehicle for six months); H. V. Funding, Inc. v. Ernest Vakkas & Sons, Inc., 531 N.Y.S.2d 484, 486 (Dist. Ct. 1988) (finding an implied retention where creditor repossessed collateral in August 1986 and had not yet sold it at time of trial in April 1988); Service Chevrolet, Inc. v. Sparks, 660 P.2d 760, 763–64 (Wash. 1983) (holding that retention of collateral for an unreasonable period of time could create a strict foreclosure, and remanding for determination whether four-week delay in informing debtors that they could reclaim their repossessed vehicle triggered an implied strict foreclosure); Swanson v. May, 697 P.2d 1013, 1015–16 (Wash. Ct. App. 1985) (concluding that creditor's retention of farm equipment for over one year was not, under the facts, sufficiently unreasonable to trigger a strict foreclosure); Durdahl v. Bank of Casper, 718 P.2d 23, 28 (Wyo. 1986) (remanding for factual determination whether creditor's continued retention of collateral at time of oral argument was so unreasonable that creditor would be deemed to have exercised its remedy of strict foreclosure). *Cf.* FDIC v. Tempest Fugat, H.L.I., Inc., 707 P.2d 81, 85 (Or. Ct. App. 1985) (failing to find an implied strict foreclosure despite 22-month delay between repossession and sale and 300 hours of unauthorized use of collateral by sales agent after "[a]ssuming that an unreasonable delay in selling repossessed collateral may imply a creditor's intent" to exercise the remedy of strict foreclosure).

579. *See, e.g., Service Chevrolet*, 660 P.2d at 763. *See also* Graff v. North Port Dev. Co., 734 N.W.2d 221, 228 (Mo. Ct. App. 1987); *Schmode's*, 361 N.E.2d at 558–59.

debt.[580] This approach borrows from the analogous concept of accord and satisfaction, which requires proof of the creditor's assent.[581]

The frequency with which the issue has been litigated, together with the inconsistent approaches taken by the courts, combined to make a response by Revised Article 9 all but a foregone conclusion. Joining the majority of courts, and following the recommendation of the PEB Study Group,[582] revised § 9-620 no longer permits constructive, implied, or involuntary strict foreclosures. Under revised § 9-620, a "purported or apparent" strict foreclosure is ineffective unless the secured party sends a proposal of strict foreclosure to the debtor (or otherwise consents, in an authenticated record, to a strict foreclosure) and all

580. *See, e.g., In re* Durastone Co., 223 B.R. 396, 404–05 (Bankr. D.R.I. 1998) (holding creditor's post-repossession behavior—using, renting, and unsuccessfully attempting to sell boom trailer held for over six years—"clearly signaled" intent to retain collateral in full satisfaction of unpaid debt; *In re* Boyd, 73 B.R. 122, 124–25 (Bankr. N.D. Tex. 1987) (finding bank employee's use of repossessed boat manifested intent to keep collateral and forgive debt); *In re* Deephouse Equip. Co., 38 B.R. 400, 403–05 (Bankr. D. Conn. 1984) (concluding evidence did not establish creditor intended to keep collateral in full satisfaction of unpaid secured debt); *Moran*, 514 P.2d at 819–21 (finding implied strict foreclosure where creditor used repossessed vehicle for his own use during four-month period between repossession and commencement of lawsuit); Nelson v. Armstrong, 582 P.2d 1100, 1107–09 (Idaho 1978) (ruling that creditor's retention of collateral for 4.5 months, without some manifestation of intent to exercise its rights under U.C.C. § 9-505(2), did not create a strict foreclosure); *Haufler*, 28 U.C.C. Rep. Serv. at 896–97 (affirming trial court's conclusion that creditor's continued possession and use of collateral for 38 months prior to sale created an implied strict foreclosure); *Schmode's*, 361 N.W.2d at 559 (holding that creditor elected to retain collateral in satisfaction of debt when, during three-year period prior to sale, it leased collateral to others who operated it for at least 204,000 miles); Wang v. Wang, 440 N.W.2d 740, 745–46 (S.D. 1989) (concluding that creditor that took collateral in July 1980, told co-maker to stay away from the storage location, and did not attempt to sell collateral until December 1984, had exercised its strict foreclosure remedy); Tanenbaum v. Economics Lab., Inc., 628 S.W.2d 769, 771–72 (Tex. 1982) (holding creditor's decision to scrap repossessed restaurant equipment amounted to strict foreclosure). *Cf.* Wisconics Eng'g, Inc. v. Fisher, 466 N.E.2d 745, 763 (Ind. Ct. App. 1984) (stating that "[t]here may be circumstances in which strict compliance with the written notice provisions of § 9-505(2) are not essential to a claim that the secured party, by his unreasonable conduct, retained the collateral in satisfaction of the debt"); Winters Nat'l Bank & Trust Co. v. Saker, 419 N.E.2d 890, 893 (Ohio. Ct. App. 1979) (stating that a "creditor may, under certain conditions, be deemed to have exercised its statutory right" of strict foreclosure).

581. *See also* RESTATEMENT (SECOND) OF CONTRACTS § 281(1) (1979) (defining an "accord" as "a contract under which an obligee *promises* to accept a stated performance in satisfaction of the obligor's existing duty") (emphasis added). *See, e.g.,* Lamp Fair, Inc. v. Perez-Ortiz, 888 F.2d 173, 176–77 (1st Cir. 1989); *Graff*, 734 S.W.2d at 228–29; *Schmode's*, 361 N.W.2d at 559.

582. *See* PEB STUDY GROUP REPORT, *supra* note 7, at 245–46.

conditions precedent to an effective strict foreclosure are met.[583] As with the three different approaches taken by various courts, the approach adopted by revised § 9-620 will have its fans and its critics. Proponents will rejoice that a creditor no longer can involuntarily waive its right to a deficiency, a most punitive result.[584] Opponents will contend that the statute effectively permits the creditor to deprive a debtor of its property for an extended period of time with impunity except in those rare situations where the debtor, already in default, has the financial ability to exert pressure on the creditor.[585] While parties may disagree on the merits of the approach taken,[586] hopefully all

583. *See* U.C.C. § 9-620(b) (1999).

584. *See, e.g.*, LAWRENCE, *supra* note 128, § 18.02[A], at 350 (1997) (describing constructive strict foreclosure as "wrong" and "nothing more than a fiction that allows a court to impose what is, in effect, an absolute bar on the secured party's right to a deficiency"). However, an unreasonable delay in disposition may support a charge that the secured party has not acted in a commercially reasonable manner. *See* U.C.C. § 9-620 cmt. 5 (1998); Solfanelli v. Meridian Bank, 230 B.R. 54, 65–67 (M.D. Pa. 1999) (finding creditor's deliberate inaction in selling shares of capital stock for eleven months commercially unreasonable).

585. *See, e.g.*, Gail Hillebrand, *The Uniform Commercial Code Drafting Process: Will Articles 2, 2B and 9 Be Fair To Consumers?*, 75 WASH. U. L.Q. 69, 130–31 (1997) (urging the retention of constructive strict foreclosure in consumer cases where the creditor's unreasonably long delay in disposing of the collateral may prejudice a consumer's ability to quantify the resulting harm); *see also* Braucher, *supra* note 422, at 95 (proposing that a creditor be barred from recovering any deficiency in a delayed disposition case because a consumer debtor has "difficulty . . . producing evidence of the loss caused by the delay").

586. Most secured parties will be pleased with the approach adopted by revised § 9-620(b), whereas most debtors will be disappointed. In a rare situation, however, the secured party may argue for, and the debtor against, a forced strict foreclosure. For example, a secured party may repossess collateral, hold it for an extended period of time, and then sell it for more than the unpaid debt. Desiring to keep the surplus proceeds, the secured party will argue that it has involuntarily elected a strict foreclosure even though it never sent notice of its intent to keep the collateral in satisfaction of the debt. The debtor will contend that the creditor, in the absence of any notice, did not elect a strict foreclosure and that the debtor is therefore entitled to the surplus proceeds. Current § 9-505(2) does not expressly address this situation. *Cf.* Gilligan v. Briar Hill Lanes, Inc., 673 N.Y.S.2d 711, 712 (N.Y. App. Div. 1998) (concluding debtor was entitled to surplus proceeds from liquidation of corporate stock held by secured party that failed to provide debtor with written notice of intent to retain stock in satisfaction of debt); Brown v. Baker, 688 P.2d 943, 951 n.5 (Alaska 1984) (refusing to relax the notice requirement of U.C.C. § 9-505 "where it is the creditor and not the debtor who argues that he opted to retain the collateral in satisfaction of the debt"); 4 WHITE & SUMMERS, *supra* note 36, § 34-9, at 429 ("But we would be generally less sympathetic when the creditor rather than the debtor advances an implied election argument, for here the debtor may not have had sufficient notice of the possible loss of its equity in the collateral."). Revised Article 9, through §§ 9-620(b) and 9-615(d)(1), would prompt a court to award any surplus proceeds to the debtor.

will agree that the decision to statutorily confront the issue should reduce litigation, promote uniformity, and provide certainty.[587] For that, the Drafting Committee deserves our applause.

---

587. *See* Braucher, *supra* note 176, at 550 (commenting on the conventional wisdom that "certainty is justice in the commercial field"); James Chareq & Anne Fortney, *An Argument for Retaining the Uniform Commercial Code*, 51 CONSUMER FIN. L.Q. REP. 315, 321 (1997) (asserting that "[t]he pillar upon which the U.C.C. rests is its promise of creating uniformity and predictability"); Corinne Cooper, *The Madonnas Play Tug of War With the Whores or Who Is Saving the UCC?*, 26 LOY. L.A. L. REV. 563, 568–69 (1993) (contending that "lawyers who have as their main goal to advance the cause of clarity, uniformity, and elegance (CUE) in commercial law . . . are the keepers of the precious flame that is the UCC"); Antonin Scalia, *The Rule of Law as a Law of Rules*, 56 U. CHI. L. REV. 1175, 1179 (1989) (observing that "[e]ven in simpler times uncertainty has been regarded as incompatible with the Rule of Law" and noting that predictability "is a needful characteristic of any law worthy of the name"); *cf.* Fred H. Miller, *Is Karl's Code Kaput?*, 26 LOY. L.A. L. REV. 703, 707 (1993) (suggesting that "rigid uniformity" is not, and probably never was, a "realistic goal" of the U.C.C.). *But see* 1 JAMES J. WHITE & ROBERT S. SUMMERS, UNIFORM COMMERCIAL CODE § 7, at 21 (Practitioner's 3d ed. 1988) (describing as "false or fanciful" the notion that a well-drafted code "will greatly reduce uncertainty, enhance predictability and diminish the volume of legal disputes").

REVISED § 9-621

NOTIFICATION OF PROPOSAL TO ACCEPT COLLATERAL

Current Article 9, through § 9-505(2), describes the parties to whom a secured party must send its notice of strict foreclosure. The parties to whom a secured party must send its "proposal"[588] of strict foreclosure under Revised Article 9 are described in § 9-621.[589]

Under current § 9-505(2), a secured party must send a written notice to a debtor that has not executed a post-default waiver

---

588. A "proposal" is "a record authenticated by a secured party which includes the terms on which the secured party is willing to accept collateral in full or partial satisfaction of the obligation it secures pursuant to §§ 9-620, 9-621 and 9-622." U.C.C. § 9-102(a)(66) (1999); see also id. § 9-102(a)(7) (defining "authenticate"); id. § 9-102(a)(69) (defining "record"). Revised Article 9 does not propose a model form or stipulate what information must be included. At a minimum, the proposal should describe the collateral to be retained, the amount of debt to be satisfied, and any applicable conditions. See id. § 9-620 cmt. 4; 2 GILMORE, supra note 2, § 44.3, at 1224; see also In re Alcom Am. Corp., 154 B.R. 97, 113 (Bankr. D.D.C. 1993) ("To fulfill the requirements of § 9-505(2), the secured party must explicitly inform the debtor that it is retaining the collateral in satisfaction of the indebtedness."); In re Leeling, 129 B.R. 637, 642 (Bankr. D. Colo. 1991) ("[W]hile it might not be necessary to use the magic words 'foreclosure' or 'retain in full satisfaction of the indebtedness' the intent to retain must be such that a reasonable person would understand that intent, and it must be clearly manifested by the secured creditor."); Patrick v. Wix Auto Co., 681 N.E.2d 98, 101 (Ill. App. Ct. 1997) ("The written notice must clearly and explicitly inform the debtor that the creditor is retaining the collateral in satisfaction of the indebtedness."). If the secured party is proposing to retain collateral in satisfaction of all of the unpaid debt, the secured party should avoid including any language in its notice that may be construed as a request for payment, which is inconsistent with the concept of full strict foreclosure and could destroy the effectiveness of the notice. See, e.g., Alcom Am. Corp., 154 B.R. at 113; Leeling, 129 B.R. at 641–42; Patrick, 681 N.E.2d at 101–02.

589. The rights and duties under revised § 9-621 cannot be waived or varied. See U.C.C. § 9-602(10) (1999).

of its right to receive the notice.[590] The debtor is nowhere to be found on the recipient list in revised § 9-621. Under revised § 9-620, however, a strict foreclosure is ineffective unless the secured party either has sent a proposal to the debtor or consents, in an authenticated record, to the debtor's acceptance.[591] It is possible, therefore, for a secured party to notify the debtor of its desire to keep the collateral and forgive all or part of the unpaid debt in a manner that is not a "proposal." But in the absence of a proposal, the debtor must agree (in an authenticated record) to the terms,[592] and the secured party must consent (also in an authenticated record) to the debtor's agreement.[593]

If the collateral consists of consumer goods, then current Article 9 does not require a creditor to send notice to anyone other than the debtor.[594] This rule is sensible because the value of most consumer goods makes them attractive as security only to one creditor, a party whose interest will often enjoy purchase-money status. Occasionally, however, a high-dollar consumer good that does not rapidly depreciate (such as a grand piano) might collateralize concurrent loans, justifying notice to any other secured party. Perhaps it is for this reason that the nature of collateral does not dictate who receives a proposal under revised § 9-621.

If the collateral is not consumer goods, current § 9-505(2) requires the creditor to send notice to any other secured party from whom the creditor has received timely written notice of its interest in the collateral.[595] Revised Article 9 significantly expands

---

590. *See id.* § 9-505(2) (1995). "Debtor" is defined at current § 9-105(1)(d) and has been construed by many courts to include guarantors. *See, e.g.,* Chrysler Credit Corp. v. B.J.M., Jr., Inc., 834 F. Supp. 813, 833 (E.D. Pa. 1993); Earl of Loveless, Inc. v. Gabele, 2 Cal. Rptr. 2d 829, 831 (Ct. App. 1991); McEntire v. Indiana Nat'l Bank, 471 N.E.2d 1216, 1223 (Ind. Ct. App. 1984); Gambo v. Maryland, 648 A.2d 1105, 1108 (Md. Ct. Spec. App. 1994); Marine Midland Bank v. CMR Indus., Inc., 559 N.Y.S.2d 892, 899 (App. Div. 1990); McChord Credit Union v. Parrish, 809 P.2d 759, 761 (Wash. Ct. App. 1991).

591. *See* U.C.C. § 9-620(b)(1) (1999).

592. *See id.* § 9-620(c)(1), (2). Observe that the debtor's consent cannot be implied, through silence, in the absence of a proposal. *See id.* § 9-620(c)(2)(A).

593. *See id.* § 9-620(b)(1).

594. *See id.* § 9-505(2) (1995).

595. *See id.* To be timely, written notice of the competing interest must be received by the foreclosing creditor before the foreclosing creditor has sent its notice of strict foreclosure to the debtor or before the debtor has renounced its rights to receive notice. *See id.*

the list of non-debtor recipients to include four categories of parties.[596] The first category includes any other person claiming an interest (whether statutory, judicial, or consensual) in the collateral from whom the secured party has received, before the debtor consents to the proposal, an authenticated notification of the competing interest.[597] The second category includes any other secured party or lienholder with a property interest that, ten days prior to the debtor's consent, was perfected by a financing statement that identified the collateral, was indexed under the debtor's then-existing name, and was filed in the then-proper place.[598] The third category includes any other secured party that, ten days prior to the debtor's consent, held a security interest perfected by compliance with any statute, regulation, or treaty referenced in revised § 9-311(a).[599] And the fourth category, which applies only if the proposal contemplates partial strict foreclosure, includes any secondary obligor.[600]

Not surprisingly, the list of non-debtor parties to whom a creditor must send its proposal closely resembles the list of

---

596. The expansion is explained as part of the analysis of revised § 9-622, discussed *infra* notes 624–46 and accompanying text.

The PEB Study Group recommended that notice should be sent to persons who timely provide the secured party with written notice of a competing property interest. *See* PEB STUDY GROUP REPORT, *supra* note 7, at 241–43. The PEB Study Group also urged the Drafting Committee to "consider seriously" whether to require a secured party to send notice to persons with recorded property interests. *See id.*

597. *See* U.C.C. § 9-621(a)(1) (1999).

598. *See id.* § 9-621(a)(2). Prior to the 1972 amendments to Article 9, U.C.C. § 9-505(2) obligated a creditor to send notice to any other person with a security interest in the collateral and who had duly filed a financing statement indexed in the name of the debtor or whose security interest was known by the creditor. *See id.* § 9-505 ("Text Prior to 1972 Amendment"), 3B U.L.A. 353 (1992). The 1972 amendments deleted these secured creditors from the recipient list to conform to concurrent amendments made to the list of recipients of a disposition notice under U.C.C. § 9-504(3). *See id.* § 9-505 ("Official Reasons for 1972 Change"). Nevertheless, a handful of states that adopted the 1972 amendments have retained language requiring a secured party to send notice of its strict foreclosure to secured parties that have filed financing statements against the collateral. *See, e.g.,* ARIZ. REV. STAT. ANN. § 47-9505B (West 1997); FLA. STAT. ANN. § 679.505(2) (West Supp. 1998); TEX. BUS. & COM. CODE ANN. § 9.505(b) (West 1992); WASH. REV. CODE ANN. § 62A.9-505(2) (West 1995); WIS. STAT. ANN. § 409.505(2) (West 1995). *See also* CLARK, *supra* note 2, ¶ 4.10[1], at 4-184 ("In any revision of Article 9, it may be wise to return to the pre-1972 rule that required notice to all secured parties of record.").

599. *See* U.C.C. § 9-621(a)(3) (1999).

600. *See id.* § 9-621(b); *see also id.* § 9-102(a)(71) (defining "secondary obligor").

non-debtor parties to whom a creditor must send its notice of disposition under revised § 9-611.[601] But three noticeable differences between revised §§ 9-611 and 9-621 are worth mentioning. First, a secondary obligor is always entitled to notice of disposition,[602] but is entitled to a proposal of strict foreclosure only if the secured party is accepting collateral in partial, rather than full, satisfaction of the unpaid debt.[603] The reason for this different treatment is both apparent and flawed. A secondary obligor usually remains liable for any deficiency following a disposition of collateral,[604] so it has an interest in receiving a disposition notice. But a deficiency survives a proposal of strict foreclosure only if the creditor proposes partial satisfaction. The statute assumes that a secondary obligor will never object to a proposal of full strict foreclosure because the obligor's liability completely disappears; therefore, requiring the creditor to send a proposal of full strict foreclosure to a secondary obligor serves no purpose, and revised § 9-621(b) acknowledges this. But this reasoning fails to recognize the existence of situations where a secondary obligor might object to an offer of full strict foreclosure. For example, SubCorp borrows $1,000,000 from Bank. Repayment of the loan is secured by a security interest in SubCorp's inventory and guaranteed by ParentCorp. SubCorp then borrows $500,000 from Lender. Repayment of the loan is secured by a subordinate security interest in SubCorp's inventory and guaranteed by ParentCorp. After SubCorp defaults on the $1,000,000 loan, Bank proposes full strict foreclosure on inventory that it believes has a fair value of $1,100,000. Bank sends its proposal to SubCorp and Lender. Bank does not send its proposal to ParentCorp, a secondary obligor, because Bank is offering to keep the inventory in full, rather than partial, satisfaction of its loan. Maybe SubCorp does not object, believing that the value of the inventory is less than $1,000,000. Maybe

601. See id. § 9-611(c).
602. See id. § 9-611(c)(2).
603. See id. § 9-620(b).
604. See id. § 9-615(d)(2); cf. id. § 9-615(e)(2) (relieving obligors of any continued liability for a deficiency, absent contrary agreement, if the underlying transaction is a sale of accounts, chattel paper, payment intangibles, or promissory notes).

Lender declines to object, knowing that it has recourse against ParentCorp. ParentCorp, believing that the inventory has a value of $1,100,000, wants to object to the offer of full strict foreclosure and preserve the excess $100,000 for the direct benefit of Lender and, in turn, its own benefit. But because Bank is offering full strict foreclosure, ParentCorp is not a party to whom Bank is required to send its proposal. Therefore, any objection by ParentCorp can be ignored by Bank.[605] The foregoing suggests that ParentCorp has an interest in the collateral sufficient to warrant veto power, and in order to protect that interest revised § 9-621 should have required a foreclosing creditor to send its proposal of any strict foreclosure, whether full or partial, to secondary obligors.[606]

Second, a creditor that intends to dispose of consumer goods must send its notice only to the debtor and any secondary obligor,[607] but a creditor that intends to keep the same consumer goods in satisfaction of the debt has a much different list of potential recipients, as the list of recipients under revised § 9-621 is not predicated on the nature of the collateral.[608] The value of most consumer goods makes them attractive as security only to one creditor (the party that either sold the goods or financed their purchase), so in many transactions this difference has no practical effect. Occasionally, however, a high-dollar consumer good retains its value and, therefore, might collateralize concurrent loans. No apparent reason explains why a second creditor is entitled to a proposal of strict foreclosure of the consumer good, but not a notice of its disposition. One can debate

---

605. *See id.* § 9-620(a)(2)(A).

606. ParentCorp can take action that will obligate Bank to send a proposal to it. ParentCorp's subrogation rights against SubCorp may provide it with a contingent property interest in the collateral. If ParentCorp timely provides Bank with an authenticated notification of this property interest, then Bank is obligated to send its proposal to ParentCorp under revised § 9-621(a)(1). Alternatively, ParentCorp can take and timely perfect a security interest in the collateral to secure SubCorp's reimbursement obligations. Without taking any further action (including sending an authenticated notification of its perfected security interest to Bank), ParentCorp becomes a party to whom Bank must send a proposal under revised § 9-621(a)(2) or (3).

607. *See* U.C.C. § 9-611(c)(1), (2) (1999).

608. *Cf. id.* § 9-505(2) (1995) (requiring a creditor to send its strict foreclosure notice only to the debtor when consumer goods will be retained).

whether non-debtors should receive notices of disposition and proposals of strict foreclosure when the collateral consists of consumer goods, but a uniform list of recipients in both situations seems best.

The third difference between revised sections 9-611 and 9-621 concerns the duty of inquiry placed on the creditor. As a result of changes made to the recipient lists in both statutes, the creditor can no longer remain passive, sending notice only to those parties that have timely informed the creditor of their competing interests.[609] Instead, in order to ensure that its notice of disposition or proposal of strict foreclosure is sent to all required parties, the creditor must order a search report from the appropriate recording office.[610] No doubt some delay will arise between ordering and receiving a U.C.C. search report, which may reflect erroneous or incomplete information. Revised § 9-611 acknowledges the possibility of delay and error and places those risks on the non-notified party.[611] But revised § 9-621 does not provide the foreclosing creditor with similar protection. Why? As explained in the Official Comments, the reason for placing the risk of filing office delays and errors on a creditor that proposes strict foreclosure is that the non-notified parties are not independently protected by the duty of commercial reasonableness (as they are in a disposition).[612] This reasoning seems weak, when in a strict foreclosure any holder of a competing property interest can protect itself from the risk of non-notification resulting from tardy or erroneous search reports by independently informing the foreclosing creditor of its competing property interest.[613]

An issue that exists under current Article 9 is whether the secured party must send *written* notice of strict foreclosure to

---

609. *Cf. id.* § 9-504(3) (stating that the only non-debtor parties to whom a secured party must send its disposition notice are parties that have timely contacted the secured party); *id.* § 9-505(2) (same).

610. *See id.* § 9-611(c)(3)(B), (C) (1999); *id.* § 9-621(a)(2), (3).

611. *See id.* § 9-611(e).

612. *See id.* § 9-621 cmt. 2; *see also* Rapson, *supra* note 4 (explaining omission of safe harbor from revised § 9-621).

613. *See* U.C.C. § 9-621 cmt. 2 (1999).

parties other than the debtor. Prior to being amended in 1972, the second sentence of § 9-505(2) read as follows:

> *Written notice* of such proposal *shall be sent to the debtor and* except in the case of consumer goods *to any other secured party* who has a security interest in the collateral and who has duly filed a financing statement indexed in the name of the debtor in this state or is known by the secured party in possession to have a security interest in it.[614]

As a result of the 1972 amendments, this sentence was revised and broken into three sentences, the first obligating the creditor to send "[w]ritten notice" to the debtor, the second excusing any other notice in the case of consumer goods, and the third requiring the creditor to send "notice" to certain other parties.[615] Neither the explanation for the amendment, nor the official comments, reveal any intent to change the existing law on the form of notice. Therefore, it seems plausible that, in crafting three sentences from one, the word "written" was accidentally omitted from the third sentence.[616] The issue disappears under Revised Article 9 through its requirement that the creditor send a "proposal,"[617] which must take the form of an authenticated record.[618] Although an oral notice of strict foreclosure can accomplish its intended purpose just as easily as a notice in the form of an authenticated record, an oral notice does expose the sender to proof problems. These proof problems are reduced, if not eliminated, if the notice is an authenticated record.

614. *Id.* § 9-505 ("Text Prior to 1972 Amendment"), 3B U.L.A. 353 (1992) (emphasis added).

615. *See* U.C.C. § 9-505(2) (1995).

616. But observe that the third sentence of current § 9-505(2) requires the recipient to object in the form of a "written notice," suggesting that the authors appreciated the difference between "notice" and "written notice." *Cf.* 9 HAWKLAND ET AL., *supra* note 15, § 9-505:06, at 861 ("Although the 1972 amendments to subsection 9-505(2) do not specifically state that the secured party's notice of a proposal of strict foreclosure to parties other than the debtor must be in writing, it is obvious, in light of the requirement of sending a written notice of strict foreclosure to the debtor and the use of the word 'send,' that a written notice of a proposed strict foreclosure to any other secured party is intended.").

617. *See* U.C.C. § 9-621(a), (b) (1999).

618. *See id.* § 9-102(a)(66); *see also id.* § 9-102(a)(7) (defining "authenticate"); *id.* § 9-102(a)(69) (defining "record").

As did its predecessor, revised § 9-621 emphasizes the act of sending, rather than receiving, the proposal.[619] If the creditor sends its proposal to the last known address with proper postage, but discovers that a party has not received the notice, is the creditor obligated to resend the proposal or attempt to contact the intended recipient and confirm its correct mailing address? The question remains unanswered.[620] The same issue exists with respect to disposition notices sent under revised § 9-611, where the accompanying comments acknowledge the issue but delegate it "to judicial resolution, based upon the facts of each case."[621] A creditor is well-advised to utilize all information readily available to it in an effort to notify the intended recipient of its desire to pursue a strict foreclosure. Otherwise, the creditor may be liable for damages[622] and, in the case of a partial strict foreclosure, have difficulty recovering any deficiency.[623]

---

619. *See id.* § 9-621(a) ("A secured party . . . shall send its proposal . . . ."); *id.* § 9-621(b) (same); *id.* § 9-505(2) (1995) (stating written notice "shall be sent to the debtor" and "notice shall be sent" to certain secured creditors); *see also* Begay v. Foutz & Tanner, Inc., 619 P.2d 551, 558–59 (N.M. Ct. App. 1979), *rev'd on other grounds*, 617 P.2d 149 (N.M. 1989) (concluding that creditor complied with notice requirements of U.C.C. § 9-505 by depositing notice in mail, even though debtor never received it).

620. *But see* MONT. CODE ANN. § 30-9-505(2)(b) (1997) (stating that notice to the debtor is reasonable when sent by certified mail to the debtor's most recent address in the loan documents or in any other writing from the debtor that is timely received by the creditor, and notice to another secured party is reasonable when sent by certified mail to the most recent address provided by the other secured party in its written notice of a competing interest in the collateral or in any other writing from the other secured party that is timely received by the creditor).

621. U.C.C. § 9-611 cmt. 6 (1999).

622. *See id.* § 9-625(b), (c).

623. *See id.* § 9-626(a)(3), (4).

REVISED § 9-622

EFFECT OF ACCEPTANCE OF COLLATERAL

Under current § 9-504, a disposition of collateral discharges security interests and liens that are subordinate to the security interest held by the foreclosing creditor.[624] Surprisingly, current § 9-505 does not state the effect of a strict foreclosure on other security interests in and liens on the collateral retained by the secured party.[625] Some scholars contend that disposition and retention are alternative methods of liquidating the relationship between the secured party and the debtor; therefore, a strict foreclosure should have the same effect on competing interests as a disposition.[626] Others, noting the express language in § 9-504(4) and the absence from § 9-505 of similar language, have expressed concern that a creditor exercising its strict foreclosure remedy may retain the collateral subject to subordinate

---

624. See id. § 9-504(4) (1995).

625. The PEB Study Group recommended that U.C.C. § 9-505 should be revised to provide that a strict foreclosure terminates all subordinate property interests. See PEB STUDY GROUP REPORT, supra note 7, at 244–45.

626. See W. Rodney Clement, Jr., Enforcing Security Interests in Personal Property in Mississippi, 67 MISS. L.J. 43, 105 & 109 (1997); 2 GILMORE, supra note 2, § 44.3, at 1225; 9 HAWKLAND ET AL., supra note 15, § 9-505:10, at 869; see also Holmes, supra note 539, at 301 (noting that a strict foreclosure terminates junior liens on personal property, whereas a deed absolute does not terminate junior encumbrances on real property). One state, through a non-uniform amendment, has revised its version of U.C.C. § 9-505 in a manner that expressly addresses the issue. See IOWA CODE ANN. § 554.9505(2) (West 1995) ("Retention of the collateral discharges the security interest of the secured party and discharges any security interest or lien subordinate to the security interest of the secured party.").

interests.[627] Revised § 9-622 removes the uncertainty by addressing the issue.[628] Once a secured party has accepted collateral in satisfaction of the unpaid obligation, the unpaid obligation is discharged in full or, if the secured party has proposed a partial strict foreclosure, in an amount approved by the debtor.[629] Additionally, all of the debtor's rights in the collateral are transferred to the secured party,[630] whose security interest is terminated.[631] Furthermore, the strict foreclosure discharges "any subordinate security interest or other subordinate lien"[632] and "any other subordinate interest."[633] By negative implication, the collateral remains subject to security interests, liens, and interests that rank equally with, or enjoy priority over, the foreclosing creditor's security interest.

A party whose interest may be adversely affected by a strict foreclosure should be entitled to notice of the secured party's intended course of action. The recipient can then protect its interest by redeeming the collateral or, alternatively, objecting to the proposal of strict foreclosure and forcing the creditor to hold a commercially reasonable disposition in which the recipient

---

627. *See* CLARK, *supra* note 2, ¶ 4.10[5], at 4-198 (suggesting that subordinate secured creditors have a "good argument" that their interests survive a strict foreclosure); Dobbs, *supra* note 389, at 142 ("While some support exists for the proposition that a strict foreclosure does extinguish junior encumbrances, there is sufficient room for doubt."); Steven O. Weise, *U.C.C. Article 9: Personal Property Secured Transactions*, 48 BUS. LAW. 1659, 1694–95 (1993) (suggesting, in reliance on real property law and express language in U.C.C. § 9-504(4), that "it seems likely from the absence of a discharge provision" in U.C.C. § 9-505 "that the retention in satisfaction does not discharge junior liens").

628. The rights and duties under revised § 9-622 cannot be waived or varied. *See* U.C.C. § 9-602(10) (1999).

629. *See id.* § 9-622(a)(1).

630. *See id.* § 9-622(a)(2); *cf. id.* § 9-617(a)(1) (stating that a post-default disposition transfers "all of the debtor's rights in the collateral" to the transferee).

631. *See id.* § 9-622(a)(3); *cf. id.* § 9-617(a)(2) (stating that a post-default disposition "discharges the security interest under which the disposition is made").

632. *See id.* § 9-622(a)(3); *cf. id.* § 9-617(a)(3) (stating that a post-default disposition "discharges any subordinate security interest or other lien"). Notwithstanding revised § 9-622(a), the secured party may wish to consult a lawyer familiar with the provisions of the Internal Revenue Code (particularly 26 U.S.C. § 7425 (1994)) to determine whether a strict foreclosure will terminate a subordinate federal tax lien.

633. *See id.* § 9-622(a)(4). Presumably subsection (a)(4) is needed to address the effect that a strict foreclosure has on an interest that is neither a "security interest" nor a "lien," both of which are the subject of subsection (a)(3).

(and, at its urging, other parties) may possibly participate.[634] Whether a recipient may find redemption or a forced disposition an attractive option will depend on several factors, including the amount of debt secured by the collateral and the perceived value of the collateral.[635]

If subordinate property interests are terminated by a strict foreclosure, then the holders of those terminated property interests should be entitled to receive the secured party's proposal of strict foreclosure. If the recipient list in revised § 9-621 was composed for the purpose of protecting the holders of interests that may be terminated, then the list is both over-inclusive and under-inclusive. The list is over-inclusive because it includes all secured parties and lienholders that have timely provided the foreclosing creditor with notice of their property interest[636] or

---

634. *See id.* § 9-623(a) (permitting "[a] debtor, any secondary obligor, or any other secured party or lienholder" to redeem the collateral); 9 HAWKLAND ET AL., *supra* note 15, § 9-505:05, at 859 (explaining the purpose of giving notice of strict foreclosure to the debtor); *id.* § 9-505:06, at 861–62 (explaining the purpose of giving notice of strict foreclosure to other secured parties); Chen v. Profit Sharing Plan, 456 S.E.2d 237, 240 (Ga. Ct. App. 1995); Herring Mining Co. v. Roberts Bros. Coal Co., 747 S.W.2d 616, 619 (Ky. Ct. App. 1988).

635. For example, Debtor defaults on a $1,000,000 loan from Bank. Debtor also defaults on a $250,000 loan from Lender. Both loans are secured by a security interest in Debtor's inventory, and Bank's interest enjoys priority. Bank proposes to retain the inventory in satisfaction of the $1,000,000 unpaid debt. In the first scenario, the inventory has a fair market value of $800,000, in the second, $1,400,000, and in the third, $1,200,000. In the first scenario, Lender will not redeem inventory worth $800,000 by paying $1,000,000 to Bank. And, under the payout scheme of revised § 9-615(a), Lender will not receive any proceeds from a forced sale of inventory worth $800,000, so it is unlikely that Lender will object to a strict foreclosure and force a sale. In the second scenario, however, paying $1,000,000 for inventory worth $1,400,000 makes redemption appealing. And because Lender may be entitled to receive proceeds under revised § 9-615(a)(3) that remain after Bank has satisfied its $1,000,000 debt and disposition-related costs, Lender may object to Bank's proposal of strict foreclosure and force a disposition. For the same reasons, redemption and disposition are attractive options in the third scenario. The attraction is not quite as bright as under the second scenario because the value of the inventory ($1,200,000) is less than both loans ($1,250,000). Whether Lender exercises its right of redemption or forces a disposition by objecting to Bank's proposal may turn on Lender's perception of Debtor's ability to pay any deficiency. If Lender opts to redeem the collateral or force a disposition, Lender can rely on excess inventory to satisfy $200,000, or 80% of the unpaid $250,000. Because Lender will lose its interest in inventory worth $200,000 if Bank keeps the inventory, Lender should either redeem the collateral or force its disposition unless Lender is confident that Debtor will pay at least 80% of Lender's unsecured deficiency claim.

636. *See* U.C.C. § 9-621(a)(1) (1999).

satisfy other statutory requirements,[637] not just secured parties and lienholders whose security interests and liens are subordinate to the security interest of the foreclosing creditor. The foreclosing creditor would undoubtedly prefer a pared list because the number of parties with veto power would decrease, but a pared list would force the foreclosing creditor to resolve priority issues prior to sending its notice. Furthermore, and perhaps more important, a party whose property interest will not be terminated (e.g., a secured creditor with a senior security interest) still benefits from receiving a proposal of strict foreclosure because the recipient, relying on the information, can then take steps to protect itself (such as accelerating the debt after enforcing a cross-default provision in the loan documents, or objecting to a proposal that puts excess value in the pockets of the foreclosing creditor which might otherwise be applied by the debtor to reduce senior debt).

The list is under-inclusive because it does not require the foreclosing creditor to send its proposal to all lienholders with subordinate liens. Instead, subordinate lienholders are entitled to a proposal only if they timely notify the foreclosing creditor of their interest[638] or "perfect" their lien "by the filing of a financing statement."[639] "Perfection" is a term of art normally associated with consensual security interests governed by Article 9, not involuntary liens created by statute or judicial process.[640] And while a lien may be evidenced by a writing filed in the public records, the writing may not qualify as a "financing statement."[641]

---

637. *See id.* § 9-621(a)(2), (3).

638. *See id.* § 9-621(a)(1).

639. *See id.* § 9-621(a)(2). A lienholder that perfects its interest by complying with a statute, regulation, or treaty described in revised § 9-311(a) is not entitled to receive a proposal under revised § 9-621(a)(3). For some unexplained reason, that provision (unlike revised § 9-621(a)(2)) fails to reference "lienholder." Lienholders receive the same treatment under revised § 9-611. *See supra* note 297.

640. *See* U.C.C. § 9-308 (1999) (indicating when a "security interest" or an "agricultural lien" is "perfected").

641. The absence of the debtor's signature, however, will not prevent the writing from being a financing statement. *See id.* § 9-502(a) (indicating that a financing statement requires the name of the debtor, the name of the secured party or its representative, and a description of collateral; *cf. id.* § 9-402(1) (1995) (requiring the name and address of the debtor and the secured party, a description of collateral, and the debtor's signature).

And even if the lien filing is a "financing statement," it may not be recorded in the same place as a financing statement filed by a secured party. The statute could have been drafted in a manner that did not apply traditional Article 9 terms and concepts to liens.[642] Apparently the drafting committee concluded that this would place on secured parties an unacceptable search-and-notify burden (a burden already made heavier by Revised Article 9[643]). Whether it is any less unacceptable to place the burden on the party whose interest will be destroyed is debatable.

Will a subordinate interest be terminated if the foreclosing creditor fails to send its proposal to the holder of that interest, even if the holder is a party entitled to notice under revised § 9-621? Revised § 9-622 answers that question affirmatively, if other conditions necessary to an effective acceptance of the proposal are met.[644] However, a person to whom the creditor is required, but fails, to send its proposal is entitled to recover damages in the amount of any loss caused by the creditor's non-compliance.[645] Damages may be non-existent unless the party is able to prove that an objection to the proposal would have forced a commercially reasonable disposition generating proceeds that would revert to the party under the payment scheme of revised § 9-615(a). For example, Bank proposes to accept inventory that it believes is worth $250,000 in satisfaction of a $300,000 debt. Bank fails to send its proposal to Lender, the

---

642. For example, revised § 9-621(a)(2) could have been drafted as follows:

(2) any other secured party or lienholder that, 10 days before the debtor consented to the acceptance, held either a security interest in the collateral perfected by the filing of a financing statement, or a lien on the collateral evidenced by a proper filing, that: (A) was indexed under the debtor's name as of that date; and (B) was filed in the office or offices in which to file a financing statement or record a lien against the debtor covering the collateral as of that date.

Original clause (A) ("identified the collateral") is deleted as unnecessary (a financing statement already must describe the collateral under revised § 9-502(a)(3)) and too limiting (a lien filing may not describe the collateral).

643. *Compare* U.C.C. § 9-505(2) (1995) (obligating a secured creditor to contact any party that has timely informed it of a competing claim), *with id.* § 9-621(a) (1999) (obligating a secured party to contact any party that has timely informed it of a competing claim, as well as any party that has a perfected interest).

644. *See id.* § 9-622(b) & cmt. 2.

645. *See id.* §§ 9-622 cmt. 2, 9-625(b).

holder of a perfected, but subordinate, security interest in the inventory. Unless Lender can introduce evidence that a commercially reasonable sale would have brought a price greater than $300,000, Lender may be unable to recover any damages for Bank's noncompliance.[646]

---

646. *See, e.g.,* McGowan v. Nebraska State Bank, 427 N.W.2d 772, 775–76 (Neb. 1988) (holding junior creditor suffered no loss from senior creditor's failure to send disposition notice to junior creditor—even if (as junior creditor argued) collateral was worth nearly $50,000 instead of $28,956 received at auction—where amount of unpaid senior debt was $372,000); River Valley State Bank v. Peterson, 453 N.W.2d 193, 195–97 (Wis. Ct. App. 1990) (concluding junior creditor suffered no loss from senior creditor's failure to send disposition notice to junior creditor—even if (as junior creditor argued) collateral was worth $10,000 instead of $6400 received at sale—where amount of unpaid senior debt exceeded $30,000). *See also* U.C.C. § 1-106 (1995) (stating that U.C.C. remedies "shall be liberally administered to the end that the aggrieved party may be put in as good a position as if the other party had fully performed"); Nickles, *supra* note 404, at 235–36 (discussing the calculation of damages under U.C.C. § 9-507(1), which provides an aggrieved party with "a right to recover from the secured party any loss caused by a failure to comply with the provisions of this Part").

REVISED § 9-623

RIGHT TO REDEEM COLLATERAL

Current Article 9 permits the debtor to redeem, or "buy back," collateral under certain conditions.[647] That right continues under Revised Article 9 and is codified at § 9-623.

Current law grants the right of redemption not only to the debtor, but also to any other secured party with a security interest in the collateral, regardless of the priority or perfection of that security interest.[648] The right of redemption, however, does not extend to nonconsensual lienholders.[649] This omission from current § 9-506 is questionable[650] for at least two reasons. First, at a minimum, a junior lienholder should be entitled to redeem the collateral because a disposition (and, perhaps, a strict foreclosure) of the collateral terminates its lien.[651] Second, unless the secured party has a post-default motive other than to be made whole,[652] it should not mind if the right of redemption is extended to any party with a property interest in the collateral. The *PEB Study Group Report* recommended that holders of judicial, statutory, and common-law

---

647. *See* U.C.C. § 9-506 (1995).

648. *See id.* § 9-506.

649. *But see* IOWA CODE ANN. § 554.9506 (West 1995) (granting redemption rights to "the debtor or any other secured party *or lienor*") (emphasis added).

650. *See, e.g.,* CLARK, *supra* note 2, ¶ 4.11[3], at 4-202 (proposing that "courts should treat the omission as a drafting error"); 2 GILMORE, *supra* note 2, § 44.2, at 1218 (suggesting that "the failure of § 9-506 to refer to other lienors must be put down to drafting inadvertence").

651. *See* U.C.C. § 9-504(4) (1995); *supra* note 626 and accompanying text.

652. An oversecured creditor might propose strict foreclosure, hoping to make a profit on any resale of the collateral. Because the creditor's desire is frustrated if the collateral is redeemed, the creditor has an interest in limiting the number of potential redeemers.

liens be given the right of redemption, concluding that to do so "would not appear to work any particular hardship on secured parties whose collateral is redeemed."[653] Revised § 9-623 adopts that recommendation.[654]

To redeem the collateral under current § 9-506, a party must tender payment of (i) all debt secured by the collateral,[655] (ii) any expenses reasonably incurred by the creditor in taking, storing, and preparing the collateral for disposition,[656] and (iii) reasonable attorneys' fees and legal expenses (but only to the extent provided in the security agreement and not otherwise prohibited by law).[657] Revised § 9-623 requires the same payment.[658] Notice

---

653. PEB STUDY GROUP REPORT, *supra* note 7, at 247.

654. *See* U.C.C. § 9-623(a) (1999).

655. *See id.* § 9-506 (1995).

656. *See id.*; *see also* Rogers v. Associates Comm. Corp., 632 P.2d 1002, 1006 (Ariz. Ct. App. 1981) (ruling debtor's payment that did not include expenses was "an insufficient tender"); Howard v. Lud, 325 N.W.2d 623, 627 (Mich. Ct. App. 1982) (noting redemption price includes "expenses reasonably incurred by the secured party in retaking the collateral"); Owens v. Automobile Recovery Bureau, Inc., 544 S.W.2d 26, 31–32 (Mo. Ct. App. 1977) (holding loan service fee was not part of redemption price); Everett v. U. S. Life Credit Corp., 327 S.E.2d 269, 269–70 (N.C. Ct. App. 1985) (concluding debtor cannot avoid paying repossession charges as part of redemption price merely because creditor failed to give notice of repossession that would allow debtor to voluntarily surrender collateral and avoid charge); Haraway v. Burnett, 33 U.C.C. Rep. Serv. 2d (West) 1256, 1267 (Tenn. Ct. App. 1997) (holding redemption price did not include expenses of $11,569.39 incurred by creditor in seizing assets not part of the collateral).

657. *See* U.C.C. § 9-506 (1995); *see also* Clark v. General Motors Acceptance Corp., 363 S.E.2d 813, 817 (Ga. Ct. App. 1987) (concluding summary judgment was premature where reasonableness of attorneys' fees had not been determined); Interstate Elec. Supply Co. v. Contractors & Eng'rs, Inc., 515 N.E.2d 182, 189 (Ill. App. Ct. 1987) (noting that U.C.C. § 9-506 permits a creditor to recover reasonable attorneys' fees and legal expenses, but concluding that implicit in the statute is "the right of a redeeming party to a hearing on the reasonableness" of those fees and expenses); *see also supra* note 384 (citing cases addressing ability to recover attorneys' fees).

658. U.C.C. § 9-623(b)(2) (1999). The secured party and the debtor should consider the merits of including a provision in the loan documents that attempts to define the "reasonableness" of fees and expenses. For example, some variation of the following might be acceptable:

> All reasonable costs, fees, and expenses (including, without limitation, attorneys' fees, legal expenses, and court costs) incurred by Secured Party incident to this transaction shall be part of the secured obligation. Costs, fees, and expenses shall be deemed "reasonable" if, in the aggregate, they do not exceed more than 25% of the sum of unpaid principal and accrued and unpaid interest thereon.

The provision should be enforceable unless a court concludes that the agreed-upon standard of "reasonableness" is "manifestly unreasonable." *See id.* § 9-603(a); *id.* § 9-501(3) (1995).

that the fair market value of the collateral is irrelevant in calculating the redemption price.[659] The presence (and exercise of) an acceleration clause will affect the calculation of "all obligations secured by the collateral"— a phrase that appears in both current § 9-506 and revised § 9-623(b). For example, Bank makes a $1,000,000 secured loan to Debtor, who agrees to repay the loan in five equal installments of $200,000 (excluding any interest). Before the first payment is due, Debtor fails to deliver an audited financial report, triggering a non-payment default. Alternatively, Debtor fails to pay the first installment, creating a payment default. Bank seizes collateral, incurring a repossession expense of $100. Is the redemption price (a) $100 (non-payment default), (b) $200,100 (payment default), or (c) $1,000,100 (both defaults)? The phrase "all obligations secured by the collateral" suggests $1,000,100. However, § 9-506 prefaces the phrase with "tendering fulfillment," language that Revised Article 9 substantially retains.[660] The official comments to revised § 9-623 shed light on the intended meaning of "tendering fulfillment":

> To redeem the collateral a person must tender fulfillment of all obligations secured, plus certain expenses. *If the entire balance of a secured obligation has been accelerated, it would be necessary to tender the entire balance.* A tender of fulfillment obviously means more than a new promise to perform an existing promise. It requires payment in full of all monetary obligations *then due* and performance in full of all other obligations *then matured.* If unmatured secured obligations

---

659. However, the collateral value does play a role in determining the redemption price in a consumer bankruptcy. The Bankruptcy Code permits an individual debtor to redeem consumer goods by paying an amount equal to the creditor's "allowed secured claim." 11 U.S.C. § 722 (1994). An "allowed secured claim" is not necessarily the amount of the unpaid debt. Rather, it is "the *lesser of* the secured debt *or* the value of the collateral." DAVID G. EPSTEIN ET AL., BANKRUPTCY § 7-39, at 562 (1993). To illustrate the difference between redemption under Article 9 and the Bankruptcy Code, assume Debtor has defaulted on a $25,000 loan secured by a boat worth $20,000. Under current § 9-506 and revised § 9-623, Debtor's redemption price is $25,000 (plus repossession and similar charges and possibly attorneys' fees and legal expenses). Under Bankruptcy Code § 722, Debtor's redemption price is only $20,000.

660. *See* U.C.C. § 9-623(b) (1999) (requiring a person to "tender: (1) fulfillment").

remain, the security interest continues to secure them (i.e.,
as if there had been no default).[661]

The emphasized language reveals that unless the secured party
has properly accelerated the debt, the redemption price is not
$1,000,100, but rather only $100 (non-payment default) or
$200,100 (payment default).[662] The foregoing example illustrates
the importance of including an acceleration clause in the loan
documents,[663] advice that many creditors already heed.[664]

661. *Id.* § 9-623 cmt. 2 (emphasis added); *see also id.* § 9-506 cmt. (1995) (similar
language).

662. *See* Williams v. Ford Motor Credit Co., 435 So. 2d 66, 68 (Ala. 1983) (holding
that creditor's acceleration of unmatured debt required debtor to redeem collateral by tendering amount equal to full contract price plus expenses, not the amount necessary to
bring contract current); Rogers v. Associates Comm. Corp., 632 P.2d 1002, 1006 (Ariz.
Ct. App. 1981) (concluding, in reliance on the official comment to U.C.C. § 9-506, that
"the accelerated balance is part of the obligation secured within the meaning of the
redemption provisions"); Black v. Peoples Bank & Trust Co., 437 So. 2d 26, 30 (Miss.
1983) (noting that U.C.C. § 9-506 requires a redeeming debtor "to pay the entire amount
due including any accelerated obligation"); Medallion Funding Corp. v. Helen Laundromat, Inc., 34 U.C.C. Rep. Serv. 2d (West) 250, 257 (N.Y. 1997) (holding that debtors who
offered to redeem collateral by paying two monthly payments, together with interest and
costs, did not make valid tender offer as all amounts due under note had been accelerated); *see also* Zubrow, *supra* note 467, at 538 n.376 ("Under Article 9, so long as the security agreement contains an adequately drafted acceleration clause redemption requires
repayment of the full amount of the antecedent debt."); *cf.* U.C.C. § 9-506 (1952 Official
Text) (permitting the debtor to reclaim collateral by "tendering payment of all sums due
under the defaulted agreement," a clause explained in the official comments: "if the agreement contains a clause accelerating the entire balance due on default in one installment,
the amount 'due under the defaulted agreement' would be the entire balance"), *reprinted
in* XV Elizabeth Slusser Kelly, Uniform Commercial Code Drafts 299–300 (1984).

663. If Bank sold the collateral before redemption, and the loan documents did not
include an acceleration clause, any proceeds in excess of $100 (non-payment default) or
$200,100 (payment default) would revert to Debtor as surplus proceeds in the absence
of any subordinate property interests in the collateral. *See* U.C.C. § 9-504(1) (1995); *id.*
§ 9-615(a), (d) (1999); *see also* Robert L. Jordan & William D. Warren, Secured Transactions in Personal Property 235 (4th ed. 1997) (discussing adverse consequences
under U.C.C. §§ 9-504(1) and 9-506 for a creditor that fails to include acceleration clause
in loan documents when debt is payable in installments).

664. *See* 2 Gilmore, *supra* note 2, § 43.4, at 1195 ("For a hundred years, it may be, no
security agreement has failed to include an acceleration clause."). If the loan documents
include an optional, rather than an automatic, acceleration clause, the creditor must properly exercise its option before accelerating the debt. For example, under Texas law a creditor cannot exercise an optional acceleration clause until it has presented the note, given
notice of its intent to accelerate the debt, and given notice of the acceleration, unless the
obligor has executed a clear and unequivocal waiver of presentment and notice. *See, e.g.,*
Shumway v. Horizon Credit Corp, 801 S.W.2d 890 (Tex. 1991) (concluding that clause
waiving "prior notice or demand" did not waive right to notice of intent to accelerate,
which creditor failed to give). And even if a creditor properly accelerates the debt, the

The phrase, "all obligations secured by the collateral," raises another, somewhat related, interpretive dilemma. Assume Bank makes a second secured loan of $500,000 to Debtor, secured by the same collateral that secures the $1,000,000 loan. The two loans are evidenced by two separate sets of loan papers and, through oversight, the first set of loan papers does not include a cross-default clause that makes a payment default on the second loan a default under the first loan. When Debtor misses a payment on the second loan, Bank repossesses the collateral and properly accelerates the full $500,000. Can Bank set a redemption price of $1,500,000, arguing that Debtor must pay "*all* obligations secured by the collateral"? Read literally, one might think so. Again, however, the official comment quoted above discourages that interpretation. Absent a default, the $1,000,000 is not "then due" or "then matured," but instead is an "unmatured secured obligation." The statutory language could have been drafted with more precision (e.g., "all obligations secured by the collateral *and then due*"), but hopefully the phrase will be interpreted as intended.

Under current Article 9, a debtor can waive its right to redeem the collateral only if the waiver is in writing and executed after default.[665] Under Revised Article 9, the right of redemption is one of the non-waivable rights referenced in revised § 9-602,[666] suggesting that no party (including the debtor) can ever waive its redemption right. However, revised § 9-602 is subject to revised § 9-624,[667] which permits redemption waivers in limited situations.[668]

accelerated part may be statutorily excluded from the redemption price. *See, e.g.,* MISS. CODE ANN. § 75-9-506 (1981) (expressly excluding from the redemption price "any sums that would not then be due except for an acceleration provision").

665. *See* U.C.C. § 9-506 (1995); *see also* Kellos v. Parker-Sharpe, Inc., 263 S.E.2d 138, 140 (Ga. 1980) ("Thus, the right to redeem collateral may be waived by an agreement in writing, after default, but cannot be waived by an agreement in writing before default."); Data Sec., Inc. v. Plessman, 510 N.W.2d 361, 365 (Neb. Ct. App. 1993) ("Under § 9-501(3)(d), a debtor's right of redemption may not be waived or varied except as provided in § 9-506, which means only in writing and *after* default."); *Medallion Funding Corp.,* 34 U.C.C. Rep. Serv. 2d (West) at 257 (finding waiver clause in promissory note "ineffective"); Indianapolis Morris Plan Corp. v. Karlen, 319 N.Y.S.2d 831, 834 (1971) (stating that a debtor's right of redemption may not be waived prior to default).

666. *See* U.C.C. § 9-602(11) (1999).

667. *See id.* § 9-602.

668. *See* discussion of U.C.C. § 9-624(c), *infra* notes 700–07 and accompanying text.

The period during which a party may redeem collateral is not statutorily prescribed in terms of a guaranteed number of days, weeks, or months.[669] Under current Article 9, the redemption period continues until the secured party disposes of the collateral, the secured party contracts for the disposition of the collateral, or the obligation is discharged by a strict foreclosure.[670] Revised Article 9 retains these termination events[671] and adds a

669. However, several states provide a minimum redemption period in transactions governed by retail installment sales statutes. *See, e.g.,* Cal. Civ. Code § 1812.2 (West 1985) (10-day redemption period following giving of notice to sell or retain goods); Conn. Gen. Stat. Ann. § 36a-785(c) (West 1996) (15-day redemption period following repossession); 815 Ill. Comp. Stat. Ann. 405/26-26 (West 1993) (15-day redemption period for selected debtors following repossession); Md. Code Ann., Com. Law § 12-625(a) (1990) (15-day redemption period following giving of statutory notice); Wis. Stat. Ann. § 425.208(1) (West 1998) (15-day redemption period following creditor's exercise of nonjudicial enforcement right). *Cf.* Unif. Conditional Sales Act § 18, 3B U.L.A. 585 (1992) (10-day redemption period following repossession). Query whether the parties can contractually agree that the debtor's right of redemption terminates after a specific period of time. For example, the security agreement might include a provision stating: "Debtor must exercise its right of redemption under Article 9 of the Texas Business and Commerce Code, as amended from time to time, no later than the 15th day following the date on which Secured Party repossesses the collateral, after which Secured Party may properly reject any offer of redemption by Debtor in its discretion." Under current § 9-501 and revised § 9-603, the secured party and the debtor may agree on standards measuring the fulfillment of rights and duties if those standards are not "manifestly unreasonable." One author believes that such a provision is enforceable if the agreed-upon period is not manifestly unreasonable. *See* 9 Hawkland et al., *supra* note 15, § 9-506:05, at 795–96. But a provision that effectively terminates the debtor's redemption rights prior to the statutory termination events appears to be a partial waiver of the redemption right, rather than an attempt to agree on permissible standards of conduct, and should not be enforceable in the absence of a statutory provision permitting the debtor to waive its redemption right. For a provision permitting waiver-of-redemption clauses in limited situations, see revised § 9-624(c), discussed *infra* notes 700–07 and accompanying text.

670. *See* U.C.C. § 9-506 (1995); *see also* Willis v. Healthdyne, Inc., 382 S.E.2d 651, 653 (Ga. Ct. App. 1989) (finding debtor's demand for redemption "untimely" when made after collateral had been sold); Korogluyan v. Chicago Title & Trust Co., 572 N.E.2d 1154, 1161 (Ill. App. Ct. 1991) (observing that debtor's redemption request "came too late" when made after court had confirmed creditor's prior sale of collateral); *Data Sec. Inc.*, 510 N.W.2d at 365 ("Under § 9-506, the debtor has a right to redeem collateral at any time before the secured party has disposed of collateral or entered into a contract for its disposition unless otherwise agreed in writing *after* default."); Cordova v. Lee Galles Oldsmobile, Inc., 668 P.2d 320, 322 (N.M. Ct. App. 1983) ("Under § 9-506 plaintiff had a right to redeem the car at any time before disposition.").

671. *See* U.C.C. § 9-623(c)(2) (1999) (disposition or disposition contract), (3) (strict foreclosure). If a secured party terminates the debtor's right of redemption under revised § 9-623(c)(2) by selling the collateral at a disposition, and the secured party failed to send a disposition notice to the debtor as required by revised § 9-611(c)(1), the debtor is entitled to recover "damages in the amount of any loss" caused by the secured party's noncompliance. *See id.* § 9-625(b). Query how a debtor quantifies damages for the loss of its redemption right. Is the debtor required to prove that it could (and would) have redeemed the collateral? If the debtor offers such proof, minimum damages might equal (i) the fair market value of a similar item in comparable shape, minus (ii) the redemption price. But what if a replacement item cannot be purchased because the item was unique?

fourth: the collection of collateral under revised § 9-607,[672] such as the receipt of a payment created by an account, a general intangible, a promissory note, or chattel paper. The fact that third-party payments of an account or a general intangible can terminate the right to redeem that account or general intangible removes any doubt that the right of redemption extends to non-possessory collateral.

How valuable is the right of redemption? For most debtors, the answer is "not very." A debtor, particularly a consumer debtor, may not be aware that it has a right of redemption. Neither current § 9-504 nor current § 9-505 requires the secured party to inform the debtor of its redemption right in the notice of disposition or offer of strict foreclosure.[673] Revised Article 9 improves the awareness of a consumer debtor by requiring a disposition notice in a consumer-goods transaction to refer to the redemption right.[674] A disposition notice sent in a non-consumer-goods transaction may improve the cognizance of other debtors by informing them that they are entitled to an accounting of the unpaid debt.[675] However, Revised Article 9 does not require a creditor to reference the redemption right in any proposal of strict foreclosure. Of course, the creditor may, on its own volition, inform the debtor of this right.[676] But even if a

672. *See id.* § 9-623(c)(1).

673. One of the stated purposes of requiring notice of a disposition or a strict foreclosure is to permit the debtor to protect its interest in the collateral by exercising its right of redemption. *See, e.g.,* Fremont Fin. Corp. v. Izzo (*In re* Rack Eng'g), 212 B.R. 98, 103 (Bankr. W.D. Pa. 1997); Friendly Fin. Corp. v. Bovee, 702 A.2d 1225, 1227 (Del. 1997); Chen v. Profit Sharing Plan, 456 S.E.2d 237, 240 (Ga. Ct. App. 1995); Herring Mining Co. v. Roberts Bros. Coal Co., 747 S.W.2d 616, 619 (Ky. 1988); Peoples Heritage Sav. Bank v. Theriault, 670 A.2d 1391, 1393 (Me. 1996).

674. *See* U.C.C. § 9-614(1)(c) (1999).

675. *See id.* § 9-613(1)(D).

676. A creditor whose notice of disposition or proposal of strict foreclosure describes, but misstates the right of redemption may find that its notice or proposal is legally defective. A common error is sending a notice that informs the debtor that its redemption rights will terminate after a specific number of days, rather than upon disposition. *See* Coones v. FDIC, 848 P.2d 783, 803 (Wyo. 1993) (concluding creditor's notice misstated debtor's redemption rights by informing debtor that it would have to competitively bid for items). *See, e.g.,* Moore v. Fidelity Fin. Servs., Inc., Nos. 94C2558, 96C4894, 1997 WL 323822, at *2 (N.D. Ill. June 11, 1997); Loyola Fed. Sav. & Loan v. Hopson, No. C.A. 92A-09-015, 1993 WL 331154, at *2 (Del. Super. Ct. July 21, 1993); Ayers v. Mellon Bank, No. 85C-DE-68, 1987 WL 8274, at *2 (Del. Super. Ct. Mar. 6, 1987); Bradford v. General Elec. Credit Corp., 359 S.E.2d 757, 758 (Ga. Ct. App. 1987); Credithrift v. Smith, 308 S.E.2d 53 (Ga. Ct. App. 1983); Topeka Datsun Motor Co. v. Stratton, 736 P.2d 82, 88–89 (Kan. Ct. App. 1987); First Nat'l Bank v. DiDomenico, 487 A.2d 646, 648-49 (Md. 1985).

debtor knows, or is informed, that it has a right to redeem the collateral, it is unlikely that the right will be exercised. A party already in default on its payment obligations is unlikely to have the financial resources to pay the statutory ransom, especially if the creditor has accelerated unmatured payments.[677] Recognizing this concern, Revised Article 9, during much of the drafting process, included a section permitting selected consumer obligors to reinstate the debt and cure a payment default by tendering an amount that excluded any accelerated payments.[678] But this

677. Professor Gilmore wrote that a defaulting debtor "never" cures a default by redeeming collateral. Whether prompted by levity, third-party comments, second thoughts, or otherwise, he modified his declaration with a footnote: "Well, almost never." *See* 2 GILMORE, *supra* note 2, § 44.2, at 1216 n.2 and accompanying text; *see also* Leonard Lakin, *Default Proceedings Under Article 9: Problems, Solutions, and Lessons to be Learned*, 8 AKRON L. REV. 1, 40 (1974) (observing that while "redemption is a right 'devoutly to be wished' by the debtor, most debtors . . . are usually unable to pay the full amount of the [accelerated] debt"); James J. White, *Representing the Low Income Consumer in Repossessions, Resales and Deficiency Judgment Cases*, 70 NW. U. L. REV. 808, 821 n.40 (1970) (referring to the number of cases in which debtors could (and would) redeem as "de minimus"); *cf.* Barkley Clark, *Default, Repossession, Foreclosure and Deficiency: A Journey to the Underworld And a Proposed Salvation,* 51 OR. L. REV. 302, 315–16 (1972) (criticizing the permitted use of acceleration clauses, which, in consumer transactions, discourage redemption and encourage deficiency judgments).

678. The section appeared as early as July 1995. *See* U.C.C. § 9-506 (Draft July 28—Aug. 4, 1995). At the time of its deletion in early 1998, the section read as follows:
SECTION 9-622. REINSTATEMENT OF OBLIGATION SECURED WITHOUT ACCELERATION.
   (a) A debtor or a secondary obligor who is a consumer obligor may cure a default consisting only of the failure to make required payment and may reinstate the secured obligation without acceleration if:
      (1) 60 percent of the cash price has been paid in the case of a purchase money security interest in consumer goods; or
      (2) 60 percent of the principal amount of the obligation secured has been paid in the case of another consumer goods secured transaction.
   (b) To cure a default under subsection (a), a person must tender:
      (1) the unpaid amount of the secured obligation due at the time of tender, without acceleration, including charges for delinquency, default, or deferral; and
      (2) reasonable expenses and attorney's fees of the type described in Section 9-614(b)(1).
   (c) A tender of payment under subsection (b) is ineffective to cure a default or reinstate a secured obligation unless made before the later of:
      (1) 21 days after the secured party sends a notification of disposition under Section 9-611(b) to the debtor and any consumer obligor who is a secondary obligor; and
      (2) the time the secured party:
         (A) disposes of collateral or enters into a contract for its disposition under Section 9-610; or
         (B) accepts collateral in full or partial satisfaction of the obligation it secures under Section 9-618.

limited right of reinstatement fell victim to heavy criticism[679] and was deleted as part of the "consumer compromise."[680]

A secondary obligor also may not redeem the collateral very often. A secondary obligor may have no objection to a disposition or a partial strict foreclosure, realizing that its potential liability for any remaining deficiency will be less than the redemption price. Alternatively, it may rely on its ability to protect its interest in the collateral by attending and participating in a public disposition or contacting the secured party and expressing a desire to participate in a private disposition. One situation where a secondary obligor may find redemption attractive is if the collateral offers sentimental value or the potential for long-term appreciation[681] and the redemption price is less than the collateral's fair market value.

> (d) A tender of payment under subsection (b) restores to the debtor and a consumer obligor who is a secondary obligor their respective rights as if the default had not occurred and all payments had been made when scheduled, including the debtor's right, if any, to possess the collateral. Promptly upon the tender, the secured party shall take all steps necessary to cause any judicial process affecting the collateral to be vacated and any pending action based on the default to be dismissed.
>
> (e) A secured obligation may be reinstated under this section only once.

U.C.C. § 9-622 (Draft Mar. 1998); *cf. id.* § 7-607(2) (Draft May 1949) ("Unless default occurred by reason of impairment of the value of the collateral or by reason of removal or other disposition of the goods the performance due shall be deemed to be the performance due as if no acceleration of the obligation had occurred."), *reprinted in* VIII KELLY, *supra* note 662, at 163–64; UNIF. CONSUMER CREDIT CODE § 5.111 (1974 Act), 7A U.L.A. 175–76 (1985) (providing consumers with a limited cure period).

679. *See, e.g.,* Miller, *supra* note 10, at 187, 213 (1997) (suggesting that the provision may actually harm consumers because it will increase the cost of credit transactions and prompt the tightening of credit standards); *id.* at 215–16 (contending that the provision does not represent a consensus position as evidenced by present state laws, harms all consumers at the expense of the few, and may delay enactment of Revised Article 9); *see also* Chareq & Fortney, *supra* note 587, at 320 (asserting that states have adequately addressed redemption and reinstatement concerns in consumer transactions through legislation that removes any need for including a reinstatement provision in Article 9); Alvin C. Harrell, *UCC Article 9 Drafting Committee March 1996 Meeting Considers Consumer-Related Collateral*, 50 CONSUMER FIN. L.Q. REP. 95, 98 (1996) (arguing that a right of reinstatement is "likely to increase the cost of a default to the lender, thereby raising overall the cost of consumer credit"); Heiser & Flemma, *supra* note 414, at 490 (referring to the reinstatement provision as "social engineering" that reflects a public policy decision best addressed in the broad context of all consumer credit transactions and not in Article 9); *cf.* Hillebrand, *supra* note 585, at 169 (observing that the "limited but useful" right of reinstatement may not be available until late in the loan period).

680. *See supra* note 548 and accompanying text.

681. Examples include rare coin collections, sports memorabilia, and other unique items.

How frequently a secured party or lienholder will redeem collateral is unknown. These parties may be in the best position to obtain the necessary funds on an expedited basis. However, not all secured parties and lienholders are entitled to a disposition notice[682] or a strict foreclosure proposal,[683] reducing the likelihood that those non-recipients will redeem the collateral. Additionally, security interests and liens not subordinate to the security interest of the foreclosing creditor survive a disposition[684] and a strict foreclosure,[685] decreasing the probability that holders of those security interests and liens will redeem the collateral. For holders of security interests and liens that will not survive a disposition or a strict foreclosure, redemption may be attractive if the value of the collateral exceeds the redemption price and the excess is more than the amount likely to be collected by the holder from the debtor in a lawsuit. Realistically, however, that attraction may be nothing more than a faint glimmer, as the senior creditor is much more likely to be undersecured, rather than over-collateralized.

---

682. *See* U.C.C. § 9-611(c) (1999) (failing to include among the parties entitled to a disposition notice any lienholder (other than a lienholder from whom the creditor has received timely notice of the lien and any lienholder that has perfected its lien by filing a financing statement in the proper place) and any unperfected secured party (other than a secured party from whom the creditor has received timely notice of the security interest)).

683. *See id.* § 9-621(a) (failing to include among the parties entitled to a strict foreclosure proposal any lienholder (other than a lienholder from whom the creditor has received timely notice of the lien and any lienholder that has perfected its lien by filing a financing statement in the proper place) and any unperfected secured party (other than a secured party from whom the creditor has received timely notice of the security interest)).

684. *See id.* § 9-617(a)(3).

685. *See id.* § 9-622(a)(3).

REVISED § 9-624

WAIVER

Under current § 9-504, a secured party usually is required to send a disposition notice to a debtor,[686] a right that the debtor cannot waive except in writing and after default.[687] Under revised § 9-611, a secured party usually is obligated to send an authenticated notification of disposition to a debtor and any secondary obligor.[688] Unlike current § 9-504, revised § 9-611 does not address the ability of a debtor or secondary obligor to waive its right to notice. Revised § 9-611, however, is included among the statutes listed in revised § 9-602 that create rights and duties that cannot be waived or varied,[689] suggesting that, in a departure from current law, a debtor and secondary obligor may never waive their right to a disposition notice. But revised § 9-602 is subject to revised § 9-624,[690] a section that permits a debtor or secondary obligor to waive its right to notification "only by an agreement to that effect entered into and authenticated after

---

686. *See id.* § 9-504(3) (1995).

687. *See id.; id.* § 9-501(3)(b); *see also In re* Huffman, 204 B.R. 562, 564 (Bankr. W.D. Mo. 1997) (stating that "a debtor's right to written notice cannot be waived or varied by any pre-default agreement"); Canadian Community Bank v. Ascher Findley Co., 280 Cal. Rptr. 521, 534 (Ct. App. 1991) ("California interpretive law is quite clear that pre-disposition notice may only be waived in writing by a debtor *after* default."); Caterpillar Fin. Servs. Corp. v. Wells, 651 A.2d 507, 520–21 (N.J. Super. Ct. Law Div. 1994) (relying on U.C.C. § 9-504(3) to conclude that waiver-of-notice provision in guaranty was ineffective); *cf. In re* Collins, 132 B.R. 491, 493 (Bankr. M.D. Fla. 1991) (observing, under North Carolina law, that a non-guarantor debtor may waive its right to a disposition notice only in writing after default, but upholding a waiver-of-notice clause in a guaranty).

688. *See* U.C.C. § 9-611(b)–(d) (1999).

689. *See id.* § 9-602(7).

690. *Id.* § 9-602 ("Except as otherwise provided in Section 9-624 . . . .").

default."[691] This provision will change the result in cases that have upheld the enforceability of the typical waiver-of-notice clauses in guaranty agreements and other loan papers executed by a secondary obligor before default.[692]

In an effort to protect a consumer debtor with significant equity in the collateral, a creditor under current Article 9 must forego its remedy of strict foreclosure and timely dispose of consumer goods in its possession if the consumer debtor has paid at least sixty percent of the cash price (or, if applicable, the principal amount).[693] Recognizing that the consumer debtor may benefit from an offer of a strict foreclosure, current Article 9 permits the debtor to waive this right to a forced sale if the waiver is in writing and executed after default.[694] Revised Article 9 imposes similar constraints on the creditor through subsections (e) and (f) of revised § 9-620,[695] neither of which suggests that the debtor retains the ability to waive its right to a forced sale.[696] As revised § 9-620 is referenced in revised § 9-602 as a statute that creates rights and duties that cannot be waived or varied,[697] one might conclude that the current law will change. But revised § 9-602 is

---

691. *Id.* § 9-624(a).

692. *See, e.g.,* Chrysler Credit Corp. v. Curley, 753 F. Supp. 611, 613–14 n.6 (E.D. Va. 1990) (citing cases enforcing waiver clauses); Gambo v. Bank of Maryland, 648 A.2d 1105, 1111 n.9 (Md. Ct. Spec. App. 1994) (same); Sigman, *supra* note 286, at 628 n.6 (same). *But see Chrysler Credit Corp.,* 753 F. Supp. at 614 n.7 (citing cases invalidating waiver clauses); *Gambo,* 648 A.2d at 1111 n.8 (same).

693. *See* U.C.C. § 9-505(1) (1995); *see also* Kelley v. Commercial Nat'l Bank, 678 P.2d 620, 623–24 (Kan. 1984) (concluding debtor renounced rights under U.C.C. § 9-505(1) to a forced sale of repossessed vehicle); Michigan Nat'l Bank v. Marston, 185 N.W.2d 47, 50 (Mich. Ct. App. 1970) (holding U.C.C. § 9-505(1) was irrelevant where debtor made no payments on note nor alleged payment of 60% of either cash price or loan amount); Press v. Purks, 32 U.C.C. Rep. Serv. 2d (CBC) 1016, 1019–20 (Va. Cir. Ct. 1997) (concluding debtor that paid more than 60% of purchase price of horse prior to default could redeem horse from creditor that failed to timely sell it under U.C.C. § 9-505(1)).

694. *See* U.C.C. § 9-505(1) (1995).

695. *See id.* § 9-620(e), (f) (1999).

696. *Cf. id.* § 9-620(a)(4) (indicating that a secured party may accept collateral and forgive all or part of the debt if "subsection (e) does not require the secured party to dispose of the collateral *or the debtor waives the requirement pursuant to Section 9-624*") (emphasis added).

697. *See id.* § 9-602(10).

698. *See id.* § 9-602 ("Except as otherwise provided in Section 9-624 . . . .").

subject to revised § 9-624,[698] a section that permits a debtor to waive its right to a forced sale under revised § 9-620(e) "by an agreement to that effect entered into and authenticated after default."[699]

Under current § 9-506, a debtor can waive its right to redeem collateral only if the waiver is in writing and executed after default.[700] Revised § 9-623 codifies the right of redemption but, unlike current § 9-506, is silent on whether a debtor or secondary obligor may waive that right. However, revised § 9-623 is referenced in revised § 9-602 as a statute that creates rights and duties that cannot be waived or varied,[701] suggesting a change in current law. But revised § 9-602 is subject to revised § 9-624,[702] a section that permits a debtor or secondary obligor to waive its redemption right in a transaction "only by an agreement to that effect entered into and authenticated after default."[703] However, in a departure from current § 9-506, a debtor or a secondary obligor may never waive its right of redemption in a consumer-goods transaction.[704]

To be effective, waivers permitted by revised § 9-624 must be authenticated.[705] In many transactions the creditor will satisfy this requirement by introducing a writing signed by the debtor or the secondary obligor.[706] As parties (particularly consumers) occasionally sign writings without reading or understanding them,

---

699. *Id.* § 9-624(b). As noted earlier, this waiver did not appear in Revised Article 9 until very late in the drafting process. *See supra* note 571.

700. *See id.* §§ 9-506, 9-501(3)(d) (1995); *see also* Kellos v. Parker-Sharpe, Inc., 263 S.E.2d 138, 140 (Ga. 1980) ("Thus, the right to redeem collateral may be waived by an agreement in writing, after default, but cannot be waived by an agreement in writing before default."); Data Security, Inc. v. Plessman, 510 N.W.2d 361, 365 (Neb. Ct. App. 1993) ("Under § 9-501(3)(d), a debtor's right of redemption may not be waived or varied except as provided in § 9-506, which means only in writing and *after* default."); Medallion Funding Corp. v. Helen Laundromat, Inc., 34 U.C.C. Rep. Serv. 2d (West) 250, 257 (N.Y. 1997) (finding waiver clause in promissory note "ineffective"); Indianapolis Morris Plan Corp. v. Karlen, 319 N.Y.S.2d 831, 834 (1971) (stating that a debtor's right of redemption may not be waived prior to default).

701. *See* U.C.C. § 9-602(11) (1999).

702. *See id.* § 9-602 ("Except as otherwise provided in Section 9-624 . . . .").

703. *Id.* § 9-624(c).

704. *See id.* ("Except in a consumer-goods transaction . . . .").

705. *See id.* § 9-624(a), (b).

706. *See id.* § 9-102(a)(7)(A).

one may question whether enforceability should turn on proof of authentication alone. The statute could have required the creditor to prove that the signatory "expressly agreed" to the waiver,[707] but that would likely create difficult, if not impossible, evidentiary hurdles. The approach taken by the Drafting Committee seems a fair compromise.

A minor quibble with revised § 9-624 is the placement of its substance apart from revised § 9-602. Revised § 9-602 provides a list of statutes that create rights and duties that cannot be waived or varied.[708] Revised § 9-624 permits limited waivers of selected rights and duties created by statutes referenced in revised § 9-602. Rather than draft a "rule" in one section (revised § 9-602) and, through a cross-reference, direct the reader to the "exception" codified in another section located nowhere nearby (revised § 9-624), the "exception" could have been strategically grafted into the "rule."[709] In this manner all waiver-related provisions would have been embodied in a single section.

Revised § 9-624 permits debtors and secondary obligors in consumer-goods transactions to waive their right to a disposition notice but not their right to redeem collateral.[710] This approach is questionable. Many debtors and secondary obligors in consumer-goods transactions are individuals who either are not aware that they enjoy a right to redeem collateral or are not in a financial

---

707. Early drafts contemplated such proof. *See id.* § 9-504(i) (Draft July 28–Aug. 4, 1995) (including bracketed language requiring a creditor to prove that a party "expressly agreed" to waive its right to a disposition notice); *id.* § 9-505(m) (requiring a creditor to prove that a party "expressly agreed" to waiving selected strict foreclosure rights); *id.* § 9-506(f) (requiring a creditor to prove that a party "expressly agreed" to waive the right to redeem collateral in a consumer secured transaction).

708. Revised § 9-624 itself is one of those statutes. *See id.* § 9-602(12) (1999).

709. For example, revised § 9-602(7) could have been drafted to read: "(7) Sections 9-610(b), 9-611, 9-613, and 9-614, which deal with disposition of collateral, except a debtor or secondary obligor may waive the right to notification of disposition of collateral under § 9-611 by authenticating an agreement to that effect after default." Similarly, revised § 9-602(10) could have been written to read: "(10) Sections 9-620, 9-621, and 9-622, which deal with acceptance of collateral in satisfaction of obligation, except a debtor may waive the right to require a disposition under revised § 9-620(e) by authenticating an agreement to that effect after default." And revised § 9-602(11) might have read: "(11) Section 9-623, which deals with redemption of collateral, except a debtor or secondary obligor may waive the right to redeem collateral in a transaction, other than a consumer-goods transaction, by authenticating an agreement to that effect after default."

710. *See* U.C.C. § 9-624 (1999).

position to exercise that right. In an effort to improve the awareness of these individuals, Revised Article 9 requires a secured creditor to include redemption information in the disposition notice.[711] Why an individual should be able to waive its right to a disposition notice that may inform the individual of its redemption right, but not waive the very right mentioned in the waivable notice, is unclear. In fact, of the four possible statutory approaches that could have been adopted with respect to the waiver of notice and redemption rights in consumer-goods transactions—(i) prohibit waiver of each right, (ii) prohibit waiver of the right to notice but permit waiver of the redemption right, (iii) prohibit waiver of the redemption right but permit waiver of the right to notice, and (iv) permit waiver of each right—the approach selected arguably makes the least sense.

The enforceability of waiver clauses in standard guaranty agreements and other loan papers executed by a secondary obligor before default was an issue considered by the PEB Study Group. The PEB Study Group received thoughtful comments from both "pro-waiver" advocates and "anti-waiver" proponents, but ultimately declined to offer a recommendation favoring one side.[712] Through revised § 9-602 and revised § 9-624, the Drafting Committee has adopted the "anti-waiver" view,[713] a choice that will be well-received by some and criticized by others. Nevertheless, by confronting the issue and resolving it statutorily the Drafting Committee has improved Article 9 by removing from potential litigation a frequently contested issue that courts have failed to resolve in a uniform manner.[714]

---

711. *See id.* § 9-614(1)(c); *see also id.* § 9-614(3) (paragraph of model form beginning "You can get . . . .").

712. *See* PEB STUDY GROUP REPORT, *supra* note 7, at 227–30.

713. The "anti-waiver" view was specifically adopted during a floor vote at NCCUSL's 1997 annual meeting. *See* Weise Memorandum, *supra* note 198.

714. *See supra* note 692 and accompanying text. Occasionally the secured debt is evidenced by a negotiable instrument governed by U.C.C. Article 3. If the instrument is executed by a guarantor and includes a typical provision by which the guarantor waives suretyship defenses, a potential conflict appears to exist between U.C.C. § 3-605(i) (permitting suretyship waivers) and revised §§ 9-602 and 9-624 (prohibiting pre-default waivers and many post-default waivers). This conflict is resolved in favor of the Article 9 provisions. *See* U.C.C. § 3-102(b) (1995); *see also id.* § 3-605 cmt. 8 (acknowledging Article 9 limitations); PEB Commentary No. 11 (Issue 11), 3B U.L.A. 120, 125 (Supp. 1998) (same).

Freedom-of-contract proponents may be disappointed that revised §§ 9-602 and 9-624 continue to limit the ability of parties to waive or modify the rights and duties created by Part 6. The disappointment may be justified, absent any empirical evidence that the majority of today's creditors engage in post-default predatory tactics. Possibly the better reason for adopting a somewhat paternalistic approach is to address the concern that the debtor's "freedom" to contract may be nonexistent in many secured transactions.[715] Usually the loan papers are drafted by creditors and their counsel, who often adopt a "take it or leave it" approach at the bargaining table. Debtors, desperate for the creditor's funds, goods, or services, may either fail to read what they sign or may read but not comprehend the significance of the legal jargon without the assistance of counsel (the cost of which may frustrate the ability to consummate the transaction).[716] Perhaps when "freedom of contract" is illusory the statutory limitations on waiver and variance are necessary to level the playing field for the various participants.

Some may criticize the contractual limitations in revised §§ 9-602 and 9-624 for being too broad. The limitations in revised § 9-602 apply to all debtors and obligors, not just those without bargaining strength.[717] Some debtors and obligors are quite

---

715. *See, e.g.,* 2 GILMORE, *supra* note 2, § 44.3, at 1221 ("No one will deny that the consumer security agreement is a contract of adhesion or that the consumer needs protection."); Miller, *supra* note 679, at 187–88 (offering several reasons why "freedom of contract" in a consumer context is "a license for the unscrupulous to take unfair advantage of the consumer"); Philip Shuchman, *Profit on Default: An Archival Study of Automobile Repossession and Resale,* 22 STAN. L. REV. 20, 52–53 (1969) ("Contract theory has long since run the full circle. The consumer's *freedom to* contract is a lie. The consumer needs *freedom from* such flexibility.").

716. *See, e.g.,* Clark, *supra* note 677, at 303 (noting that a consumer "is as likely to read (let alone understand) [a security agreement] as he is to run windsprints in Red Square"); Greenfield, *supra* note 550, at 300 (contending that a consumer's waiver of a statutory right at the time of contract formation "is highly suspect" and that the "small-print boilerplate" language of the waiver makes a consumer's assent "a fiction"). *But see* Heiser & Flemma, *supra* note 414, at 493 (contending that "[t]he idea that a consumer debtor is unsophisticated and completely at the mercy of secured parties ignores reality"); James J. White, *Work and Play in Revising Article 9,* 80 VA. L. REV. 2089, 2095 (1994) (urging the Drafting Committee to "purge the idea of the noble consumer who borrows in ignorance, who is surprised by repossession and deficiency judgment, and who claims incredible promises by his creditor" because "the consumer class overflows with liars and cheats").

· 717. *See* U.C.C. § 9-602 (1999).

sophisticated and knowledgeable in commercial matters. They can adequately protect themselves against any attempted over-reaching and intimidation by their creditors and have no need to be rescued from their own errors by a statutory white knight. These parties should be permitted to waive or vary their rights and the duties imposed on their creditors if they so desire.

Redrafting revised §§ 9-602 or 9-624 in a manner that extends protection only to those parties in need of it is a noble goal, but drafting language that furthers that goal is a daunting challenge. How does one discern whether a party can adequately handle its commercial affairs? Should Article 9 create the term, "sophisticated party"?[718] And if so, how should the term be defined? What factors should dictate the inclusion of natural persons? Education? Net worth? Adjusted gross income on the most recent tax return? And when is a business entity a "sophisticated party"? If its capital stock is traded on a national exchange? If it is audited by a "Big Five" accounting firm? If it has had net income of at least "x" dollars for at least "y" consecutive years? Should the term include some built-in exclusions (e.g., the term excludes all natural persons and any party to a transaction involving principal of less than "x" dollars)? One may criticize revised §§ 9-602 and 9-624 for limiting the contractual freedom of parties that can take care of themselves, but the criticism pales in comparison to the drafting nightmares triggered when one contemplates how and where to statutorily draw the line between those parties who need its protection and those who do not.

---

718. Federal securities laws have adopted a similar approach, excluding from coverage selected transactions involving "accredited investors." *See, e.g.,* 15 U.S.C. § 77b(a)(15) (1994) (defining "accredited investor"); *id.* § 77d (exemption); *id.* § 80a-6(a)(5)(A)(iii) (exemption).

REVISED § 9-625

REMEDIES FOR SECURED PARTY'S FAILURE TO COMPLY WITH ARTICLE

A secured party may breach the peace while repossessing collateral, forget to send a disposition notice to the debtor, fail to dispose of collateral in a commercially reasonable manner, or otherwise falter in carrying out its statutory obligations. Under current Article 9, the secured party's liability for noncompliance is addressed in § 9-507(1).[719] Revised Article 9 deals with the same concern in § 9-625.[720]

Current law provides injunctive relief by authorizing a court to order or restrain a disposition if the secured party "is not proceeding in accordance with the [default] provisions of this Part [5]."[721] For example, if a secured party has held collateral for an unreasonable period of time without attempting to sell it or offering to keep it in satisfaction of the debt, a court may order a disposition. And if a secured party has repossessed collateral prior to a default, a court may restrain any scheduled disposition.

Revised § 9-625 makes two modifications to this remedy. First, the remedy applies when the secured party fails to comply with any provision of Article 9, not just the default provisions.[722] Therefore, injunctive relief may be available if the secured party is breaching its statutory duties that arise under a section of

---

719. *See* U.C.C. § 9-507(1) (1995).
720. The rights and duties under revised § 9-625 cannot be waived or varied. *See id.* § 9-602(13) (1999).
721. *See id.* § 9-507(1) (1995).
722. *See id.* § 9-625(a) (1999) ("If it is established that a secured party is not proceeding in accordance with *this article* . . . .") (emphasis added).

166

Revised Article 9 other than those sections in Part 6, such as the statutory duty to release collateral in its control[723] or to file or send (or cause to be filed or sent) a termination statement.[724] And second, the remedy has been expanded to permit a court to order or restrain "collection" and "enforcement" of collateral, in addition to its disposition.[725] For example, a court may enjoin a secured party from collecting payments from account debtors[726] if a default has not occurred and the secured party is not otherwise contractually permitted to collect the payments. Also, a court might order a hesitant secured party to initiate litigation to protect the debtor's interest in intellectual property against unlawful infringement[727] if the loan documents prohibit the debtor from initiating the litigation.

The introductory phrase in both current § 9-507(1) and revised § 9-625(a) is identical: "If it is established . . . ."[728] This language places the burden of establishing noncompliance on the party seeking injunctive relief. Neither statute, however, indicates who is eligible to seek relief. Elsewhere both statutes permit recovery of damages by specific parties.[729] Presumably the absence of any prescribed list of potential litigants permits a court to grant injunctive relief at the request of any party that establishes that the creditor is failing to comply with Article 9 and otherwise convinces the court that injunctive relief is warranted.[730]

Other remedies for noncompliance are available in addition to injunctive relief. Under current Article 9, a secured party is

723. *See id.*

724. *See id.* § 9-513.

725. *See id.* § 9-625(a).

726. A secured party enjoys this post-default remedy under current and Revised Article 9. *See id.* § 9-502(1) (1995); *id.* § 9-607(a) (1999).

727. Under Revised Article 9, a secured party enjoys the statutory right to initiate litigation aimed at protecting and preserving collateral consisting of intellectual property against unlawful infringement. *See id.* § 9-607(a)(3) & cmt. 3 (1999).

728. *See id.* § 9-525(1) (1995); *id.* § 9-625(a) (1999).

729. *See id.* § 9-501(1) (1995) (permitting "the debtor or any other person entitled to notification or whose security interest has been made known to the secured party prior to the disposition" to recover damages); *id.* § 9-625(c)(1) (1999) (awarding damages to "a person that . . . was a debtor, was an obligor, or held a security interest in or other lien on the collateral").

730. At least one source suggests that the normal conditions for injunctive relief need not be satisfied, as the relief is statutorily authorized. *See* LAWRENCE ET AL., *supra* note 128, § 19.01[A], at 377.

liable for "any loss" caused by its noncompliance.[731] However, the loss must be caused by the secured party's noncompliance with the default provisions, and no loss is recoverable until the collateral has been disposed.[732] Parties eligible to recover damages include the debtor, any person entitled to notification of a disposition, and any party whose security interest in the collateral was known by the secured party before disposition.[733] The priority rank of the security interest held by an injured party is irrelevant. Noticeably absent from the list of parties entitled to damages are parties holding liens in the collateral (including subordinate liens destroyed by the disposition[734]).

Under Revised Article 9, a secured party is liable "for damages in the amount of any loss" caused by its noncompliance with *any* provision of Revised Article 9, whether or not the collateral has been disposed.[735] The revised list of potential claimants includes any debtor, any obligor (whether primary or secondary), and any party holding a security interest in *or other lien on* the collateral (regardless of priority and whether or not the party was entitled to receive a disposition notice or the secured party knew of the party's property interest).[736] However, the party must enjoy that status "at the time of the failure."[737]

---

731. *See* U.C.C. § 9-507(1) (1995).

732. *See id.* Because § 9-507(1) permits recovery of any loss only if "the disposition has occurred," the reader may conclude that an aggrieved party has no remedy under § 9-507(1) if the secured party has breached its duties under the strict foreclosure provision of § 9-505. However, comment 2 to § 9-505 reveals that a party can recover damages under § 9-507(1) caused by a secured party's failure to comply with § 9-505. *See also* 4 WHITE & SUMMERS, *supra* note 36, § 34-19, at 463-64 n.2.

733. *See* U.C.C. § 9-507(1) (1999); *see also id.* § 9-504(3) (indicating which parties are entitled to a disposition notice).

734. *See id.* § 9-504(4).

735. *Id.* § 9-625(b) (1999). The ability to recover these damages is "[s]ubject to subsections (c), (d), and (f)." *Id.* Subsection (c) places limits on who can recover damages and incorporates the limitations of revised § 9-628, discussed *infra* notes 833–53 and accompanying text. Subsection (d) is discussed *infra* notes 757–62 and accompanying text. Subsection (f), not discussed herein, applies when a person fails to comply with revised § 9-210.

736. *See* U.C.C. § 9-625(b), (c)(1) (1999); *cf.* PEB STUDY GROUP REPORT, *supra* note 7, at 205–06 (recommending that U.C.C. § 9-507(1) be revised to provide a remedy to all junior claimants, not just junior claimants entitled to a disposition notice or whose property interest is known by the secured party before disposition).

737. U.C.C. § 9-625(c)(1) (1999).

A secured party's failure to comply with a provision of Article 9 may create an obvious loss. For example, a creditor may repossess equipment from a debtor that is not in default, forcing the debtor to lease replacement equipment until it can persuade the creditor (or a court) that the original equipment should be returned. At a minimum, the debtor has sustained a loss equal to the amount of its lease expense.[738] In other instances, a party in whose favor the breached duty runs may suffer no loss. For example, a senior secured party with an unpaid debt of $100,000 may sell collateral without sending the requisite disposition notice to a subordinate secured creditor.[739] The collateral is sold for $75,000. Unless the subordinate creditor can prove that the value of the collateral was worth more than $100,000, it has suffered no loss as a result of the senior secured creditor's noncompliance. Why? Because the subordinate secured party is entitled to receive proceeds only after the senior secured creditor has recouped its reasonable expenses and satisfied its debt.[740]

In many consumer transactions, the financial resources of the debtor, the costs of litigation, and little (if any) actual damage collectively permit a creditor to breach its statutory duties with impunity. Recognizing that potential liability for actual damages

---

738. An aggrieved party may claim a different measure of damages in tort. *See id.* § 9-625 cmt. 3. Query whether a party should have the option to pursue a tort remedy for a creditor's breach of an Article 9 provision. Comment 3 to § 9-625 references § 1-103, which permits principles of law (e.g., tort law) to supplement the U.C.C. provisions "[u]nless displaced by the particular provisions of this Act." Is § 9-625 not a remedy provision? If so, is a tort remedy not displaced by a particular provision? If one overlooks this tension between § 1-103 and comment 3 to § 9-625 and concludes that an aggrieved party can pursue a tort remedy, then the party should determine whether a tort remedy will provide a greater recovery than an action under § 9-625 for actual damages. For example, after Debtor defaults, Lender unlawfully repossesses equipment with a fair market value of $100,000 and sells it in a commercially unreasonable manner for $70,000. Evidence reveals that a commercially reasonable sale should have rendered a bid of $80,000. Under statutory principles, Debtor is entitled to a credit of $80,000 (the sales price at a commercially reasonable sale). In a conversion action, Debtor is entitled to a credit of $100,000 (the fair market value of the collateral at the time of the unlawful repossession). Suing in tort permits Debtor to recover an additional $20,000. Debtor also may be able to recover punitive damages. *See, e.g.,* Chrysler Credit Corp. v. Turner, 553 So. 2d 64, 67 (Ala. 1989); Truck Center of Tulsa, Inc. v. Autrey, 836 S.W.2d 359, 365–66 (Ark. 1992); Star Bank, N.A. v. Laker, 637 N.E.2d 805, 807 (Ind. 1994); Zimprich v. Harvestore Sys., Inc., 461 N.W.2d 425, 430–31 (N.D. 1990).

739. *See* U.C.C. § 9-611(b), (c)(3) (1999).

740. *See id.* § 9-615(a); *see also supra* note 646 and accompanying text.

may not adequately discourage creditor misconduct, current Article 9 imposes a minimum penalty in selected transactions. The penalty, equal to "an amount not less than the credit service charge plus ten per cent of the principal amount of the debt or the time price differential plus ten per cent of the cash price," can be recovered by any debtor that has granted a security interest in consumer goods.[741] The same minimum award is available under revised § 9-625 to a party that was a debtor or a secondary obligor at the time of noncompliance.[742] A party need not prove any actual damages in order to recover the minimum award[743] (which, in some cases, has significantly reduced, if not completely eliminated, the debtor's liability for any deficiency[744]). A

741. U.C.C. § 9-507(1) (1995). This minimum civil penalty has been described as "probably the most glittering nugget of consumer protection found in all of Article 9." CLARK, *supra* note 2, ¶ 4.12[4], at 4-214; *see also* Wirth v. Heavey, 508 S.W.2d 263, 268 (Mo. Ct. App. 1974) (noting that debtor was not entitled to statutory minimum award because collateral consisted of business equipment, not consumer goods); Joyce v. Cloverleaf Homes, Inc., 344 S.E.2d 58, 60–61 (N.C. Ct. App. 1986) (concluding trial court properly invoked third sentence of § 9-507(1) as mobile home was a consumer good); *cf.* CAL. COM. CODE § 9507(1) (West 1990) (deleting remedy from statute); OR. REV. STAT. § 79.5070(1) (Supp. 1996) ("If the collateral is consumer goods, the debtor has a right to recover in any event an amount not less than $350.").
   Some courts have held that the bankruptcy trustee inherits the debtor's cause of action. *See, e.g.,* Jones v. Star Bank (*In re* Angel), 142 B.R. 194, 198 (Bankr. S.D. Ohio 1992); *In re* Reed, 102 B.R. 243, 246 (Bankr. E.D. Okla. 1989).
   742. *See* U.C.C. 9-625(c)(2) (1999). Three stylistic changes have been made to the statutory language: the revised statute references "10 percent" rather than "10 per cent" or "ten per cent," "obligation" rather than "debt," and "time-price differential" instead of "time price differential."
   This minimum award can be recovered only when the secured party has "failed to comply with this part [6]" (as contrasted with "this article"). *Id.*
   743. *See* Ogletree v. Brokers South, Inc., 383 S.E.2d 900, 902 (Ga. Ct. App. 1989); Davenport v. Chrysler Credit Corp., 818 S.W.2d 23, 31 (Tenn. Ct. App. 1991); First City Bank—Farmers Branch v. Guex, 659 S.W.2d 734, 740 (Tex. App.—Dallas 1983, writ granted), *aff'd*, 677 S.W.2d 25 (Tex. 1984).
   744. *See, e.g.,* Reed, 102 B.R. at 243 (indicating a $2763.28 deficiency and a $2590 penalty); *In re* Hamby, 19 B.R. 776, 779, 784 (Bankr. N.D. Ala. 1982) (indicating a $3017.07 deficiency and a $2997.22 penalty); Gulf Homes, Inc. v. Gonzales, 676 P.2d 635, 640–41 (Ariz. Ct. App. 1983) (indicating a $1621.29 *surplus* and an $8250 penalty), *aff'd & vacated in part*, 676 P.2d 629 (Ariz. 1984); Gulf Homes, Inc. v. Goubeaux, 664 P.2d 183, 185, 189 (Ariz. 1983) (indicating a $2416.72 deficiency and a $10,916.60 penalty); Conti Causeway Ford v. Jarossy, 276 A.2d 402, 405 (N.J. Dist. Ct. 1971) (indicating a $258.12 deficiency and an $872.00 penalty), *aff'd*, 288 A.2d 872 (N.J. Super. Ct. App. Div. 1972) Kruse v. Voyager Ins. Cos., 648 N.E.2d 814, 815, 819 (Ohio 1995) (indicating a $2477.44 deficiency and a $2461.91 penalty); Fidelity Fin. Servs., Inc. v. Wilson, 635 N.E.2d 92, 93 (Ohio Mun. Ct. 1994) (indicating a $4913.48 deficiency and a $5359.35 penalty); *Davenport*, 818 S.W.2d at 23 (indicating a $6774.00 deficiency and a $6727.52 penalty).

party, however, that can prove its actual damages exceed the statutory minimum can collect the greater amount.

Whether the "credit service charge" formula or the "time-price differential" formula applies to a particular transaction is unclear. The statute offers no direction, and the accompanying comments leave "construction and application to the court."[745] Case law and scholarly commentary reveal that application depends on whether the debtor received credit from the seller or a third-party financer. If the seller extended credit to the buyer, then the statutory minimum equals the time-price differential plus ten percent of the cash price. If the debtor received credit from a third-party financer, such as a bank, then the minimum award equals the credit service charge plus 10% of the principal.[746] A simple example may be helpful. Consumer desires to buy a piano, but cannot pay the $5000 cash price. Seller agrees to sell the piano to Consumer on credit if Consumer agrees to make twelve monthly payments of $500. Alternatively, Bank agrees to finance the purchase if Consumer agrees to pay $5750 on the one-year anniversary date of the loan. If Seller finances the purchase and breaches a statutory duty, Consumer can recover $1500 (time-price differential of $1000 [total payments of $6000 minus cash price of $5000] plus $500 [10% of $5000 cash price]). If Bank finances the purchase and breaches a statutory duty, then Consumer is entitled to recover $1250 (credit service charge of $750 [total payment of $5750 minus borrowed amount of $5000] plus 10% of the $5000 principal).

---

745. U.C.C. § 9-625 cmt. 4 (1999).

746. *See* 9 HAWKLAND ET AL., *supra* note 15, § 9-507:06, at 901–02; LAWRENCE ET AL., *supra* note 128, § 19.03, at 384–85; *see also Angel*, 142 B.R. at 198–99 (using "credit service charge" formula to calculate damages recoverable from third-party financer); *Gulf Homes*, 676 P.2d at 640 (using "time price differential" formula to calculate damages recoverable from seller); Jacobs v. Healey-Ford Subaru, Inc., No. CV 900031301S, 1996 WL 87600 (Conn. Super. Ct. Feb. 7, 1996) (using "time price differential" formula to calculate damages recoverable from seller after noting that "it appears to be more appropriate to interpret [the third sentence of U.C.C. § 9-507(1)] as requiring a 'credit service charge' calculation when there is a third party creditor, such as a bank, and to require a calculation of the 'time-price differential' when the original seller demands a premium representing the difference between the cash and credit price"); *Kruse*, 648 N.E.2d at 819 (using "credit service charge" formula to calculate damages recoverable from third-party financer); Western Nat'l Bank v. Harrison, 577 P.2d 635, 642 (Wyo. 1978) (using "credit service charge" formula to calculate damages recoverable from third-party financer).

Is the "cash price" (as that term is used in the "time-price differential" formula) reduced by any down payment paid by Consumer out of its own funds? The same term also appears in the redemption statute,[747] where it is distinguished from the amount financed. If the term is intended to have a uniform meaning throughout the default provisions of Article 9, then a Consumer's down payment has no impact on the damages calculation. However, three reasons for a contrary interpretation could trump the desire for a uniform meaning. First, the redemption statute uses "cash price" in a calculation that attempts to preserve the debtor's equity in the collateral; the damages statute uses "cash price" in a calculation that attempts to penalize a creditor for breaching its statutory duty. As the term appears in statutes that accomplish different purposes, then perhaps the term need not be interpreted in a uniform manner.[748] Second, ignoring the effect of a down payment seems to result in a windfall for a debtor that has funded the down payment with third-party funds rather than its own money. In fact, in the unlikely (but not impossible) event that a seller and a third-party lender both finance part of the purchase and breach their statutory duties,[749] failure to subtract the down payment from the cash price results in an inflated aggregate penalty.[750] Third, failing to reduce the cash price by any down payment may elevate form over substance. Debtor wants to buy a new car that costs $25,000. Debtor will make a $5000 down payment. Both Dealer and Bank have offered to finance the $20,000 balance on terms requiring Debtor to repay the loan in 60 equal payments (each of which includes a "time-price differential" or "credit service charge" component). From Debtor's perspective, the two proposals are identical. The only discernible difference is whose name appears on the payee line of the monthly check. But if the "cash price" component is $25,000

---

747. *See* U.C.C. § 9-505(1) (1995); *id.* § 9-620(e)(1) (1999).

748. *See* LAWRENCE ET AL., *supra* note 128, § 19.03, at 385.

749. For example, the third-party financer may receive full payment of the funded down payment but fail to timely file a termination statement (a breach of U.C.C. § 9-513(a) (1999)), and the seller, after a default, may dispose of the collateral in a manner not commercially reasonable (a breach of U.C.C. § 9-610(b)).

750. *See* 9 HAWKLAND ET AL., *supra* note 15, § 9-507:06, at 902.

rather than $20,000, Debtor may recover additional damages of $500 (10% of the $5000 down payment) by accepting Dealer's offer. No persuasive reason justifies different penalties for substantively identical credit transactions.

Certainly some guidance on whether the "cash price" excludes any down payment would have been welcome.[751] But that is not the only question that arises under revised § 9-625(c). Why does the statute permit only secondary obligors to recover the statutory penalty[752] when any obligor is allowed to recover actual damages?[753] And if the minimum statutory penalty is a form of consumer protection, should not the penalty provision be both expanded to apply when a consumer debtor grants a security interest in any collateral (rather than just consumer goods) and modified to protect, in addition to debtors, all (but only) consumer obligors?[754]

---

751. Guidance was requested in the Zinnecker Memorandum, *supra* note 102, at 5. Another, less troublesome, issue is whether the "principal amount" as referenced in the "credit service charge" formula is measured at the inception of the loan or the time of noncompliance. Most, if not all, sources have concluded that the term refers to the original amount of the loan. *See, e.g.,* 9 HAWKLAND ET AL., *supra* note 15, § 9-507:06, at 901 ("The principal amount of the debt, of course, means the original amount of the debt without any additions for interest or deductions for payment made."); 4 WHITE & SUMMERS, *supra* note 36, § 34-19, at 465 (observing that "the penalty is computed on the basis of the original principal amount"). *See also* Fidelity Fin. Servs., Inc. v. Wilson, 635 N.E.2d 92, 95 (Ohio Mun. Ct. 1994); Knights of Columbus Credit Union v. Stock, 814 S.W.2d 427, 432 (Tex. App.—Dallas 1991, writ denied); Garza v. Brazos County Fed. Credit Union, 603 S.W.2d 298, 300–01 (Tex. Civ. App. 1980, no writ). The specific reference to "at the time a secured party failed to comply" elsewhere in revised § 9-625(c)(2), and the omission of the same or similar language in the formula itself, further supports the conclusion reached by scholars and the case law. Furthermore, using the amount of the loan principal at the time of the noncompliance, which frequently will be less than the amount originally borrowed, effectively punishes the borrower and rewards the third-party financer through a reduced penalty.

752. *See* U.C.C. § 9-625(c)(2) (1999).

753. *See id.* § 9-625(c)(1). The official comments attempt to limit the breadth of the statute by stating that "a principal obligor who is not a debtor may recover damages only for noncompliance with Section 9-616, inasmuch as none of the other rights and duties in this Article run in favor of such a principal obligor." *See id.* § 9-625 cmt. 3. For much of the drafting process, only secondary obligors were allowed to recover actual damages. *See id.* § 9-507(b) (Draft Nov. 15, 1995). *But see id.* § 9-625(c)(1) (undated draft marked to reflect changes to the ALI Proposed Final Draft dated Apr. 15, 1998) (changing reference from "a secondary obligor" to "an obligor").

754. The reference to "consumer obligor" in subsection (e) suggests that the use of "secondary obligor" in subsection (c)(2) was a deliberate choice.

The minimum statutory penalty may have the unintended consequence of providing consumer creditors with an extra incentive to proofread their notices for accuracy and otherwise scrutinize their compliance with the provisions of Article 9. Although a creditor's noncompliance may not trigger a material statutory penalty in any single transaction, noncompliance that is widespread (e.g., a wrong telephone number on a standard, computer-generated, disposition notice[755]) could prompt one or more class actions with significant and adverse financial consequences.[756] Query whether creditors will attempt to mitigate this risk by increasing the cost, or limiting the availability, of consumer credit.

A debtor continues to enjoy the ability to pursue damages for the loss of any surplus proceeds.[757] However, if its deficiency is reduced or eliminated under revised § 9-626, revised § 9-625 prevents a debtor or secondary obligor from recovering *any* actual damages (other than damages for loss of surplus proceeds) triggered by the secured party's failure to comply with default provisions relating to collection, enforcement, disposition, or acceptance.[758] The goal of awarding damages is to restore the aggrieved party to the position it occupied before the secured party breached its statutory duties.[759] The limitation found in subsection (d) attempts to further that goal by eliminating the possibility

---

755. *See* U.C.C. § 9-614(1)(C), (D) (1999) (requiring a secured party in a consumer-goods transaction to include in its disposition notice a telephone number from which the recipient can discover the redemption price and additional information about the disposition and the secured obligation).

756. For a while, a proposed provision capped the aggregate statutory penalty payable by a secured party in one or more class actions prompted by the same noncompliance, but the provision was deleted as part of the "consumer compromise." *See infra* notes 852–53 and accompanying text.

757. *See* U.C.C. § 9-625(d) (1999).

758. *See id.* The relevant provisions presumably include at least revised §§ 9-607 to 9-616, 9-620, and 9-621. These statutes, or their substantive counterparts codified at a different address, were expressly referenced before being deleted and replaced with "the provisions of this part relating to collection, enforcement, disposition, or acceptance." *See id.* § 9-624(d) (Draft Apr. 6, 1998). If the secured party fails to comply with a provision not concerning collection, enforcement, disposition, or acceptance, then an injured party whose deficiency is reduced or eliminated under revised § 9-626 should pursue damages under revised § 9-625.

759. *See id.* § 9-625 cmt. 3; *id.* § 1-106(1) (1995).

of double-recovery or over-compensation.[760] Yet, the limitation on recovery may frustrate the goal of restoration if the aggrieved party proves damages in an amount that exceeds that portion of the deficiency reduced or eliminated under revised § 9-626. For example, Creditor fails to send the requisite disposition notice to Debtor. Under local law, Creditor's noncompliance bars recovery of a $2000 deficiency. Debtor can prove actual damages resulting from Creditor's noncompliance. Debtor has improved its position by $2000, less its actual damages. If those damages are not greater than $2000, then a court can deny recovery of actual damages and yet place Debtor in a position no worse (and probably better) than it would have enjoyed if Creditor had sent a disposition notice.[761] If actual damages, however, exceed $2000 (for example, $2400), then a court should permit recovery of the amount ($400) by which the damages ($2400) exceed the discharged deficiency ($2000). Only by doing so can Debtor be restored to its proper place. To best advance the restoration goal of damage awards, revised § 9-625(d) should be interpreted in a manner that prohibits recovery of actual damages only *to the extent that* (rather than *if*) the deficiency is reduced or eliminated.[762]

Because revised § 9-626 does not apply to consumer transactions,[763] the limitation in revised § 9-625(d) also does not apply to consumer transactions.[764] If the aggrieved party in a consumer transaction seeks to recover *actual* damages, then the restoration goal is best achieved if those damages are netted against any unadjusted deficiency claim or reduced, dollar for

760. *See id.* § 9-625 cmt. 3.
761. *See, e.g.,* Coones v. FDIC, 894 P.2d 613, 615–16 (Wyo. 1995) ("Since the amount of Coones's alleged damages did not exceed the amount of the deficiency, a judgment for damages would be an impermissible double recovery.").
762. This concern was raised in the Zinnecker Memorandum, *supra* note 102, at 5. Revised § 9-625(d) would advance the proposed interpretation if the second sentence were revised to read as follows: "However, a debtor or secondary obligor may not otherwise recover under subsection (b) for noncompliance with the provisions of this part relating to collection, enforcement, disposition, or acceptance to the extent that its deficiency is eliminated or reduced under Section 9-626."
763. *See* U.C.C. § 9-626(a) (1999) (stating that the rules therein apply "[i]n an action arising from a transaction, *other than a consumer transaction*") (emphasis added).
764. *See id.* § 9-625(d) (stating that the first sentence applies only if a "deficiency is eliminated under Section 9-626" and the second sentence applies only if a "deficiency is eliminated or reduced under Section 9-626").

dollar, by that part of the creditor's deficiency claim reduced or eliminated under local law for noncompliance. Should the same relationship exist between a reduced or eliminated deficiency claim and the minimum civil penalty? Some cases have held that a creditor must pay the minimum civil penalty to the injured consumer even if noncompliance bars or reduces the deficiency claim,[765] while other cases have concluded that an injured consumer cannot recover minimum damages if those damages are less than the discharged deficiency.[766] During most of the drafting process, the secured party could offset against the minimum statutory penalty that part of its deficiency claim reduced or eliminated under Revised Article 9, together with any other damages payable to the aggrieved party.[767] However, these offsets fell by the wayside as part of the "consumer compromise."[768] Whether

765. *See, e.g.,* Wilmington Trust Co. v. Conner, 415 A.2d 773, 781 (Del. 1980) (denying $2262.19 deficiency and awarding statutory damages of $1445.32); Randolph v. Franklin Inv. Co., 398 A.2d 340, 352 (D.C. 1979) (ruling creditor's noncompliance barred deficiency recovery and permitted debtor to pursue relief under § 9-507(1)); Georgia Cent. Credit Union v. Coleman, 271 S.E.2d 681, 684 (Ga. Ct. App. 1980) (holding creditor could not recover deficiency of $1892.55 and must pay debtor minimum damages of $366.37); Staley Employee Credit Union v. Christie, 443 N.E.2d 731, 732 (Ill. App. Ct. 1982) (denying deficiency and awarding statutory damages of $2647.38); Kruse v. Voyager Ins. Cos., 648 N.E.2d 814 (Ohio 1995) (awarding $2461.91 statutory damages and denying deficiency of $2477.44 deficiency); Wilkerson Motor Co. v. Johnson, 580 P.2d 505, 509–10 (Okla. 1978) (concluding creditor must pay minimum damages of $982.82 to debtor and forego deficiency). One scholar describes this approach as "the no-deficiency-PLUS rule." *See* Steve H. Nickles, *Rethinking Some U.C.C. Article 9 Problems—Subrogation, Equitable Liens; Actual Knowledge; Waiver of Security Interests; Secured Party Liability for Conversion Under Part 5,* 34 ARK. L. REV. 1, 172–73 (1980); *cf.* PEB STUDY GROUP REPORT, *supra* note 7, at 203–04 (recommending that a debtor not recover statutory minimum damages if a deficiency is discharged).

766. *See, e.g.,* Northwest Bank & Trust Co. v. Gotshall, 274 N.W.2d 713, 718–19 (Iowa 1979) (holding discharge of $1078.32 deficiency precluded debtor from recovering statutory damages of either $394.03 or $514.75); Topeka Datsun Motor Co. v. Stratton, 736 P.2d 82, 84 (Kan. Ct. App. 1987) (concluding debtor could not recover statutory damages of $3192.66 after court discharged $3083.51 deficiency under Kansas version of Uniform Consumer Credit Code); Bank of Chapmanville v. Workman, 406 S.E.2d 58, 65 (W. Va. 1991) (indicating that a hypothetical debtor cannot recover minimum damages of $10,000 if the court denies a $50,000 deficiency). *See also* LAWRENCE ET AL., *supra* note 128, § 19.03, at 385 (contending that awarding penalty damages after a deficiency has been reduced or eliminated "would violate the spirit of the Code" and "would be adding a penalty on top of a penalty").

767. *See, e.g.,* U.C.C. § 9-507(g) & cmt. 10 (Draft July 28–Aug. 4, 1995); *id.* § 9-624(d) & cmt. 7 (Draft Jan. 1998).

768. *See id.* § 9-624(c)(2) (underlined as new language), (d) (lined through as deleted language), and "Changes from Prior Draft" (Draft Mar. 1998); *supra* note 548 (discussing "consumer compromise").

the end result is favorable depends on one's perspective of the minimum civil penalty. If the formulaic damage award bears no relationship to the nature of the misconduct or the actual harm suffered, the award should be viewed as a penalty, not an attempt to make the injured party whole, and should be fully recoverable even if the creditor's noncompliance reduces or eliminates its deficiency.[769] But if statutory damages exist solely as a substitute for actual, but non-quantifiable, damages, and the creditor's non-compliance also reduces or eliminates its deficiency claim, then the dollar amount of that reduction or elimination should serve as the debtor's "actual damages" and render unnecessary any award of statutory damages (at least if the "actual damages" exceed the statutory damages).

Some statutes impose on a secured party a duty (such as releasing collateral in its control after the transaction has concluded,[770] filing or sending a termination statement after the transaction has ended,[771] or sending an explanation of the calculated deficiency or surplus[772]) that, if breached, may not result in quantifiable damages. To provide the obligated party with an incentive to carry out specific duties, revised § 9-625 permits a party for whose benefit the duty exists to recover $500 for each breach of that duty.[773] This $500 is a supplement to, not in lieu of, any other damages awarded under revised § 9-625[774] and is not reduced or eliminated if, as a result of the breach, a deficiency claim is reduced or eliminated.[775]

---

769. In a jurisdiction that follows this approach and yet reduces actual damages by the amount of any forfeited deficiency claim, a debtor that incurs actual damages greater than the minimum statutory damages may find it economically attractive to forego the larger claim and pursue the smaller claim. For example, assume Creditor's noncompliance bars recovery of a $5000 deficiency claim, Debtor's actual damages are $3500, and its minimum statutory damages are $2000. If Debtor attempts to recover its actual damages, it improves its position by $1500 ($5000 deficiency claim minus $3500 actual damages). But if Debtor opts for the statutory minimum, it improves its position by $3500 ($5000 deficiency claim minus $3500 actual damages plus $2000 statutory damages).

770. See U.C.C. § 9-208 (1999).

771. See id. § 9-513.

772. See id. § 9-616.

773. See id. § 9-625(e).

774. See id. ("In addition to any damages recoverable under subsection (b) . . . .").

775. See id. § 9-625(d) (limiting recovery "under subsection (b)" but not other provisions).

REVISED § 9-626

Action in Which Deficiency or Surplus Is in Issue

Whether intentionally or through oversight, a secured party may dispose of the collateral in a commercially unreasonable manner, fail to send a disposition notice to a debtor, or otherwise breach one of its statutory duties. Current Article 9 does not expressly state the effect that noncompliance has on a secured party's ability to pursue a deficiency claim.[776] As a result, three judicial responses have emerged: (i) a secured party's noncompliance absolutely bars recovery of a deficiency claim, (ii) a secured party's noncompliance creates a rebuttable presumption that the value of the collateral equals the amount of unpaid debt, effectively negating a deficiency claim absent contrary proof by the secured party that a deficiency would remain even if the secured party had complied with its duties,[777] and (iii) a secured party's noncompliance permits the aggrieved party to recover damages under § 9-507(1) that can be applied against the secured party's deficiency claim. A legion of cases and articles have analyzed the

---

776. Professor Gilmore noted that the effect of a secured party's noncompliance on the debtor's continuing liability for a deficiency "seems to have escaped the conscious attention of the Article 9 draftsmen." 2 GILMORE, *supra* note 2, § 44.9.4, at 1264.

777. Courts have disagreed on the degree of proof required to rebut the presumption. *See, e.g.,* Warnaco, Inc. v. Farkas, 872 F.2d 539, 545–46 (2d Cir. 1989) (preponderance); Fedders Corp. v. Taylor, 473 F. Supp. 961, 978 (D. Minn. 1979) (preponderance); United Bank Alaska v. Dischner, 685 P.2d 90, 93 (Alaska 1984) (clear and convincing); Connecticut Bank & Trust Co., N.A. v. Incendy, 540 A.2d 32, 38–39 (Conn. 1988) (preponderance); Caterpillar Fin. Servs. Corp. v. Wells, 651 A.2d 507, 519 (N.J. Super. Ct. Law Div. 1994) (preponderance); Associates Capital Servs. Corp. v. Riccardi, 408 A.2d 930, 934 (R.I. 1979) (clear and convincing); McChord Credit Union v. Parrish, 809 P.2d 759, 762 (Wash. Ct. App. 1991) (clear and convincing).

various approaches, lauding the merits and criticizing the defects of each.[778] As one can readily surmise, the existing law on this issue is anything but consistent.

The PEB Study Group acknowledged the present nonuniformity and recommended adoption of the rebuttable presumption rule.[779] The Drafting Committee accepted that recommendation. Revised § 9-626[780] states, in relevant part, that if a secured party fails to comply with the default provisions pertaining to collection, enforcement, disposition, or acceptance, then the liability for a deficiency "is limited to an amount by which the sum of the secured obligation, expenses, and attorney's fees exceeds the greater of: (A) the proceeds of the collection, enforcement, disposition, or acceptance; or (B) the amount of proceeds that

---

778. Relevant cases are cited in most of the literature. *See, e.g.,* CLARK, *supra* note 2, ¶ 4.12[5][a]–[d]; 9 HAWKLAND ET AL., *supra* note 15, § 9-507:07; 4 WHITE & SUMMERS, *supra* note 36, § 34-20; Alan Aronowitz, Comment, *Secured Creditor's Right to a Deficiency Judgment After Misbehavior Under U.C.C. § 9-504(3): Which Judicial Approach Should Texas Adopt?*, 21 HOUS. L. REV. 359 (1984); Elizabeth Dalton, Note, *The Consequences of Commercially Unreasonable Dispositions of Collateral: Haggis Management, Inc. v. Turtle Management, Inc.,* 1986 UTAH L. REV. 813; Norma G. Formanek, Comment, *The California Article 9 No-Deficiency Rule: Undermining the Secured Party's Security,* 34 HASTINGS L.J. 153 (1982); Howard Foss, Comment, *The Noncomplying Secured Party's Right to a Deficiency,* 21 UCC L.J. 226 (1989); Benjamin N. Henszey, *A Secured Creditor's Right to Collect a Deficiency Judgment under UCC Section 9-504: A Need to Remedy the Impasse,* 31 BUS. LAW. 2025 (1976); Elaine P. Lariviere, Comment, *Reevaluating Section 9-504(2) of the Uniform Commercial Code: Deficiency Actions After Commercially Unreasonable Collateral Sales,* 2 W. NEW ENG. L. REV. 493 (1980); Lloyd, *supra* note 279, at 695; Douglas M. Mancino, Note, *Denial of Deficiency: A Problem of Reasonable Notice Under UCC § 9-504(3),* 34 OHIO ST. L.J. 657 (1973); Note, *The Right to an Article 9 Deficiency Judgment Without 9-504 Notice of Resale,* 7 VAL. U. L. REV. 465 (1973); Joseph J. Ortego, *Collateral Disposition: Creditor Concerns,* 113 BANKING L.J. 726 (1996); Kathryn Page, *A Secured Party's Right to a Deficiency Judgment After Noncompliance with the Resale Provisions of Article 9,* 60 N.D. L. REV. 531 (1984); Michelle Rowe, Comment, *Failure of Notice in the Disposition of Collateral: Its Effect on Debtor and Creditor Rights Under the Alabama Uniform Commercial Code,* 14 CUMB. L. REV. 181 (1984); Gary D. Spivey, Annotation, *Uniform Commercial Code: Failure of Secured Creditor to Give Required Notice of Disposition of Collateral as Bar to Deficiency Judgment,* 59 A.L.R.3d 401 (1975 & 1996 Supp.); Richard C. Tinney, Annotation, *Failure of Secured Party to Make "Commercially Reasonable" Disposition of Collateral Under UCC § 9-504(3) as Bar to Deficiency Judgment,* 10 A.L.R.4th 413 (1981); Erika L. Weinberg, Comment, *An Equitable Approach to Creditor Noncompliance with Section 9-504(3) of New York's Uniform Commercial Code: Siemens Credit Corp. v. Marvik Colour, Inc.,* 70 ST. JOHN'S L. REV. 373 (1996).

779. *See* PEB STUDY GROUP REPORT, *supra* note 7, at 199–201.

780. The rights and duties under revised § 9-626 cannot be waived or varied. *See* U.C.C. § 9-602(13) (1999).

would have been realized" if the secured party had complied
with the relevant provisions.[781]
The decision to adopt the rebuttable presumption rule should
not come as a surprise, as it is the law in the majority of states.[782]
The rebuttable presumption rule also represents a fair compromise of the two other positions, both of which suffer from serious
flaws. The absolute bar rule often renders a punitive result that
bears no relationship to the actual harm caused by the noncompliance and also provides the defaulting debtor with a windfall.[783]

---

781. *Id.* § 9-626(a)(3). The amount of proceeds that would have been realized in the
absence of the secured party's noncompliance "is equal to the sum of the secured obligation, expenses, and attorney's fees unless the secured party proves that the amount is less
than that sum." *Id.* § 9-626(a)(4).
    If the secured party has failed to comply with a provision not pertaining to "collec-
tion, enforcement, disposition, or acceptance" (*e.g.*, repossessing a motor vehicle prior to
default), then revised § 9-626 does not apply. Instead, the secured party is liable for damages under revised § 9-625. *See id.* § 9-626 cmt. 2.
    782. *See* Joseph P. Cook, *The Secured Party's Right to a Deficiency Judgment After Violating
UCC Section 9-504(3): A Tabular Approach*, 49 CONSUMER FIN. L.Q. REP. 242, 245–55 (1995).
    783. *See* Aronowitz, *supra* note 778, at 377 ("The absolute bar approach may frequently
be 'harsh and punitive' because it is not premised on the debtor's actual loss caused by the
creditor's noncompliance."); Formanek, *supra* note 778, at 176 (criticizing the absolute bar
rule for "inflicting direct harm on the secured party and awarding an unjustified benefit to
the debtor"); Foss, *supra* note 778, at 238–39 ("Especially when the debtor is not damaged
by the secured party's noncompliance or is damaged less than the amount of the deficiency,
it is argued that the absolute bar approach will result in a windfall to the debtor and a penalty
to the secured party . . . ."); Heiser & Flemma, *supra* note 414, at 491 (criticizing the rule for
allowing a debtor "to escape a valid obligation on the basis of a harmless infraction" and
encouraging a debtor "to look for technical violations of the law . . . where the alleged infraction had no adverse impact on the debtor whatsoever"); Lloyd, *supra* note 279, at 701 (contending that the absolute bar rule "encourages the waste of resources," is "unjust," and
"results in higher deficiencies for most debtors while giving an undeserved windfall to a lucky
few"); Mancino, *supra* note 778, at 662 ("On the negative side, denial of any deficiency may
give a 'windfall' to the debtor."); Robert S. Minetz, *May a "Wrongdoer" Recover a Deficiency
Judgment, or Is Section 9-507(1) a Debtor's Exclusive Remedy?*, 6 UCC L.J. 344, 363 (1974)
(concluding that the absolute bar rule "may punish a secured party guilty of only a technical
harmless error and unjustly reward certain debtors"); Page, *supra* note 778, at 553 (contending that the absolute bar rule "is a harsh, punitive, and unwarranted measure"); Rowe,
supra note 778, at 192 (observing the "penalizing effect of the absolute bar rule when the
debtor's damages do not equal or exceed the amount of the deficiency"); Sigman, *supra* note
286, at 631 (describing the absolute bar rule as "arbitrary, unfair and wasteful"); Weinberg,
supra note 778, at 392 (concluding that "the absolute bar rule often arbitrarily deprives creditors of the deficiency"); *see also* Security Pacific Nat'l Bank v. Kirkland (*In re* Kirkland), 915
F.2d 1236, 1237–38 (9th Cir. 1990) (affirming application of absolute bar rule to deny deficiency of $1,303,882.78 to secured party that failed to send disposition notice to guarantor-
debtor); *In re* Excello Press, Inc., 890 F.2d 896, 904 (7th Cir. 1989) (observing that the
absolute bar rule "produces a penalty out of line with the gravity of the omission"); Siemens
Credit Corp. v. Marvik Colour, Inc., 859 F. Supp. 686, 692 (S.D.N.Y. 1994) ("The absolute
bar rule is disproportionately harsh to the creditor because it deprives the creditor of money
to which it is entitled, often as punishment for a relatively minor oversight. . . . An absolute
bar can result also in a windfall for the debtor, who is relieved of the obligation to pay a

And while the setoff rule strives to measure the actual harm triggered by the creditor's noncompliance, it places the burden of proof not on the creditor, but on a party that may have neither the financial resources nor the access to information necessary to pursue its remedy.[784] By permitting the noncomplying secured party to recover a deficiency only after proving that a commercially reasonable disposition would have generated proceeds in an amount less than the unpaid debt, the rebuttable presumption rule balances the interests of both parties without penalizing either.[785]

legitimate debt."); Bank of Chapmanville v. Workman, 406 S.E.2d 58, 64 (W. Va. 1991) (describing the absolute bar rule as "a judge-made punitive provision" that imposes a penalty in the amount that "bears no relation to the degree of commercial unreasonableness of the secured creditor's conduct, but depends solely upon the amount of the deficiency").

784. See Aronowitz, supra note 778, at 381 (observing that the setoff approach penalizes the debtor for the creditor's misbehavior by placing on the debtor "the very arduous task of proving the debtor's actual loss, which may be impossible to perform"); Lloyd, supra note 279, at 723 (noting that "the setoff rule gives the secured party an unfair advantage" because "[t]he facts necessary to prove the debtor's damage claim are much more readily available to the secured party than they are to the debtor"); Page, supra note 778, at 553 (contending that the setoff rule is "an inequitable solution because it requires the debtor to submit evidence proving a loss"); Rowe, supra note 778, at 198–99 (arguing that the setoff approach "is the least popular of the three approaches because the debtor bears the burden of proof"); Weinberg, supra note 778, at 394 ("The problem inherent in this approach is that it places the burden of proving damages upon the debtor, often the party least able to prove such damages."); see also Commercial Credit Equip. Corp. v. Parsons, 820 S.W.2d 315, 324 (Mo. Ct. App. 1991) ("The impediment of this [setoff] rule is that the burden to prove damages rests on the debtor."); Bank of Chapmanville, 406 S.E.2d at 64 ("The main problem with this [setoff] rule is that the debtor has the burden of proving his losses under U.C.C. § 9-507, and will usually have a hard time proving that the fair market value was higher than what the collateral actually sold for at the repossession sale.").

785. But the rebuttable presumption rule is not without its critics. See, e.g., Braucher, supra note 422, at 85 (observing that the rule prompts the debtor to raise the issue of noncompliance, "which as a practical matter requires having an attorney," and then respond to the secured party's evidence with proof, the cost of which is "usually prohibitive . . . particularly in consumer cases"); Clark, supra note 677, at 320 (describing the presumption as "highly fictional"); Comment, Remedies for Failure to Notify Debtor of Disposition of Repossessed Collateral Under the UCC, 44 U. COLO. L. REV. 221, 232 (1972) (observing that "there seems to be no basis under the language of the Code for placing the burden on the creditor to prove [the fair market value of the collateral]"); see also Wilmington Trust Co. v. Conner, 415 A.2d 773, 779–80 (Del. 1980) (rejecting the rebuttable presumption rule and adopting the absolute bar rule after noting the "minimal" burdens placed on the creditor and the "very onerous" results that noncompliance may place on the debtor); Randolph v. Franklin Inv. Co., 398 A.2d 340, 347–48 (D.C. 1979) (rejecting the rebuttable presumption rule and adopting the absolute bar rule after noting "the substantial prejudice to debtors in the absence of notice of resale, especially when compared to the ease with which any creditor can comply with the notice requirements"); Tanenbaum v. Econs. Lab., Inc., 628 S.W.2d 769, 772 (Tex. 1992) (contending that the rebuttable presumption rule can "rob the debtor" of "express protections the Code provides"); cf. Zubrow, supra note 467, at 529 ("Ordinarily, in tort or contract cases alleging a similar failure to perform a duty of care, the burden of proof is placed on the injured party to establish the violation of duty and the resulting loss sustained.").

Another issue not expressly addressed by current Article 9 concerns the allocation of the burdens of pleading and proving compliance with the statutory requirements associated with collecting, enforcing, disposing of, or accepting collateral. In the absence of a roadmap, courts have traveled different paths. Some require the secured party to plead and prove compliance,[786] others require the debtor to raise an issue in its pleadings as a counterclaim or a defense before the secured party is required to prove compliance,[787] and a few treat noncompliance as an affirmative defense.[788] Revised Article 9 provides clarity on the burden of proof.

Under revised § 9-626, a secured party need not prove compliance unless a debtor or a secondary obligor places the secured party's compliance in issue.[789] If the creditor's compliance is placed in issue, then the secured party bears the burden of establishing its compliance.[790] If the secured party disposed of the collateral to itself, a person related to itself, or a secondary obligor, then a debtor or an obligor wishing to contest the propriety of such a sale has the burden of establishing that the amount of proceeds yielded at the actual disposition is significantly below the range of prices that a proper disposition to a party outside those three categories would have yielded.[791]

This allocation of proof is reasonable, although not free from debate. The secured party's compliance may not be disputed in a deficiency suit. To require proof of compliance in such a case would be, as one court observed, "an unreasonable burden on the judicial process."[792] Revised § 9-626 avoids a waste of judicial resources by requiring a secured party to prove that it has satisfied its statutory obligations only when a debtor or a secondary obligor

---

786. *See* Greathouse v. Charter Nat'l Bank-Southwest, 851 S.W.2d 173, 174–75 n.4 (Tex. 1992) (citing cases).

787. *See id.* at 174–75 n.5 (citing cases).

788. *See id.* at 175 n.6 (citing cases).

789. *See* U.C.C. § 9-626(a)(1) (1999).

790. *See id.* § 9-626(a)(2).

791. *See id.* § 9-626(a)(5). The reason for placing the burden of proving low proceeds on the objecting party, rather than the secured party, is to discourage price challenges every time the collateral is disposed to one of the suspect parties. *See id.* § 9-626 cmt. 5.

792. *See Greathouse,* 851 S.W.2d at 176.

challenges the secured party's conduct.[793] But once the creditor's compliance is challenged, the appropriateness of placing the burden of proof on the creditor, rather than the party challenging the compliance, is debatable. Some may argue that revised § 9-626 departs from established legal principles that place the burden of proof on the injured party, not the wrongdoer.[794] If a debtor or a secondary obligor alleges that the secured party has failed to satisfy its obligations, and that allegation is true, then the challenger receives a benefit (no deficiency) through the statutory presumption. Why not place the burden of proving noncompliance on the party that benefits from the truth of its allegation?[795] There are two likely responses. First, a creditor's noncompliance should not go unpunished; the law should provide the creditor with an incentive to satisfy its statutory obligations.[796] Revised § 9-626 creates that incentive by requiring the creditor to prove its compliance when challenged by a debtor or a secondary obligor. Second, evidence of compliance is more accessible to the secured party than others;[797] therefore, the burden of proof should be placed on the secured party. To each response is a plausible reply. The rebuttable presumption (which becomes relevant only after the secured party's

---

793. See U.C.C. § 9-626(a)(1). This will change the law in jurisdictions that presently require a secured party to prove compliance if its pleadings are specific, rather than general. Texas is such a jurisdiction. See *Greathouse*, 851 S.W.2d at 77.

794. See RESTATEMENT (SECOND) OF CONTRACTS § 360 cmt. b (1981); W. PAGE KEETON ET AL., PROSSER AND KEETON ON THE LAW OF TORTS § 30, at 165 (5th ed. 1984); 2 MCCORMICK ON EVIDENCE § 337, at 427 (4th ed. 1992) ("In most cases, the party who has the burden of pleading a fact will have the burdens of producing evidence and of persuading the jury of its existence as well."); Zubrow, *supra* note 467, at 529.

795. See Michael P. Donaldson, *The Commercially Reasonable Disposition of Collateral Under Article 9 of the UCC: The Question of the Burden of Proof*, 20 UCC L.J. 307, 325 (1988) (proposing that whichever party benefits from the truth of a proposition of fact should bear the burden of proof as to that proposition); *see also* 2 GILMORE, *supra* note 2, § 44.5, at 1235 ("Allegations of fraud or of failure to exercise a required degree of diligence are easily made; the burden of bringing forward convincing proof should be on the party who makes the allegations.").

796. See Norton v. National Bank of Commerce, 398 S.W.2d 538, 542 (1966) (noting it would be "manifestly unfair" for a creditor to benefit from its own misbehavior). *Norton* was the first case to apply the rebuttable presumption approach. Donaldson, *supra* note 795, at 821. Whether (and when) the rebuttable presumption rule applies in Arkansas is the subject of some debate. See First State Bank v. Hallett, 722 S.W.2d 555, 555–57 (Ark. 1987) (applying absolute bar rule); Cheshire v. Walt Bennett Ford, Inc., 788 S.W.2d 490, 492 (Ark. Ct. App. 1990) (applying rebuttable presumption rule).

797. See Aronowitz, *supra* note 778, at 371; Dalton, *supra* note 778, at 834; Foss, *supra* note 778, at 246; *see also Greathouse*, 851 S.W.2d at 176.

noncompliance has been established) provides a secured party with an adequate incentive to comply with its statutory obligations through the denial of a deficiency absent proof *by the secured party* that rebuts the presumption. Therefore, the creditor's noncompliance does not necessarily go unpunished. Additionally, while the secured party may have better access to some evidence (e.g., whether, and to whom, a disposition notice was sent and its contents), other evidence may be easier for a debtor or a secondary obligor to access, especially when the secured party did not sell the collateral to the debtor.[798] And so the arguments go, back and forth, like tennis balls at Wimbledon. Revised § 9-626 brings the argument to a close by placing the burden of proof on the secured party.[799] Mindful of the statutory allocation, a creditor should anticipate the possibility that its conduct will be questioned and, as a result, carefully monitor and document its post-default behavior with a view towards litigation.

The effect of a secured party's noncompliance on its ability to recover a deficiency in a consumer-goods transaction was the subject of much thought during the drafting process.[800] An early draft proposed a modified absolute bar rule that permitted a noncomplying creditor to recover only that part of its deficiency claim that exceeded a statutory (but undetermined) dollar amount.[801] The same draft also either mandated or allowed a court to award reasonable attorneys' fees and the costs of the action to a consumer debtor or consumer obligor that prevailed on the issue of noncompliance.[802] A subsequent draft proposed two alternatives if the secured party failed to comply with the relevant statutes. Under

---

798. *See* Zubrow, *supra* note 467, at 529.

799. U.C.C. § 9-626(a)(2) (1999).

800. The PEB Study Group invited discussion of this issue through a "teaser" recommendation. *See* PEB STUDY GROUP REPORT, *supra* note 7, at 201 ("The Drafting Committee should consider defining one or more special classes of transactions to which the 'absolute bar' rule would be applied (e.g., those in which the collateral is consumer goods or those in which the secured debt is less than a specified amount). . . . The Committee reached no consensus on the appropriate scope of this special class.").

801. *See* U.C.C. § 9-507(c)(2)(i) & cmt. 4 (Draft July 28–Aug. 4, 1995). The proposed rule only applied if no other collateral remained to secure the obligation. *See id.* The same draft barred a deficiency claim, *even if the secured party satisfied all of its statutory obligations,* if the secured party took possession of collateral consisting of consumer goods and the secured debt did not exceed a statutory (but undetermined) dollar amount at the time of default. *See id.* § 9-504A.

802. *See id.* § 9-507(h).

the first alternative, the absolute bar rule would apply in consumer secured transactions (and the rebuttable presumption rule would apply in all other transactions).[803] Under the second alternative, the rebuttable presumption rule would apply in all transactions, including consumer secured transactions.[804] The same draft retained the provision mandating or allowing a court to award reasonable attorneys' fees and the costs of the action to a consumer debtor or consumer obligor that prevailed on the issue of noncompliance.[805] As with other consumer-oriented provisions, the first alternative (favoring consumers through adoption of the absolute bar rule), together with the provision permitting consumers to recover legal fees and expenses, was deleted near the end of the drafting process as part of the "consumer compromise."[806] *Ultimately, a decision was made to exclude consumer transactions from the coverage of revised § 9-626.*[807]

So which rule applies in consumer transactions? The absolute bar rule? The rebuttable presumption rule? The setoff rule? And who bears the burden of pleading and proof on compliance issues in consumer transactions? The answers (or lack thereof) are found in subsection (b), which states:

> The limitation of the rules in subsection (a) to transactions other than consumer transactions is intended to *leave to the court the determination of the proper rules in consumer transactions.* The court may not infer from that limitation the nature of the proper rule in consumer transactions and may continue to apply established approaches.[808]

803. *See* U.C.C. § 9-625 (Alternative A) (Draft Oct. 1996). Under Alternative A, the absolute bar rule would apply in a consumer secured transaction only if no other collateral remained to secure the obligation. *See id.* If other collateral remained, the secured party's sole recourse would be to that collateral, and a consumer obligor would have no personal liability for any deficiency. *See id.*
804. *See id.* § 9-625 (Alternative B).
805. *See id.* § 9-628.
806. *See id.* § 9-625 (deleting Alternative A); *id.* § 9-628 (deleting provision); *see also supra* note 548 (discussing "consumer compromise").
807. *See* U.C.C. § 9-626(a) (1999) (stating that the rules apply "[i]n an action arising from a transaction, *other than a consumer transaction*") (emphasis added).
808. *Id.* § 9-626(b) (emphasis added); *see id.* § 9-102(a)(26) (defining" consumer transaction"); Rapson, *supra* note 4 (discussing drafting evolution of revised § 9-626(b)); Braucher, *supra* note 422, at 97 ("Translated into plain language, this means: 'We won't tell you what the rules are,' or, 'We punt.'").

Whether the rules of revised § 9-626 should apply to consumer transactions, whether a different set of rules applicable to consumer transactions should have been drafted, or whether a court should apply, or depart from, the rules of revised § 9-626 in consumer transactions are all questions worthy of debate to a degree greater than the confines of these pages.[809] Suffice it to say that nonuniformity is a foregone conclusion.[810] That may be a not-so-small (but nevertheless acceptable) price to pay, if the inclusion of rules governing deficiency claims in consumer transactions would delay enactment of Revised Article 9 by state legislatures.[811]

809. Some authors already have fueled the debate. *See, e.g.,* CLARK, *supra* note 2, ¶ 4.12[5][d], at 4-224 (suggesting that courts apply the absolute bar rule in cases involving consumer goods); Braucher, *supra* note 422, at 87 (contending that, in the absence of a rule calculating deficiencies on the basis of wholesale value, consumers "would have preferred codification of the 'absolute bar' approach"); Hillebrand, *supra* note 370, at 208–11 (advocating an anti-deficiency rule for all consumer goods other than well-defined luxury goods); Lloyd, *supra* note 279, 701 n.33 (declining to take a position on whether the absolute bar rule should be retained in consumer cases but offering several reasons for its retention); James J. White, *UCC Proposals Concerning Consumer Transactions*, SC36 ALI-ABA 253, 256 (1997) ("What policy requires the rebuttable presumption rule for all commercial transactions but would allow states to adopt the absolute bar rule for consumer transactions?").

810. Even if Revised Article 9 adopted a rule applicable to consumer transactions, some nonuniformity would likely result from the enactment of nonuniform amendments enacted by state legislatures unhappy with the rule selected by the Drafting Committee. *Cf.* Alvin C. Harrell, *Commentary: The Case for Nonuniformity in State Law*, 51 CONSUMER FIN. L.Q. REP. 294, 327 (1997) (suggesting that "it serves the interests of the uniform law process to steer clear of uniform rules for issues that are subject to widespread disagreement"); Discussion, *Uniform State Laws: A Discussion Focused on Revision of the Uniform Commercial Code*, 22 OKLA. CITY U. L. REV. 257, 269 (1997) (Julianna J. Zekan, panelist) (observing that "the paramount goal should be to improve the law, not to maintain perfect uniformity"); Miller, *supra* note 75, at 727 (asserting that adding consumer protection provisions to the Code increases the risk of delayed enactment and nonuniformity); *see also* Richard A. Elbrecht, *The NCCUSL Should Abandon Its Search for Consensus and Address More Difficult and Controversial Issues Applying "Process" Concepts*, 28 LOY. L.A. L. REV. 147, 152 (1994) (contending that "NCCUSL is not serving the interests of either the business community or the consumers" when it "focus[es] on writing statutes that will have the consensus needed to guarantee their adoption in almost every state").

811. *Cf.* Julian B. McDonnell, *The Code Project Confronts Fundamental Dilemmas*, 26 LOY. L.A. L. REV. 683, 688 (1993) (observing that drafters "must produce a product that has a good chance of being sold to all of the state legislatures" if the goal of uniformity is to be advanced); Memorandum of Article 9 Drafting Committee, Consumer Issues Subcommittee (May 29, 1996), *reprinted in* Fred H. Miller, *UCC Proposals Concerning Consumer Transactions (Article 2 and 9)*, SC36 ALI-ABA 185, 201 (Dec. 11, 1997) ("A major goal in the revision process is maintenance of uniformity and quick acceptance of Revised Article 9 and the final decision regarding the extent of special consumer provisions in Article 9 must take into account enactability of the statute."); Woodward, *supra* note 75, at 1522 (observing that "[e]nactability operates as the great leveling agent in the reform process").

REVISED § 9-627

DETERMINATION OF WHETHER CONDUCT WAS COMMERCIALLY REASONABLE

Current Article 9 does not define "commercially reasonable." Although the term "is a vague and fluctuating one, which cannot be meaningfully described except in terms of particular fact situations,"[812] a secured party can avoid the peril often associated with the term by sailing into one of several safe harbors in current § 9-507.[813] Similar safety exists under Revised Article 9 and is codified at § 9-627.[814]

Under current § 9-507(2), the mere fact that a better price could have been achieved if the secured party had sold collateral at a different time or in a different method will not, by itself, establish that the secured party failed to sell the collateral in a commercially reasonable manner.[815] Revised § 9-627 retains the

---

812. *See* 2 GILMORE, *supra* note 2, § 44.5, at 1234–35.

813. *See* U.C.C. § 9-507(2) (1995).

814. In addition to the protection afforded by revised § 9-627, a secured party is advised to take advantage of revised § 9-603(a), which permits parties to adopt standards defining "commercial reasonableness" if the standards are not manifestly unreasonable. *See id.* § 9-603(a) (1999).

815. *See id.* § 9-507(2) (1995); *see also id.* § 9-504(3) (requiring all aspects of a collateral disposition to be commercially reasonable); *see also* FDIC v. Lanier, 926 F.2d 462, 467 (5th Cir. 1991) (refusing to infer commercial unreasonableness of private sale that yielded $100,000—an amount $400,000 less than the distributor's cost and approximately $80,000–$150,000 less than an independent distributor alleged he was willing to pay—absent proof of "procedural irregularities, allegations of bad faith, or other reasons to explain the allegedly low price"); Leasing Serv. Corp. v. Diamond Timber, Inc., 559 F. Supp. 972, 979 (S.D.N.Y. 1983) ("Commercial reasonableness of a sale depends on the procedures employed in the sale, not on the proceeds it generates."), *aff'd*, 729 F.2d 1442 (2d Cir. 1983); *In re* Marshall, 219 B.R. 687, 690 (Bankr. M.D.N.C. 1997) (ruling that

same concept and expands it beyond just collateral sales to also include collateral acceptance, collateral collection, collateral disposition, and collateral enforcement.[816] Rarely, if ever, will post-default activity yield maximum proceeds, making this safe harbor "necessary to prevent every disgruntled debtor from making a jury case by talking price."[817] Although the rule suggests that the court should shine its spotlight on the procedures followed by the creditor, rather than the amount of proceeds yielded by those procedures, it would be imprudent for a creditor to believe that a court will completely ignore allegations of an inadequate price when reviewing the propriety of the creditor's actions.[818]

Under current § 9-507(2), a secured party can claim a conclusive presumption of commercial reasonableness by selling collateral of a type customarily sold on a recognized market either in the "usual manner" or at "the price current in such market at

foreclosure sale of motor home for $2650, a price much less than the fair market value of $5500 estimated by the creditor's expert, did not make the sale commercially unreasonable); *In re* Whatley, 126 B.R. 231, 236 (Bankr. N.D. Miss. 1991) (holding creditor's foreclosure sale of collateral to itself for $25,000 was not rendered commercially unreasonable merely because creditor subsequently sold same collateral at auction for $39,748.29); Daniel v. Ford Motor Credit Co., 612 So. 2d 483, 485 (Ala. Civ. App. 1992) (declining to rule that dealer's wholesale auction was commercially unreasonable solely because vehicle sold for $3500, instead of $5775 as suggested by national appraisal guidebook); Commercial Credit Equip. Corp. v. Parsons, 820 S.W.2d 315, 322 (Mo. Ct. App. 1991) (noting the disparity between the $6600 sales price and the $27,000 value ascribed to collateral by expert "is a factor important, but not decisive, to commercial reasonableness").

816. *See* U.C.C. § 9-627(a) (1999); *see also id.* § 9-607(c) (obligating the secured party to proceed in a commercially reasonable manner in its collection and enforcement efforts); *id.* § 9-608(a)(3) (requiring a secured party to apply noncash proceeds in a commercially reasonable manner); *id.* § 9-610(b) (stating every aspect of a collateral disposition must be commercially reasonable).

817. Nadler v. Baybank Merrimack Valley, N.A., 733 F.2d 182, 184 (1st Cir. 1984); *see also* Hall v. Owen County State Bank, 370 N.E.2d 918, 929 (Ind. Ct. App. 1977) (observing that the first sentence of U.C.C. § 9-507(2) recognizes that "only on rare occasions will a repossession sale bring the highest bids or the highest value for the collateral and therefore such sales could always be vulnerable to attack by a showing that a higher price might have been obtained under different circumstances"); 9 HAWKLAND ET AL., *supra* note 15, § 9-507:08, at 915 (noting that "the drafters apparently did not want the secured party to be second-guessed after the fact").

818. *See, e.g.,* Mercantile Fin. Corp. v. Miller, 292 F. Supp. 797, 801 (E.D. Pa. 1968) (noting that a discrepancy between a price received and a price obtainable, "if substantial, is relevant to a determination of whether a challenged sale [is] 'commercially reasonable'"); McMillian v. Bank South, N.A., 373 S.E.2d 61, 63 (Ga. Ct. App. 1988) (reducing

the time of his sale."[819] Revised § 9-627 retains the same rule.[820] The reason for this rule is not hard to glean. Market forces independent of the secured party's behavior dictate the price of collateral sold on a recognized market. If the creditor disposes of such collateral in its usual manner, then any disparity between the market price and the disposition price did not result from creditor misconduct. And if the creditor disposes of collateral at its then-current market price, the commercial reasonableness of procedures followed by the creditor is irrelevant.

Current Article 9 states that the sale of collateral sold "in conformity with reasonable commercial practices among dealers in the type of property sold" is a commercially reasonable sale.[821]

deficiency judgment by $150, the difference between the $500 appraised value at repossession and the $350 yielded at the foreclosure sale); Auto Credit, Inc. v. Long, 971 P.2d 1237, 1239–40 (Mont. 1998) (concluding foreclosure sale of auto for $150 in August was not commercially reasonable when debtor had purchased auto for $2,795 in April and had not devalued auto by 95% by driving it 3500 miles); FDIC v. Herald Square Fabrics Corp., 439 N.Y.S.2d 944, 953–55 (1981) (concluding that proof of discrepancy between original sale price of $85,200 and foreclosure sale price of $8393.14 was sufficient to deny creditor's motion for summary judgment even though no issues existed on adequacy of notice or sales procedures); Meadows, *supra* note 457, at 2446–47 ("While the Code does not require the price to be maximized, the creditor is expected to make choices regarding the conduct of the sale with the expectation that they will result in a fair price.") (footnotes omitted); Miller, *supra* note 811, at 224–25 (contending that if evidence suggests that the price obtained by the creditor is unreasonable in light of information concerning prices generally obtained for similar property, then the creditor should be required to introduce a commercially reasonable justification for carrying out the sale as it did and accepting the particular price); *see also* U.C.C. § 9-627 cmt. 2 (1999) ("While not itself sufficient to establish a violation of this Part, a low price suggests that a court should scrutinize carefully all aspects of a disposition to ensure that each aspect was commercially reasonable.").

819. U.C.C. § 9-507(2) (1995); *see also supra* notes 248–57 and accompanying text (discussing "recognized market"); Ford Motor Credit Co. v. DeValk Lincoln-Mercury, Inc., 600 F. Supp. 1547, 1551 (N.D. Ill. 1985) (finding sale of vehicle at dealers-only auction—"a well-recognized market for automobiles in the Chicago metropolitan area"—to be commercially reasonable); Washburn v. Union Nat'l Bank & Trust Co., 502 N.E.2d 739, 742–43 (Ill. App. Ct. 1986) (concluding creditor was entitled to summary judgment on issue of commercial reasonableness after selling Ginnie Mae bonds in usual manner on recognized market); Ford Motor Credit Co. v. Russell, 519 N.W.2d 465–66 (Minn. Ct. App. 1994) (affirming trial court's grant of creditor's motion for summary judgment on issue of commercial reasonableness where creditor sold vehicle at wholesale, dealers-only, auction—a "well-recognized market"); Ford Motor Credit Co. v. Potts, 548 N.E.2d 223, 228 (Ohio 1989) (finding public sale of repossessed vehicle was conducted "in the usual manner in any recognized market therefor").

820. *See* U.C.C. § 9-627(b)(1), (2) (1999).

821. *See id.* § 9-507(2) (1995); *see also* Piper Acceptance Corp. v. Yarbrough, 702 F.2d 733, 735 (8th Cir. 1983) (holding creditor's sale of aircraft in accordance with industry

The same principle continues under revised § 9-627.[822] The premise is that, in the absence of a recognized market, the collateral will bring a fair (if not the best) price if it is disposed by reasonable commercial practices through normal channels,[823] thus negating any need to review the commercial reasonableness of the secured party's actions. However, the reasonableness of a dealer's commercial practices remains subject to judicial scrutiny.[824]

A disposition of collateral under current Article 9 that has been approved (i) in a judicial proceeding, (ii) by any bona fide creditors' committee, or (iii) by any representative of creditors is commercially reasonable[825] (although the absence of such approval does not necessarily prevent a disposition from being

practice was commercially reasonable); Chrysler Credit Corp. v. B.J.M., Jr., Inc., 834 F. Supp. 813, 835 (E.D. Pa. 1993) (concluding sale of dealer's motor vehicle inventory at wholesale, dealers-only, auction was commercially reasonable in absence of any evidence that method utilized did not conform to reasonable commercial practices in auto dealership industry); Daniel v. Ford Motor Credit Co., 612 So. 2d 483, 484–85 (Ala. Civ. App. 1992) (concluding sale of vehicle at wholesale dealer auction—"the usual manner of sale of repossessed automobiles . . . in conformity with the reasonable commercial practices among dealers in repossessed automobiles"—was commercially reasonable); Davis v. Concord Commercial Corp., 434 S.E.2d 571, 576 (Ga. Ct. App. 1993) (affirming trial court's directed verdict on issue of commercial reasonableness in favor of creditor that retained expert dealer to dispose of used heavy equipment); McMillian, 373 S.E.2d at 62–63 (upholding trial court's conclusion that method and manner of vehicle sale was commercially reasonable where vehicle was sold at private auction by recognized automobile auction company according to standard practice and procedures followed weekly for eleven years); Carter v. First Fed. Savs. & Loan Ass'n, 347 S.E.2d 264, 268 (Ga. Ct. App. 1986) (concluding creditor's sale of repossessed motor home by same method and manner followed by similar creditors was commercially reasonable).

822. See U.C.C. § 9-627(b)(3) (1999).

823. See id. § 9-507 cmt. 2 (1995); 2 GILMORE, supra note 2, § 44.5, at 1236.

824. See U.C.C. § 9-507 cmt. 2 (1995) ("Such a method of sale, *fairly conducted*, is recognized as commercially reasonable . . . .") (emphasis added).

825. See id. § 9-507(2); *see also* Maryland Nat'l Bank v. Traenkle, 933 F. Supp. 1280, 1286–87 (D. Md. 1996) (holding borrowers could not challenge commercial reasonableness of court-ordered marshal's sale of yacht); Geiger v. Tokheim, 191 B.R. 781, 796 (N.D. Iowa 1996) (ruling commercial reasonableness of stock sale approved by bankruptcy court in judicial proceeding could not be challenged); FBS AB Credit, Inc. v. Estate of Walker, 906 F. Supp. 1427, 1432 (D. Colo. 1995) (finding bank's sale of collateral pursuant to bankruptcy court order was conclusively deemed commercially reasonable); National Westminster Bank v. Ross, 130 B.R. 656, 678 (S.D.N.Y. 1991) (holding trustee was estopped from challenging commercial reasonableness of sale expressly approved by bankruptcy court); Bryant v. American Nat'l Bank & Trust Co., 407 F. Supp. 360, 367 (N.D. Ill. 1976) (concluding borrowers could not challenge commercial reasonableness of

commercially reasonable[826]). Other than extending the conclusive presumption to dispositions approved by an assignee for the benefit of creditors, the law remains unchanged under Revised Article 9.[827] One court explained the purpose of this principle as follows:

> [A] judicial approval of a disposition of collateral is given conclusive effect not because the tribunal necessarily scrutinized all aspects of the disposition and found them reasonable, but because the hearing allowed the parties to voice their objections and to comment upon the proposed transaction. If the parties have had an opportunity for thorough discussion of the sale's terms, it is appropriate to give the court's determination of reasonableness a conclusive effect.[828]

Although the time and expense necessary to qualify for the presumption may limit the frequency of its use, a secured party may overlook those impediments if the collateral is atypical or the monetary risks of failing to act in a commercially reasonable manner are great. Once the necessary approval has been obtained, the secured party should adhere to the pre-approved procedures; a departure may result in a loss of the presumption.[829]

---

court-ordered stock sale absent proof of noncompliance, fraud, or overreaching by creditor); Cramton v. Altus Bank, 596 So. 2d 902, 906 (Ala. 1992) (holding guarantor could not challenge commercial reasonableness of court-ordered sale of barge in absence of evidence that court proceedings were procedurally defective or creditor was guilty of malfeasance); *Davis*, 434 S.E.2d at 574 (ruling trustee's auction sale of machine was conclusively deemed to be commercially reasonable).

826. *See* U.C.C. § 9-507(2) (1995).

827. *See id.* § 9-627(c), (d) (1999).

828. *Bryant*, 407 F. Supp. at 364; *see also In re* Zsa Zsa Ltd., 352 F. Supp. 665, 672 (S.D.N.Y. 1972).

829. *See, e.g.,* Leasing Serv. Corp. v. Appalachian Pocohontas Coal Co. (*In re* Appalachian Pocahontas Coal Co.), 31 B.R. 579, 580–81 (S.D. W. Va. 1983) (concluding that even if bankruptcy court order was "judicial approval" under U.C.C. § 9-507(2), creditor that failed to comply with express terms and implied provisions of order could not invoke conclusive presumption that disposition was commercially reasonable). *Cf.* Carlton Mfg., Inc. v. Bauer, 429 S.E.2d 329, 331 (Ga. Ct. App. 1993) (holding creditor could not invoke conclusive presumption as bankruptcy court order "merely authorized plaintiff to conduct a commercially reasonable sale; it did not declare the manner in which plaintiff ultimately conducted the sale to be commercially reasonable").

Noticeably absent from revised § 9-627 (and its predecessor) is a safe harbor for dispositions of collateral of a type that is the subject of widely distributed standard price quotations.[830] The same reasons that justify a conclusive presumption of commercial reasonableness when collateral is disposed on a recognized market support enactment of a similar presumption when collateral subject to widely distributed standard price quotations is disposed. In many instances collateral subject to such quotations also is sold on a recognized market, so the need for an additional safe harbor may not be great.[831] Nevertheless, the statutory references to both "recognized market" and "widely distributed standard price quotations" discourage any suggestion that collateral subject to the latter will always fall within the former.[832] Therefore, an additional safe harbor would provide some benefit. The desired result could be accomplished if revised § 9-627(b) were amended in a manner that created a conclusive presumption of commercial reasonableness for any disposition of collateral "at the price current at the time of disposition of property subject to widely distributed standard price quotations."

---

830. An explanation was requested in the Zinnecker Memorandum, *supra* note 102, at 5.

831. A secured party disposing of such collateral also might avail itself of revised § 9-627(b)(3), as collateral subject to widely distributed standard price quotations is likely to be disposed by dealers.

832. *See, e.g.,* U.C.C. § 9-504(3) (1995) (excusing disposition notice if collateral is sold on recognized market but not excusing disposition notice if collateral is subject to widely distributed standard price quotations; also permitting secured party to buy at private sale if collateral is sold on recognized market or the subject of widely distributed standard price quotations); *id.* § 9-610(c)(2) (1999) (permitting secured party to purchase at private disposition if collateral is sold on recognized market or the subject of widely distributed standard price quotations); *id.* § 9-611(d) (excusing disposition notice if collateral is sold on recognized market but not excusing disposition notice if collateral is subject to widely distributed standard price quotations).

REVISED § 9-628

Nonliability and Limitation on Liability of Secured Party; Liability of Secondary Obligor

Revised § 9-628 has no predecessor under current Article 9. Through its five provisions, revised § 9-628 limits a secured party's liability for noncompliance in specific situations.

As noted earlier, a secured party owes no duty to a debtor or an obligor (or a secured party or a lienholder that has filed a financing statement against a debtor) unless the secured party knows (i) that the person is either a debtor or an obligor, (ii) the identity of the person, and (iii) how to communicate with the person.[833] If a secured party owes no duty to a person in the absence of the requisite knowledge, then it seems only fair that the secured party's acts or omissions should neither trigger liability to, nor reduce or eliminate any deficiency claim against, such a person. An exculpatory clause to that effect is codified in revised § 9-628.[834]

Many of the duties created by the default provisions of Revised Article 9 require a secured party to determine whether the transaction is a consumer-goods transaction or a consumer

---

833. *See id.* § 9-605 (1999), discussed *supra* notes 99–108 and accompanying text.
834. *See* U.C.C. § 9-628(a). A casual reading of subsections (a)(1) and (b) may prompt the reader to question whether any substantive difference exists between the two provisions. Subsection (a)(1) exculpates the secured party from liability for failing to comply with Article 9. Subsection (b) relieves the secured party from liability for breaching a duty arising under other law (e.g., suretyship or tort law) if that duty is imposed on the secured party in its capacity as such. Regrettably, this difference is not explained in revised § 9-628, but in revised § 9-605. *See id.* § 9-605 cmt. 2 (last sentence).

transaction or if the collateral includes consumer goods.[835] A secured party may breach its duty only because its determination is erroneous. For example, a secured party may erroneously conclude that all collateral offered by an individual is a consumer good (whereas it may be something else, such as equipment or investment property) or any secured loan made to an individual creates a consumer-goods transaction or consumer transaction (when it may be a loan not incurred primarily for person, family, or household purposes). Revised § 9-628 relieves a secured party from liability to, and preserves its deficiency claim against, any person for any breach predicated on a reasonable (but erroneous) belief concerning the type of transaction or collateral.[836] The protection is available to a secured party whose reasonable belief is based on its "reasonable reliance" on either "a debtor's representation concerning the purpose for which collateral was to be used, acquired, or held" or "an obligor's representation concerning the purpose for which a secured obligation was incurred."[837] Accordingly, a secured party's standard loan documents should include representations concerning the use of collateral and the purpose of the debt. And the provisions of Revised Article 9 should be applied as if the facts reasonably believed and reasonably relied upon by the secured party were true.[838]

To provide the secured party with some incentive to comply with its statutory obligations, revised § 9-625(c) permits a debtor or a secondary obligor to recover minimum statutory damages in

---

835. *See, e.g., id.* § 9-611(c)(3) (requiring secured party to send disposition notice to parties other than the debtor and any secondary obligor only if collateral is other than consumer goods); *id.* § 9-612(b) (indicating disposition notice sent after default and no less than ten days before disposition is timely; rule applies only if transaction is not consumer transaction); *id.* § 9-613 (describing contents and form of disposition notice to be sent in transaction other than consumer-goods transaction); *id.* § 9-614 (describing contents and form of disposition notice to be sent in consumer-goods transaction); *id.* § 9-616(b) (obligating secured party to send written calculation of surplus or deficiency in consumer-goods transaction); *id.* § 9-620(a)(3) (prohibiting secured party from accepting collateral in full or partial satisfaction of unpaid debt if collateral is consumer goods not in debtor's possession when debtor consents to acceptance); *id.* § 9-620(e) (forcing secured party to dispose of consumer goods in its possession if significant payments have been made); *id.* § 9-620(g) (prohibiting secured party from accepting collateral in partial satisfaction of unpaid debt in consumer transaction).

836. *See id.* § 9-628(c).

837. *See id.*

838. *See id.* § 9-628 cmt. 2.

an amount equal to "not less than the credit service charge plus 10 percent of the principal amount of the obligation or the time-price differential plus 10 percent of the cash price" when the collateral consists of consumer goods.[839] Revised § 9-628 limits a secured party's liability for minimum statutory damages in two instances. First, minimum statutory damages cannot be awarded to punish a secured party that breaches its duty under revised § 9-616 to timely send a written calculation of a surplus or deficiency to a debtor or a consumer obligor.[840] However, the secured party remains liable for "damages in the amount of any loss" caused by its noncompliance[841] and, in appropriate situations, may be assessed a $500 penalty.[842]

Second, a secured party cannot be liable for the minimum statutory penalty "more than once with respect to any one secured obligation."[843] For example, if a secured party fails to send a disposition notice to the debtor and a secondary obligor[844] and then sells the collateral in a manner not commercially reasonable,[845] it cannot be required to pay the minimum statutory penalty four times (two breaches, two parties). But can the secured party be forced to write two checks—one to the debtor and another to the secondary obligor?[846] Probably not. (So who is entitled to the single check?[847]) The language in the statute ("once with respect to any one secured obligation") and the relevant comment ("Subsection (e) ensures that a secured party will incur statutory damages only once in connection with any one secured obligation."[848]) suggests that a secured party is liable

839. *Id.* § 9-625(c)(2). This provision is discussed *supra* notes 741–69 and accompanying text.
840. *See* U.C.C. § 9-628(d) (1999); *see also id.* § 9-625(c) (stating that minimum statutory damages may be awarded "[e]xcept as otherwise provided in Section 9-628").
841. *Id.* § 9-625(b).
842. *See id.* § 9-625(e)(5), (6).
843. *Id.* § 9-628(e).
844. *See id.* § 9-611(c)(1), (2) (obligating a secured party to send a disposition notice to the debtor and any secondary obligor).
845. *See id.* § 9-610(b) (requiring all aspects of a disposition to be commercially reasonable).
846. This question was posed in the Zinnecker Memorandum, *supra* note 102, at 5.
847. To avoid answering that question, the secured party may wish to deposit the appropriate amount with the court and bring an interpleader action against all potential claimants.
848. U.C.C. § 9-628 cmt. 4 (1999).

"once per transaction" rather than "once per person per transaction." Furthermore, the phrase "not liable to any person" in the preceding subsection[849] strongly implies that the Drafting Committee appreciated the difference in meaning between "once per transaction" and "once per person per transaction." Nevertheless, that interpretation seems wrong, especially if a debtor and a secondary obligor each can establish a violation unique to itself[850] for which actual damages do not exceed the statutory penalty. To adequately compensate multiple parties that each suffer unique injuries, while also providing the secured party with an incentive to comply with its statutory duties, subsection (e) should be interpreted in a manner that obligates a secured party to pay the statutory penalty no more than "once per person per transaction" rather than "once per transaction." And if the statutory language of revised § 9-628 and its accompanying comments discourage such an interpretation, legislatures may wish to consider the following non-uniform amendment (new language italicized): "(e) A secured party is not liable *to any person* under § 9-625(c)(2) more than once with respect to any one secured obligation."

At one time or another, the Drafting Committee considered two additional exculpatory provisions. One proposed provision relieved a secured party from liability for the minimum statutory penalty if the secured party established that its noncompliance resulted from an unintentional good-faith error.[851]

---

849. *See id.* § 9-628(d).

850. For example, the secured party may breach the peace while repossessing a vehicle from the debtor (creating a cause of action under revised § 9-609 in favor of the debtor) and then may fail to send a disposition notice to the guarantor (creating a cause of action under revised § 9-611(c)(2) in favor of the guarantor).

851. *See id.* § 9-627(d) (Draft Oct. 1996). The proposed provision read as follows (brackets in original):

(d) A secured party is not liable to any person under Section 9-624(c) if the secured party meets the burden of establishing that its failure to comply with this [part] [article] was not intentional and resulted from a good-faith error notwithstanding the secured party's maintenance of procedures reasonably adapted to avoid the failure. [Examples of a good-faith error include clerical, calculation, computer malfunction and programing, and printing errors, except that an] [An] error of legal judgment concerning the secured party's rights and duties under this [part] [article] is not a good faith error.

Id. Draft § 9-624(c) was a predecessor of revised § 9-625(c)(2). The provision was based on the bona fide error defense in the Truth-in-Lending Act. *See* 15 U.S.C. § 1640(c) (1994).

Another provision capped a secured party's liability for the minimum statutory penalty in a class action or series of class actions arising out of the same noncompliance (e.g., its standard disposition notice sent to multiple parties in numerous transactions contains a seriously misleading error).[852] Unfortunately for secured creditors, neither provision survived the final cut; both were deleted as part of the "consumer compromise."[853]

852. *See* U.C.C. § 9-627(e) (Draft Aug. 7, 1997). The proposed provision read as follows:

(e) The total recovery under Section 9-624(c) in a class action or a series of class actions arising out of the same noncompliance by the same secured party shall not be more than the lesser of $500,000 or one percent of the net worth of the secured party.

Id. Draft § 9-624(c) was a predecessor of revised § 9-625(c)(2).

853. *See id.* § 9-627 (Draft Mar. 1998) (deleting the good-faith error defense to statutory damages and the limitation on recoveries in class actions); *see also supra* note 548 (discussing the "consumer compromise").

CONCLUSION

As evidenced by the foregoing analysis, the default provisions of Revised Article 9 are much more detailed than their counterparts under current Article 9. With additional detail comes increased statutory complexity. But the additional guidance should improve the efficiency of secured financing through greater certainty and less judicial intervention.

Professor Elizabeth Warren once wrote: "[d]efault is a distasteful idea . . . . Getting the money paid is a matter of course, or of honor, or—if it should come to that—of grubby technical steps."[854] Distasteful or not, defaults do occur. For that reason, secured parties, debtors, other obligors, and their respective counsel should be familiar with the revised default provisions (which often are "technical" and, in places, perhaps even "grubby").

Although the revised default provisions may not be embraced with unbridled enthusiasm by all interested parties in every post-default situation, the provisions do constitute a notable improvement in the law. The provisions specifically address many current concerns, provide detailed procedures that should provide clarity and reduce litigation, expand the post-default rights available to the secured party, and attempt to fairly balance the desires of foreclosing creditors and the interests of debtors and third-party claimants. Because the provisions are quite extensive and introduce several new terms (or utilize current, but redefined, terms), the significance of the improvement may best be appreciated by taking an exhaustive statutory journey. Hopefully this volume will serve as a welcome traveling companion.

---

854. Elizabeth Warren, *Bankruptcy Policy*, 54 U. Chi. L. Rev. 775, 779 (1987).

ABOUT THE AUTHOR

Tim Zinnecker is an associate professor at South Texas College of Law, where he teaches secured transactions, payment systems, and banking law. He chaired the Texas state bar Revised Article 9 Task Force from its inception through enactment of Revised Article 9 by the Texas legislature in 1999. His previous scholarship has appeared in the SMU, Tennessee, Missouri, Richmond, and Mercer law reviews.

Professor Zinnecker graduated with honors from the J. Reuben Clark Law School, Brigham Young University, in 1986, where he served as lead note and comment editor of the law review and was a member of Order of the Coif. He then served as a judicial clerk for the Hon. Frank X. Gordon, chief justice of the Arizona Supreme Court, and the Hon. Edith H. Jones, United States Court of Appeals (Fifth Circuit). He practiced commercial law in Dallas and Houston for five years before joining the faculty at South Texas in 1994.

Order additional copies of
The Default Provisions of Revised Article 9
and other essential guides

Yes, please send me:

_____copies of *The Default Provisions of Revised Article 9* (PC# 5070350)
$29.95 each (1-25 copies) / $23.95 each (26-50 copies) / $17.95 each (51+ copies)
_____copies of *The New Article 9* (PC# 5070346)
$39.95 each (1-25 copies) / $29.95 each (26-50 copies) / $23.95 each (51+ copies)
_____copies of *The Portable UCC, 2nd Edition* (PC# 5070294)
$29.95 each (1-25 copies) / $23.95 each (26-50 copies) / $17.95 each (51+ copies)

$_____Subtotal

$_____Tax (DC residents add 5.75%, IL residents add 8.75%, MD residents add 5%)

$_____Handling (orders up to $49.99 add $5.95, $50-$99.99 add $7.95, $100+ add $9.95)

$_____Total

Payment:

☐ Bill me   ☐ Check enclosed payable to the ABA   ☐ VISA   ☐ MasterCard

Acct #_____Exp.Date_____

Signature_____

Name_____

Firm/Org_____

Address_____

City/State/Zip_____

Phone number (in case we have a question about your order)_____

Mail to: ABA, Publication Orders, P.O. Box 10892, Chicago, IL 60610-0892

Phone: 1-800-285-2221 (M-F, between 7:30 am and 5:30 pm Central Time)

Fax: 312-988-5568

E-mail: abasvcctr@abanet.org

source code: BOOK